KAPLAN

Other Kaplan Books for College-Bound Students:

College Admissions and Financial Aid

Parent's Guide to College Admissions
Straight Talk on Paying for College: Lowering the Cost of Higher Education
The Unofficial, Unbiased Guide to the 328 Most Interesting Colleges

Test Preparation

ACT
AP Biology
AP Calculus AB: An Apex Learning Guide
AP Chemistry: An Apex Learning Guide
AP English Language & Composition: An Apex Learning Guide
AP English Literature & Composition
AP Macroeconomics/Microeconomics: An Apex Learning Guide
AP Physics B: An Apex Learning Guide
AP Psychology
AP Statistics: An Apex Learning Guide
AP U.S. Government & Politics: An Apex Learning Guide
AP U.S. History
AP World History
Domina el SAT: Preparate para tomar el examen para ingresar a la universidad
Frankenstein: A Kaplan SAT Score-Raising Classic
PSAT
Ring of McAllister: A Score-Raising Mystery Featuring 1,046 Must-Know SAT Vocabulary Words
SAT
SAT Math Mania
SAT Math Workbook
SAT Vocab Velocity
SAT Verbal Workbook
SAT Vocabulary Flashcards Flip-O-Matic
SAT II: Biology E/M
SAT II: Chemistry
SAT II: Literature
SAT II: Mathematics Levels IC and IIC
SAT II: Physics
SAT II: Spanish
SAT II: U.S. History
SAT II: World History
SAT II: Writing
What Smart Girls Know About the SAT

KAPLAN®

SAT* 1600

2004 Edition

by Gretchen VanEsselstyn, Ingrid Multhopp, Michael Palmer,
and the Staff of Kaplan, Inc.

Simon & Schuster

New York · London · Sydney · Toronto

Kaplan Publishing
Published by Simon & Schuster
1230 Avenue of the Americas
New York, NY 10020

For bulk sales to schools, colleges, and universities, please contact:
Order Department, Simon & Schuster, 100 Front Street, Riverside, NJ 08075
Phone: (800) 223-2336, Fax: (800) 943-9831

Contributing Editor: Jon Zeitlin
Project Editor: Charli Engelhorn
Cover Design: Cheung Tai
Interior Page Design and Production: Renée Mitchell
Production Manager: Michael Shevlin
Managing Editor: Déa Alessandro
Executive Editor: Del Franz

Special thanks to Josh Weill, Eric Goodman, Ed Logue, David Stuart, Larissa Shmailo, and Laurel Douglas

Manufactured in the United States of America
Published simultaneously in Canada

February 2004
10 9 8 7 6 5 4 3 2 1
ISBN: 0-7432-5198-9

Table of Contents

www.kaptest.com/publishing

The material in this book is up-to-date at the time of publication. However, the College Entrance Examination Board may have instituted changes in the test or test registration process after this book was published. Be sure to carefully read the materials you receive when you register for the test.

If there are any important late-breaking developments—or any changes or corrections to the Kaplan test preparation materials in this book—we will post that information online at **www.kaptest.com/publishing**. Check to see if there is any information posted there for readers of this book.

About the Authors

Ingrid Multhopp seemed predestined for life as a test-prep master. For over a decade she has been likened to a colossus striding the test-prep stage, shredding standardized tests with her powerful intellect, and using this knowledge to prepare legions of students for scholastic success, through face-to-face teaching and countless books and online courses. Ingrid lives in New York City, where, when not agonizing over how to enable test takers to wring another point out of the test, she enjoys writing acerbic poetry and watching old movies.

Michael Palmer has been working for Kaplan since 1997. In addition to test preparation, he enjoys poker, cat-sitting, and acting as spiritual adviser to Kaplan's basketball squad, the Scorelords. He dwells in New York City where he likes to "kick it old-school style" while "laying low" and "keeping it real."

Gretchen VanEsselstyn has worked for Kaplan for 11 years. During that time, she has written books, course materials, and software for nearly every exam. As Director of Distance Education, she established Kaplan's highly successful online learning division. A graduate of New York University and Teachers College, Columbia University, Gretchen lives in Brooklyn, New York. She is also a fiction writer, a food writer, and a professional chef. Gretchen VanEsselstyn doesn't like "funny bios."

The Perfect Score

SHOOTING FOR 1600

If you've bought this book, you must think you've got the right stuff to kick proverbial butt on the SAT. Kudos to you! Confidence and ambition are invaluable to upper echelon SAT performance.

But it doesn't stop there. It takes the right mix of determination, preparation, and moxie to launch you into the SAT stratosphere.

That's where we come in. Over the years, we've taught hundreds of students like you. And we realize that most SAT books aren't really written with high scorers like you in mind. Rather than the standard review of concepts you've already mastered mixed with strategies for questions you can knock off in seconds, this book targets the tricky concepts and tough questions that stand between the good score you know you can get and the great score you're shooting for. We'll move fast and push you hard to raise your score as high as it can go.

But what is it with this quest for a perfect score? No college requires a perfect score on the SAT. Getting a perfect score on the SAT won't guarantee success in all your future endeavors. It probably won't make you the center of attention at parties. And if you've ever had an unrequited crush, it most likely won't make that past or present object of your affections realize what a fool he or she has been. The only thing a perfect score—or even a very high score—will get you is a good chance to get into the school of your dreams. And that's no small thing. We understand your quest for perfection. We salute your desire to shoot for the moon. We find your goal to be perfectly laudable, and we think we have written the perfect book for you.

HOW TO USE THIS BOOK

We should warn you up front: This book is not for the faint of heart. It is comprised exclusively of the toughest material you're likely to see on the SAT and the strategies designed for cracking the tough stuff. Unlike some of the other SAT test prep books we publish, we don't review every single math concept that could appear or the SAT or provide you with lengthy study lists of SAT vocabulary and word roots. If you want a more fundamental introduction to the SAT and practice with questions ranging from easy to difficult, we recommend that you work your way through some of our more traditional test-prep materials, such as *SAT 2004 Spring Edition* (with or without CD-ROM), *SAT Math Workbook*, *SAT Verbal Workbook*, *SAT Math Mania*, or *SAT Vocab Velocity*. If you find any deficiencies in your SAT knowledge base as you go through this book, you should get your hands on one or more of these books.

Basically, we are assuming that you already have some other SAT test-prep materials in the form of practice tests, either those found in the books we've just mentioned, or those straight from the horse's mouth itself, the College Board's own *10 Real SATs*. This is because the best course of test preparation for a high scorer like yourself involves a combination of taking real or simulated SATs under testlike conditions, which is what the aforementioned books provide, and studying the tips and techniques for acing the hard questions, which is what this book is all about.

This book is divided into six sections. The three verbal sections correspond to the three verbal question types: Critical Reading, Sentence Completion, and Analogies. The three math sections use a different structure. The first math section, "SAT 1600 Math—The Basics," introduces you to the tricky nature of difficult math questions on the SAT and reveals all of our favorite strategies for handling the toughest math questions, whatever their format. The next math section deals with the very trickiest "straight math" questions found on the SAT—that is, the really tough questions that are not word problems. The final math section deals with ugly SAT math word problems of every stripe, size, and flavor. Each of the "Strategy" chapters in the book—Chapters Two, Five, Eight, and Eleven—concludes with a recap of all our favorite 1600-level strategies for handling the different SAT question types. Finally, at the end of every section is a practice set of questions that allows you to apply the tips and strategies you've just been studying, along with detailed explanations for every question. Unlike the practice sets found in our other books, these are composed of only the most difficult questions.

You can either work your way through the sections in the order presented, or jump right into the section that gives you the most trouble. You'll notice that the habits and thought processes of top test takers are highlighted throughout the book, as are our favorite strategy tips. Study these thoroughly, and strive to make these effective techniques your own. No matter what you do, try not to overload. Remember that this is dense, complicated material and not representative of the range of difficulty you'll see on test day. One thing is for sure, if you can ace this stuff, the real thing will be a breeze.

Have fun, and good luck!

A New SAT in 2005

The SAT is getting a major overhaul. A new version of the SAT will replace the current test beginning in March 2005. The changes are designed to align the test more closely to high school curricula and college skills, thus making the test a more accurate predictor of college performance. There will be changes not only in the content tested but also in the types of questions used. Here are the most important changes.

The New Writing Section

The biggest change in the SAT will be the addition of a writing test. The SAT Writing Section will include multiple choice questions and a written essay. The multiple choice questions will test the students ability to identify sentence errors and to make improvements in sentences and paragraphs. The essay section will assess the student's writing ability. Plans call for the student to be asked to write a persuasive essay taking a position on a particular issue given them in the test and support their position with reasons and evidence. The Writing section of the SAT will be 50 minutes in length.

Changes to the Verbal Section

First, the Verbal section is getting a new name to reflect its new focus: Critical Reading. The Analogies questions, which required test takers to understand the meanings of specific words and analyze the relationship between them (see chapter 5 for examples) are being dropped. In their place there will be short reading passages added with one or two multiple-choice questions after each passage. The new Critical Reading section will be 70 minutes instead of the 75 minutes currently allocated for the Verbal section.

Changes to the Math Section

Some questions of greater difficulty will be added to the SAT Mathematical section; these will cover the topics usually taught in algebra II in U.S. high schools. In addition, the Quantitative Comparison questions, which require a comparison of a quantity in column A to a quantity in column B to determine which is larger, are being eliminated entirely (see chapter 12 for examples). They will be replaced by additional regular multiple-choice questions and Grid-in questions. The Math section in the new SAT will be 70 minutes—five minutes shorter than it currently is.

Scoring the New Test

The new writing test will be scored on a scale 200-800, the same scale currently used for the Mathematical and Verbal sections of the SAT. The composite scores on the new test will be between 600-2400, instead of the 400-1600 now used.

SAT Changes in a Nutshell

	Current SAT	Changes for New SAT
Verbal	Critical Reading (long passages), Sentence Completion, Analogies	Analogies eliminated, Short Critical Reading passages added
Math	5-Answer Multiple Choice, Quantitative Comparisons, Grid-Ins	Quantitative Comparisons eliminated, Advanced Algebra added
Writing	Does not exist	Multiple-Choice Grammar, 20–25 minute essay
Time	3 hours	Now 3 hours and 35 minutes
Scoring	Math: 200-800 Verbal 200-800	Math: 200-800 Critical Reading 200-800 Writing: 200-800

Frequently Asked Questions

Which test should I take?

Students in the class entering college in 2005 will take the current SAT, and students in the class of 2007 will take the new test. However, if you are in the class of 2006, most colleges plan to accept the higher of the scores from the current SAT and the new SAT. Check with the colleges you are considering to find out about their policies. Kaplan recommends that students in the class of 2006 take both tests.

Will the new test be harder?

Yes, most students will find the new test to be harder. The new writing section will test students' knowledge of grammar and require them to write an essay in 20–25 minutes. The new SAT math section will include more advanced algebra. The test itself will be longer and require more stamina. However, keep in mind that your score is based on how well you did compared with other students. Therefore, even though it's harder, your score on the new SAT may be better than your score on the current test.

How will the essays on the new SAT be graded?

Essay graders hired by the test makers will assign a score of 1 to 6 to each essay based on a rubric, or scoring, scale. Each essay will be graded by two readers. If the essay readers' scores differ by more than two points, the essay will be graded by a third reader, and all the readers' scores will be averaged together.

Will many colleges still require the SAT II: Writing test?

No. Since writing will be tested on the new SAT, there is no reason for colleges to require the SAT II: Writing test. In fact, the College Board has announced plans to discontinue this test.

For More Information

The latest information about the new SAT is available at kaptest.com/newsat.

section one

CRITICAL READING

CHAPTER ONE

The Critical Reading Challenge

- Learn Kaplan's Five-Step Method for Critical Reading
- Practice the five Kaplan Reading Principles for working with Critical Reading passages.
- Get to know the Critical Reading question types.

If you're already a top scorer, you may find Critical Reading easy, like browsing through an article in your favorite magazine, and then having a pleasant chat about its contents with one of your more intellectual friends. Right. Most SAT takers, even high scorers, have trouble with Critical Reading. The passages are usually very dull, and the questions are either impossibly broad or way too picky.

As with all the other SAT question types, practice helps. Reading lots of dull books in your spare time may help you to get prepped for those zone-out passages. However, there's something much more helpful that you can do right now if you want to improve your Critical Reading performance. Let's say that again, in bold this time, in case you missed it.

One Thing You Can Do to Improve in SAT Critical Reading:

Learn how to spend less time reading the passage and more time researching the questions and attacking the answer choices.

> A 1600 test taker manages time wisely, especially when tackling tough passages.

Time management is a critical issue in SAT Critical Reading. Most students spend far too much time reading the passage, and not enough time researching the passage for the answers to specific questions, attacking the answer choices, and choosing the best response. To help you manage your time more efficiently, Kaplan has developed the following approach.

ATTACKING SAT CRITICAL READING STRATEGICALLY

Step 1: When you first encounter the passage, read enough of it to figure out the author's "Big Idea" and get a general sense of how the passage is organized.

Step 2: Read the question; if a question seems hard, go back to it after you've answered the other questions in the set.

Step 3: As necessary, go back into the passage to locate the answer to a specific question.

Step 4: Put the answer in your own words.

Step 5: Attack the answer choices, and choose the one that comes closest to the answer you found.

This is the approach that you should internalize as you work through the Critical Reading passages in this book. We'll talk more about how to work with the passage and questions in the following sections, but this process should stay with you, no matter what.

WORKING WITH THE PASSAGE: STEP 1

Step 1: When you first encounter the passage, read enough of it to figure out the author's "Big Idea" and get a general sense of how the passage is organized.

How you approach reading the passage may vary depending on how difficult the passage is and whether you are running into time trouble. For instance, when you're not running into time trouble and the passage itself doesn't present serious obstacles, you'll want to read the entire passage. Here are some reading principles that will allow you to do so with maximum efficiency.

A 1600 test taker follows the Kaplan Reading Principles in order to focus and save time.

Principle 1: Focus on the author.

Principle 2: Don't sweat the details.

Principle 3: Read the first third closely.

Principle 4: Note paragraph topics and make a roadmap.

Principle 5: Stop to sum up.

Let's try this on the following passage.

The following passage is excerpted from the catalog of a museum exhibition on arms and armor. The passage provides examples of the connections between art and weaponry throughout the ages.

From the beginning, arms and art were essential and interrelated elements in the life of mankind. Weapons for the hunt were necessary tools in the daily struggle for survival. Art, meanwhile, seems to have begun primarily as hunting magic. By painting images of game animals on cave walls and carving them on spear-throwers and arrow straighteners, hunters attempted to use supernatural means to secure an abundant supply of meat and hides for food and clothing.

Because arms were literally a matter of life and death, either as weapons designed to kill or as armor designed to protect, it was crucial that they be constructed for maximum effect and with the greatest technical efficiency; in many cases, this process also resulted in functional beauty. To further enhance the aesthetic and ideological values of arms—and to increase their cachet as status symbols—arms of all periods were embellished with a wide range of designs in every technique known to the decorative arts.

In classical antiquity, too, there was a close relationship between art and arms. The patron deity of the arts in ancient Greece, for instance, was Pallas Athena, who was represented as helmeted, armored, and carrying a shield and a spear. Significantly, there was also one among the Olympian gods who worked with his hands at a human craft, the divine smith Hephaestos—known as Vulcan to the Romans—who not only created dazzling jewelry for the goddesses but also manufactured impenetrable and splendidly decorated armor for the god of war Ares, or Mars, as well as for the mortal hero Achilles.

Evidence of the artistry brought to weapons in ancient times is abundant. In *The Iliad*, Homer describes the shield of Achilles as a mirror of the world "in imperishable bronze, some tin, and precious gold and silver." When Mycenae was excavated in 1875 by Heinrich Schliemann, he found swords and daggers decorated with superb multicolored inlays in the technique vividly described by Homer. They were of such artistic finesse that they would have met with the approval even of Hephaestos.

Under the influence of Christianity, the idea of the divine craftsman was transformed into a human figure: the legendary Wayland the Smith. Wayland worked in gold as well as in steel, fashioning jewels so temptingly beautiful as to sway the virtue of princesses, and forging sword blades painstakingly wrought from interwoven strands of iron and steel. The craft of the smith was believed to hold a powerful magic, and the prestige of even the greatest of Celtic or Germanic heroes was enhanced if they were apprenticed to smiths.

For centuries, master craftsmen remained nameless, but when awakening artistic self-esteem in the Renaissance let artists step out of the shadows of anonymity, the greatest names, such as Leonardo da Vinci, Hans Holbein, Albrecht Durer, and Benvenuto Cellini, were found quite matter-of-factly among those of designers and manufacturers of arms.

Principle 1: Focus on the Author

SAT Critical Reading tests your understanding of what the author is thinking and doing. Therefore, your focus as you read must always be on the author. The test writers may want you to draw conclusions about *why* the passage is organized the way it is and *what* the author's purpose is in writing it.

> ***Inside your brain***
>
> "Okay, this passage doesn't seem so bad. It appears to be about the relationship between art and weaponry in human history. In fact, the italicized information tells me that much and also tells me that the passage was written for an art catalog. The author's tone is descriptive and neutral."

This is a good way to begin. Get the gist of the author's tone and his or her purpose in writing the passage.

Principle 2: Don't Sweat the Details

Details are in the passage only to illustrate what the author is thinking or doing. Therefore, read over details quickly. Trying to comprehend all of the content is a waste of time. Always boil down the passage to its basics.

> ***Inside your brain***
>
> "'. . . Pallas Athena, who was represented as . . . In *The Iliad*, Homer describes . . .When Mycenae was excavated . . .' These are details. I don't need to memorize them. They might ask me questions about them later but that's okay, because I can always go back to the passage."

It's okay to recognize details. Just don't obsess over them.

Principle 3: Read the First Third Closely

You should read the first third more closely than the rest of the passage. Why? Because the passage's topic is revealed here, and—quite often—so is the author's purpose, as well as his or her attitude towards the subject. This is what you want to know to get a sense of the "Big Picture."

> ***Inside your brain***
>
> "Since the beginning of mankind, art and weaponry have been very closely allied human activities. The very first sentence here gives me the big idea of the whole passage. The rest of this paragraph applies this big idea to prehistoric man. The second discusses how a wide range of decorative arts were used in each period and how art could even make weaponry a status symbol."

Good. Recognizing the topic and supporting details is key to understanding the passage.

Principle 4: Note Paragraph Topics and Make a Roadmap

Paragraphs are the fundamental building blocks of a passage. Therefore, as you read, you should take note of paragraph topics and make a mental roadmap. Ask yourself: "What's the point of this paragraph? How does it fit into the overall structure of the passage?"

Inside your brain

"The first paragraph discusses art and weaponry in the stone age, and subsequent paragraphs carry this discussion up through the Renaissance (¶1: the stone age, ¶2: background, general about each period, ¶¶3 and 4: classical antiquity, ¶5: early Christianity, and ¶6: the Renaissance)."

Principle 5: Stop to Sum Up

After you've read through the passage, take a moment to think about how the passage was put together. Sum up the main idea of the passage in your own words.

Inside your brain

"The passage was amazingly straightforward. It's about the close relationship between art and weaponry throughout history. It carries this discussion up through the Renaissance."

That's a clear, concise summary of the passage.

All the work that you've done to read and understand the passage in Step 1 will serve you well as you move on to Step 2: Attacking the Questions.

WORKING WITH THE QUESTIONS: STEP 2

As soon as you've read through the passage, you're ready to focus on the questions. Understanding the different types of Critical Reading questions can help you cut down on the amount of time you spend answering them. Each type of question calls for a slightly different plan of attack. Let's take a look at the different types of Critical Reading questions.

"Big Picture" Questions

Big picture questions relate to the passage as a whole. They may ask about the main idea or primary purpose of the passage. You should be able to answer these questions based on your initial reading of the passage.

Correct answers to Critical Reading questions tend to be fairly inconspicuous, whereas incorrect answers always contain some sort of wording that makes them definitely wrong. Therefore, the process of elimination is essential on this question type.

What does this mean to me?

You should concentrate your efforts on *attacking* and *eliminating* wrong answer choices. Common wrong answer choices to big picture questions include those that do the following:

- Don't relate to the main idea of the passage
- Contradict the passage
- Are too specific (deal with just one part of the passage)
- Are too general (go beyond the scope of the passage)
- Are too extreme

A 1600 test taker has the Big Picture—the author's main idea and purpose—in mind before attacking the questions.

Keeping this in mind, give this big picture question a try.

The following passage is excerpted from the catalog of a museum exhibition on arms and armor. The passage provides examples of the connections between art and weaponry throughout the ages.

From the beginning, arms and art were essential and interrelated elements in the life of mankind. Weapons for the hunt were necessary tools in the daily struggle for survival. Art, meanwhile, seems to have begun primarily as hunting magic. By painting images of game animals on cave walls and carving them on spear-throwers and arrow straighteners, hunters attempted to use supernatural means to secure an abundant supply of meat and hides for food and clothing.

Since arms were literally a matter of life and death, either as weapons designed to kill or as armor designed to protect, it was crucial that they be constructed for maximum effect and with the greatest technical efficiency; in many cases this process also resulted in functional beauty. To further enhance the aesthetic and ideological values of arms—and to increase their cachet as status symbols—arms of all periods were embellished with a wide range of designs in every technique known to the decorative arts.

In classical antiquity, too, there was a close relationship between art and arms. The patron deity of the arts in ancient Greece, for instance, was Pallas Athena, who was represented as helmeted, armored, and carrying a shield and a spear. Significantly, there was also one among the Olympian gods who worked with his hands at a human craft, the divine smith Hephaestos—known as Vulcan to the Romans—who not only created dazzling jewelry for the goddesses but also manufactured impenetrable and splendidly decorated armor for the god of war Ares, or Mars, as well as for the mortal hero Achilles.

Evidence of the artistry brought to weapons in ancient times is abundant. In *The Iliad*, Homer describes the shield of Achilles as a mirror of the world "in imperishable bronze, some tin, and precious gold and silver." When Mycenae was excavated in 1875 by Heinrich Schliemann, he found swords and daggers decorated with superb multicolored inlays in the technique vividly described by Homer. They were of such artistic finesse that they would have met with the approval even of Hephaestos.

Under the influence of Christianity, the idea of the divine craftsman was transformed into a human figure: the legendary Wayland the

Smith. Wayland worked in gold as well as in steel, fashioning jewels so temptingly beautiful as to sway the virtue of princesses, and forging sword blades painstakingly wrought from interwoven strands of iron and steel. The craft of the smith was believed to hold a powerful magic, and the prestige of even the greatest of Celtic or Germanic heroes was enhanced if they were apprenticed to smiths.

For centuries master craftsmen remained nameless, but when awakening artistic self-esteem in the Renaissance let artists step out of the shadows of anonymity, the greatest names, such as Leonardo da Vinci, Hans Holbein, Albrecht Durer, and Benvenuto Cellini, were found quite matter-of-factly among those of designers and manufacturers of arms.

1. The central purpose of the passage is to

    (A) compare the relative importance of art and of arms-making in various eras

    (B) describe the high level of artistry brought to arms-making throughout history

    (C) show how the influence of Christianity affected the practice of arms-making

    (D) analyze the interplay between Renaissance ideals of beauty and function in the design of arms

    (E) trace the artistic growth of arms-making artisans throughout human history

This is a classic big picture question stem, one that you'll see often on the SAT. The answer should be summed up by the purpose and main idea of the passage.

(B) gives the most accurate paraphrase of the passage. **(A)** is wrong because the passage never says or implies that art and arms-making were more or less important in one era than in another. **(C)** is too narrow; the influence of Christianity is mentioned as one chapter in a lengthy history. **(D)** is also too specific; the Renaissance is only mentioned in the final paragraph. **(E)** is off because the passage is about the relationship between arms-making and artistry, not the "artistic growth" of arms-making artisans.

STRATEGY HIGHLIGHT

To answer this Big Picture question, we relied on our paraphrase of the passage's topic and scope. You may have also eliminated choices that were too specific or outside the scope of the passage.

Detail Questions

Detail questions ask about a specific part of the passage. On these questions, you may have to go back into the passage to research the answer.

The key is to know where to look for the answer. Also, note that common wrong answer choices to detail questions include those that:

- Refer to the wrong part of the passage—in other words, they don't answer the question being asked
- Use similar wording to the passage but distort what was said
- Contradict the passage
- Go outside the scope of the passage, stating things that aren't said
- Use extreme wording

STRATEGY TIP

The correct answers to detail questions will almost always be paraphrases of information found in the passage.

Line Reference Questions

> **STRATEGY TIP**
>
> Reading just the sentence that contains the line reference may not be sufficient; you may have to read a few lines before and after the reference to get a sense of the context.

Sometimes the test maker is kind enough to tell you exactly where to look in the passage to research the answer. Because you are told exactly where to go in the passage, go ahead and reread the sentence containing the line reference. Try to formulate your own answer to the question before looking at the answer choices.

Take a look at the following question. Refer to the passage as necessary to find the answer.

2. It is most likely that the author mentions Pallas Athena (line 18) and Hephaestos (line 21) in order to demonstrate

   (A) the close association between the tools of war and the arts

   (B) the difference between human and divine arts

   (C) the classical ideals of beauty and craftsmanship

   (D) the notion of artists as divinely inspired

   (E) the technical advances in the artistry of weapon-making

This detail question gives us a line reference, so to answer the question, we can go directly to the cited lines. Rereading the sentence before the referenced line will point to the best answer. "In classical antiquity, too, there was a close relationship between art and arms" (lines 16–17). Athena and Hephaestos are then used as examples of the connection between weaponry and the arts, so **(A)** is the correct answer.

> **STRATEGY HIGHLIGHT**
>
> We were able to paraphrase the cited lines, which helped us identify the correct choice. We also used elimination strategies to get rid of choices that contradicted or went beyond the scope of the passage.

Choice **(B)** isn't right because the paragraph isn't about divine arts. You can eliminate **(C)** because not enough description of Athena's weaponry is provided to qualify as a demonstration of the classical ideals of beauty and craftsmanship. **(D)** is out because the examples have nothing to do with artists being inspired. Finally, **(E)** is completely off base, as the paragraph in question has nothing to do with "technical advances."

Inference Questions

Inference questions can deal with either the big picture or details in the passage, but because of the way they are worded, they present a unique challenge for test takers. This is because inference questions require you to conclude something that is not explicitly stated in the passage. To some extent, they require you to "read between the lines."

> A 1600 test taker draws reasonable inferences that are within the scope of the passage.

We'll talk more about inference questions in a later section, but let's try one that fits with this passage.

3. In lines 12–15, the author implies that arms were decorated as a way of

    (A) lending legitimacy to the causes for which wars were fought
    (B) distinguishing them from purely ceremonial objects
    (C) enhancing their effectiveness in battle
    (D) identifying strategic military alliances
    (E) suggesting the importance of those who possessed them

The word *implies* in the question stem signals that this is an inference question, and you may need to think outside the passage a bit in order to find the answer.

This question asks you to make an inference from information in the passage: Why were arms decorated in ancient times? Lines 12–15 give several reasons: it enhanced their aesthetic and ideological value and made them more valuable as status symbols. (**E**) captures the second of these ideas—decorating arms helped suggest the status or importance of the arms-bearer.

(**A**) is too broad: Arms decorating couldn't really make a war seem more legitimate. (**B**) distorts the passage: Distinguishing arms from purely ceremonial objects (vases, statues, etc.) doesn't seem to have been a problem. (**C**) is simply not mentioned, nor is (**D**).

STRATEGY HIGHLIGHT

For some inference questions, you'll need to draw conclusions based on information in the passage. But here we were once again able to answer the question by paraphrasing what we found in the passage.

Vocabulary-in-Context Questions

Vocabulary-in-context questions ask you about the usage of a single word. You won't need to define the word, but you'll need to glean the meaning of the word from context.

Here's our recommended method for handling vocabulary-in-context questions:

Step 1: Read the sentence through looking for clues.

Step 2: Predict a word that could replace the vocabulary word.

Step 3: Check the answer choices for a word that matches.

Step 4: Plug your selection into the sentence to make sure it makes sense.

4. In line 6, *secure* most nearly means

    (A) create
    (B) make safe
    (C) obtain
    (D) guard
    (E) attach

STRATEGY HIGHLIGHT

We used the Sentence Completion strategy of predicting a replacement for the word in question to get this one right.

This is a straightforward vocabulary-in-context question, so the first thing to do is go back to the passage and do a little research. According to lines 6–7, "Hunters attempted to use supernatural means to *secure* an abundant supply of meat and hides for food and clothing." In other words, they were trying to *obtain* a supply.

It doesn't make sense that they would **(A)** *create* a supply of animals. **(B)** and **(D)** don't work because the sentence is not about *making safe* or *guarding* the supply—it's about getting it in the first place. Finally, **(E)** makes no sense; why would anyone *attach* a supply of animals?

A 1600 test taker predicts the answer before checking out the answer choices to nail vocabulary-in-context questions.

Now that you've got the overview, let's go on to some hard—really hard—passages and look at what makes them hard. In the next chapter, we'll examine the different passage types and give you strategies to crack the toughest ones.

CHAPTER TWO

Strategies for Tough Critical Reading

- Find out what makes hard Critical Reading passages hard and how to handle them.
- Get to know the four Critical Reading passage types.
- Tackle extra-hard Science and Narrative passages.
- Learn the secrets of Paired passages.

WHAT MAKE HARD CRITICAL READING PASSAGES HARD

Some Critical Reading passages are born bad. The vocabulary is grueling, the sentence structure is torturous, and the tone, scope, and focus are nowhere to be found. In fact, you're not even sure that it's in English.

Give up? Not if you want that 1600 you don't. In this section, we'll talk about how to deal with tough passages of all kinds. We'll also review certain passage types that many test takers find difficult and give you special strategies to help you tackle them.

The Passage Types

As you may already know, SAT Critical Reading Passages come in four flavors: Humanities, Social Science, Science, and Narrative. Usually Humanities and Social Science passages are manageable, though you'll find some extra-tough ones in the Practice chapter at the end of this section. The passage types that tend to strike the most fear into the hearts of high school students everywhere are the latter two, the tag team of Science and Narrative. Most students dread one or the other. To apply some gross stereotypes, Physics Club members usually eat Science passages for breakfast, but a few dense fiction paragraphs will send them running for the solace of their bug collections. English major types will incisively pick through the most complex Narrative passages with a quick glance, but the merest hint of a chemistry symbol may induce sweating, gasping, and a tendency to quote soliloquies from *Hamlet.*

Nonetheless, the same approach can help you with any type of hard passage, and we'll talk you through it step by step. We'll then tackle a hard Science and a hard Narrative passage together. Finally, we'll confront one other passage type that tends to send test takers into a panic: the Paired passages.

ATTACKING HARD PASSAGES: THE APPROACH

As we noted in the last chapter, if you're not running low on time, and if the passage itself is not overly difficult, you'll want to read the entire passage. But if you are running into time trouble, or if the passage is extraordinarily dense and hard to get through, you'll want to try a different approach.

When the going gets tough, here's what we recommend: Read the first third of the passage carefully, then read the first sentence of each subsequent paragraph and the last sentence of the passage. As with all passages, focus on the Big Picture, not the details. Apply the following reading principles:

- Read with the author in mind: Ask yourself, "What is the author trying to convey? Why is the passage structured as it is?"
- Even in the first third that you will be reading in its entirety, focus on the big idea(s), not the supporting details.

> 1600 test takers read hard passages selectively, focusing on topic sentences and the sections that provide the most relevant information.

If you're still unsure about the main idea of the passage from the first third of the passage, pay especially close attention to the last sentence of the passage; this is where many authors tie together the loose ends and clarify the main idea of the passage.

Science Passages

Let's try this approach on a tough Science passage.

The following passage was excerpted from a geology text book.

The basic theory of plate tectonics recognizes two ways in which continental margins can grow seaward. Where two plates move away from a midocean rift that separates them, the continental margins on those plates are said to be passive. Such continental margins grow slowly from the accumulation of riverborne sediments and from the carbonate skeletons of marine organisms. Since most sequences of such accretions, or miogeoclinal deposits, are undeformed, passive margins are not associated with mountain building.

Along active margins continents tend to grow much faster. At an active margin an oceanic plate plunges under a continental plate, fragments of which then adhere to the continental margin. The process is met with extensive volcanism and mountain-building. A classic example is the Andes of the west coast of South America.

In the original plate-tectonic model western North America was described as being initially passive and then active. It was assumed that the continent grew to a limited extent along this margin as oceanic rocks accreted in places such as the Coast Ranges of California. The model was successful in explaining such disparate features as the Franciscan rocks of the California Coast Ranges, created by subduction, and the granite rocks of the Sierra Nevada that originated in volcanoes.

The basic plate-tectonic reconstruction of the geologic history of western North America remains unchanged in the light of microplate tectonics, but the details are radically changed. It is now clear that much more crust was added to North America in the Mesozoic era than can be accounted for by volcanism and by the simple accretion of sediments. Further, some adjacent terranes are not genetically related, as would be expected from simple plate tectonics, but have almost certainly traveled great distances from entirely different parts of the world.

What makes this passage hard? A quick glance will show you that it's an esoteric, difficult topic with its own unique lingo and a mass of technical details. Now's the time for all you science-phobes to take a deep breath. Hang on, and we'll talk you through it.

A 1600 test taker approaches science passages with a clear head and isn't phased by technical vocabulary.

The first third

This passage has four paragraphs, so let's read the first two carefully. In Paragraph 1, the first line gives us the topic: the basic theory of plate tectonics. This theory, we're told "recognizes two ways in which continental margins can grow seaward." The phrase *two ways* is key here; it tells us that we should be looking out for a comparison or contrast. The paragraph goes on to describe one of the two ways, a mechanism known as passive margins. There are many details about passive margins, but we can let those pass for now and move on.

In Paragraph 2, the author describes the other way that continental margins can grow, and that's along active margins. We're told what actually happens at active margins, the results of such activity (volcanoes and mountains), and an example of these results (the Andes). Take in what you can, but don't obsess over the details.

The first sentence of each subsequent paragraph

The beginning of Paragraph 3 talks about " the original model," which is a clue that we'll probably get information about some kind of new model. In this sentence, we find that western North America was seen as first passive, then active. We can move on to the next paragraph with confidence, assuming that the rest of Paragraph 3 consists of details to support the first sentence.

Paragraph 4 begins with more information about the plate-tectonic model of western North America. Here we're told that the basic reconstruction of geologic history remains the same, but the details are radically different, in the light of something called "microplate tectonics."

The last sentence of the passage

In this case, the last sentence gives further detail about the plate-tectonics of western North America. From this detail, we get the gist that information about "microplate tectonics" is undermining the credibility of the basic theory of plate tectonics. Did you miss this? The sentence explains that adjacent terranes (whatever they are) aren't genetically related as would be expected from simple plate tectonics.

Often an author will conclude a passage with a rousing send-off summary, which can be very useful when you attack the questions. Even when the final sentence isn't so blatantly helpful, you can usually get some good information.

What have we got?

The author's purpose is to describe the basic theory of plate tectonics. Passive and active margins are discussed. Microplate tectonics are introduced, and it seems that the basic theory of plate tectonics falls short of explaining all the phenomena of growing continental margins.

Not so bad, considering that we didn't even read the whole passage. Let's try some questions.

The following passage was excerpted from a geology text book.

The basic theory of plate tectonics recognizes two ways in which continental margins can grow seaward. Where two plates move away from a midocean rift that separates them, the continental margins on those plates are said to be passive. Such continental margins grow slowly from the accumulation of riverborne sediments and from the carbonate skeletons of marine organisms. Since most sequences of such accretions, or miogeoclinal deposits, are undeformed, passive margins are not associated with mountain building.

Along active margins continents tend to grow much faster. At an active margin an oceanic plate plunges under a continental plate, fragments of which then adhere to the continental margin. The process is met with extensive volcanism and mountain-building. A classic example is the Andes of the west coast of South America.

In the original plate-tectonic model western North America was described as being initially passive and then active. It was assumed that the continent grew to a limited extent along this margin as oceanic rocks accreted in places such as the Coast Ranges of California. The model was successful in explaining such disparate features as the Franciscan rocks of the California Coast Ranges, created by subduction, and the granite rocks of the Sierra Nevada that originated in volcanoes.

The basic plate-tectonic reconstruction of the geologic history of western North America remains unchanged in the light of microplate tectonics, but the details are radically changed. It is now clear that much more crust was added to North America in the Mesozoic era than can be accounted for by volcanism and by the simple accretion of sediments. Further, some adjacent terranes are not genetically related, as would be expected from simple plate tectonics, but have almost certainly traveled great distances from entirely different parts of the world.

1. Which one of the following best expresses the main idea of the passage?
   (A) The margin of the west coast of North America developed through a combination of active and passive mechanisms.
   (B) The growth of continental margins is only partially explained by the basic theory of plate tectonics.
   (C) Continental margins can grow seaward in two ways: sedimentation or volcanism.
   (D) The introduction of microplate tectonics poses a fundamental challenge to the existing theory of how continental margins are formed.
   (E) Continental margins grow more rapidly along active margins than along passive margins.

Here's a classic big picture question. In our quick summary, we said that, whereas the basic theory of plate tectonics explains much about the growth of continental margins, the fourth paragraph suggests that it cannot fully explain certain geologic details. Choice **(B)** best captures this idea, and it's correct.

Choices **(A)** and **(E)** both represent true statements, but they're details from the passage, not the passage's main idea. Choice **(C)** distorts the notion of the two ways that continental margins can grow. We don't know that sedimentation and volcanism are the two ways, and even if we did, this is too specific to be the main point of the passage.

Choice **(D)** is incorrect because it's too extreme. The first sentence of paragraph 4 states that the basic plate tectonic theory remains unchanged in the light of microplate tectonics; it's the details that are radically changed, not the basic theory.

2. The author mentions the Franciscan rocks of the California Coast Ranges in order to make which of the following points?
   (A) The basic theory of plate tectonics accounts for a wide variety of geologic features.
   (B) The original plate tectonic model falls short of explaining such features.
   (C) Subduction processes are responsible for the majority of the geologic features found along the west coast of North America.
   (D) Passive margins can take on many geologic forms.
   (E) The concept of microplate tectonics was first introduced to account for such phenomena.

In our quick reading of the passage, we missed this detail about the Franciscan rocks. No matter; we can simply scan the passage for the detail, then read the lines around it to get the answer. Scan for the phrase *Franciscan rocks*. You'll find it there towards the end of paragraph 3. Read that sentence, and you'll find that the Franciscan rocks are an example of a geologic feature that is successfully explained by the model discussed in the topic sentence of that paragraph, i.e., the original plate-tectonic model. Choice **(A)** is an excellent paraphrase of just what we're looking for.

Choice **(B)** is wrong because it directly contradicts paragraph 3; the problems with the basic plate tectonic model are discussed in paragraph 4, a paragraph in which the California Coast Ranges are never mentioned. **(C)** is a distortion of the facts. We don't know if subduction processes are responsible for the *majority* of the west coast's geologic features. We're told only that they're responsible for some, such as the Coast Ranges. **(D)** is wrong because the Coast Ranges were formed by local subduction processes, according to paragraph 3, not by the actions of passive margins. The concept of microplate tectonics was introduced to account for phenomena that the basic model couldn't explain. But the Coast Ranges are features that the basic model *can* account for, so **(E)** is incorrect.

A 1600 test taker knows that the key to answering most Science passage questions is simply locating the answer in the passage and then finding a paraphrase of that answer among the answer choices.

---

3. Which one of the following does the author mention as evidence for the inadequacy of the original plate tectonic model to describe the formation of continental margins?

   (A) Accreted rock formations have been found along some continental margins where there are granite mountains farther inland.

   (B) Sediments and fragments from the depths of the ocean accumulate along continental margins.

   (C) Large pieces of the Earth's crust that appear to be completely unrelated are found in the same area today.

   (D) Undeformed miogeoclinal deposits are usually not linked to mountain building.

   (E) Oceanic plates drop beneath continental plates along active margins.

To answer this detail question, go straight to the final paragraph. That's where the inadequacy of the plate tectonic model is finally discussed. There we're told that genetically distinct pieces of the Earth's crust are found in the same area, a fact that the original plate tectonic model can't explain. **(C)** gets at this issue.

The original plate tectonic model can account for **(A)**—see the description of the California Coast Ranges in the third paragraph. **(B)**, **(D)**, and **(E)** are true statements—see the first and second paragraphs—but none of these statements has a direct bearing on the issue of the inadequacy of the original plate tectonic model, which is only discussed in the final paragraph.

A 1600 test taker realizes that she doesn't have to completely understand everything in an SAT Science passage in order to answer all the questions correctly.

Narrative Passages

On the SAT, you will encounter at least one Narrative passage. Narratives are like stories. Sometimes they come from memoirs and reminiscences; other times they come from works of fiction. In either case, your goal is to figure out the main point of the story.

Narrative passages can appear either in the paired-passages section or as stand-alone passages in any Critical Reading section.

For those of you who haven't voluntarily read a work of fiction since *Charlotte's Web*, we'll take it nice and slow.

Narrative passages are pretty similar to other passages. You still see big picture, detail, and vocabulary-in-context questions, and you still want to read for structure. There is one important difference, though.

The Big Idea in a Narrative Passage

In Narrative passages, the Big Idea is a little different than in other passages. The test maker wants you to understand *why people do what they do or why people feel a particular way.*

To figure out the author's opinion in a Narrative passage, you may have to read between the lines or draw conclusions from what is not stated. With a Narrative passage you will most likely get several questions that ask you to infer or surmise the characters' opinions or intentions. This is actually easier than it sounds.

> A 1600 test taker reads Narrative passages with an eye toward characters' personalities and motivations.

Reading for inferences—three questions to ask yourself

As you read a narrative passage, you should ask yourself three questions:

Who are the character(s), and how does the author describe them?

- What do the characters want?
- What are the characters doing?
- Can you think of adjectives to describe each character?

What do the characters think of each other or themselves?

- Do they like each other? Hate each other?
- Why does each character make a particular decision or take a particular course of action?
- What do these decisions or actions tell you about a character?

What's the "point" of the story?

- What are the "turning points" in the passage?
- Is there a "moral" to the story?

Keep these questions in mind as you read this semitough Narrative passage.

The following passage, excerpted from a classic Victorian novel first published in 1871, focuses on the reactions by both the groom-to-be and his chief rival to the former's engagement to a young woman.

Mr. Casaubon, as might be expected, spent a great deal of his time at the Grange in these weeks, and the hindrance which courtship occasioned to the progress of his great work—the Key to all Mythologies—naturally made him look forward the more eagerly to the happy termination of courtship. But he had deliberately incurred the hindrance, having made up his mind that it was now time for him to adorn his life with the graces of female companionship, to irradiate the gloom which fatigue was apt to hang over the intervals of studious labor with the play of female fancy, and to secure in this, his culminating age, the solace of female tending for his declining years. Hence he determined to abandon himself to the stream of feeling, and perhaps was surprised to find what an exceedingly shallow rill it was. As in droughty regions baptism by immersion could only be performed symbolically, Mr. Casaubon found that sprinkling was the utmost approach to a plunge which his stream would afford him; and he concluded that the poets had much exaggerated the force of masculine passion. Nevertheless, he observed with pleasure that Miss Brooke showed an ardent submissive affection which promised to fulfill his most agreeable previsions of marriage. It had once or twice crossed his mind that possibly there was some deficiency in Dorothea to account for the moderation of his abandonment; but he was unable to discern the deficiency, or to figure to himself a woman who would have pleased him better; so that there was clearly no reason to fall back upon but the exaggerations of human tradition.

It was wonderful to Sir James Chettam how well he continued to like going to the Grange after he had once encountered the difficulty of seeing Dorothea for the first time in the light of a woman who was engaged to another man. Of course the forked lightning seemed to pass through him when he first approached her, and he remained conscious throughout the interview of hiding uneasiness; but, good as he was, it must be owned that his uneasiness was less than it would have been if he had thought his rival a brilliant and desirable match. He had no sense of being eclipsed by Mr. Casaubon; he was only shocked that Dorothea was under a melancholy illusion, and his mortification lost some of its bitterness by being mingled with compassion.

Nevertheless, while Sir James said to himself that he had completely resigned her, since with the perversity of a Desdemona she had not affected a proposed match that was clearly suitable and according to nature, he could not yet be quite passive under the idea of her engagement to Mr. Casaubon.

Middlemarch: **the recap**

If you're a literature fan, you may have recognized this as a selection from *Middlemarch* by George Eliot. If not, don't worry. As with the other SAT Critical Reading passage types, you don't need any outside knowledge to do well.

We start out with a short italicized blurb, which gives us some good clues about the content of the selection. From the blurb, we know that we'll have three main characters: a young woman, her fiance, and the fiance's rival.

Let's break down the passage in terms of these three main characters and ask the first two of our three Narrative passage questions.

Who are the character(s), and how does the author describe them? What do the characters think of each other or themselves?

Mr. Casaubon: This character is Dorothea's fiance. He has decided to become engaged because he believes that it is the correct time in his life to do so, yet he finds himself lacking in passion. He wonders whether it's Dorothea's fault that he isn't more passionate toward her but concludes that romance is an exaggerated notion.

Dorothea Brooke: We don't know much about her, except with regard to her relationship to the two men. She shows "an ardent submissive affection" to Mr. Casaubon. From Sir James's perspective, she has made a mistake by becoming engaged to Mr. Casaubon, and the match is not suitable.

Sir James Chettam: Sir James believes that Mr. Casaubon is not a worthy rival for Dorothea's affections. He is clearly smitten by Dorothea, and is "not quite passive" about the engagement.

Finally, we can address the third Narrative question:

What's the "point" of the story?

The passage focuses on the different views of the characters toward the recent engagement. We get a great deal of information about Mr. Casaubon's thoughts and feelings, some details on Sir James's feelings, and very little knowledge about Dorothea's perspective on the matter.

The passage paints a picture of a struggle that is about to occur. We aren't told what happens next, but we get a sense of foreboding, based on the feelings of the two rivals.

This passage has a great deal of flowery language and some tough vocabulary, but when you break it down, it has the same plot line that you might find on your favorite soap opera or TV drama. Let's check out the questions.

The following passage, excerpted from a classic Victorian novel first published in 1871, focuses on the reactions by both the groom-to-be and his chief rival to the former's engagement to a young woman.

Mr. Casaubon, as might be expected, spent a great deal of his time at the Grange in these weeks, and the hindrance which courtship occasioned to the progress of his great work—the Key to all Mythologies—naturally made him look forward the more eagerly to the happy termination of courtship. But he had deliberately incurred the hindrance, having made up his mind that it was now time for him to adorn his life with the graces of female companionship, to irradiate the gloom which fatigue was apt to hang over the intervals of studious labor with the play of female fancy, and to secure in this, his culminating age, the solace of female tending for his declining years. Hence he determined to abandon himself to the stream of feeling, and perhaps was surprised to find what an exceedingly shallow rill it was. As in droughty regions baptism by immersion could only be performed symbolically, Mr. Casaubon found that sprinkling was the utmost approach to a plunge which his stream would afford him; and he concluded that the poets had much exaggerated the force of masculine passion. Nevertheless, he observed with pleasure that Miss Brooke showed an ardent submissive affection which promised to fulfill his most agreeable previsions of marriage. It had once or twice crossed his mind that possibly there was some deficiency in Dorothea to account for the moderation of his abandonment; but he was unable to discern the deficiency, or to figure to himself a woman who would have pleased him better; so that there was clearly no reason to fall back upon but the exaggerations of human tradition.

It was wonderful to Sir James Chettam how well he continued to like going to the Grange after he had once encountered the difficulty of seeing Dorothea for the first time in the light of a woman who was engaged to another man. Of course the forked lightning seemed to pass through him when he first approached her, and he remained conscious throughout the interview of hiding uneasiness; but, good as he was, it must be owned that his uneasiness was less than it would have been if he had thought his rival a brilliant and desirable match. He had no sense of being eclipsed by Mr. Casaubon; he was only shocked that Dorothea was under a melancholy illusion, and his mortification lost some of its bitterness by being mingled with compassion.

Nevertheless, while Sir James said to himself that he had completely resigned her, since with the perversity of a Desdemona she had not affected a proposed match that was clearly suitable and according to nature, he could not yet be quite passive under the idea of her engagement to Mr. Casaubon.

1. In line 15, *approach* most nearly means

(A) method
(B) likeness
(C) path
(D) attitude
(E) objective

This is a particularly tough section of the passage, but you just need to decode the language in order to get this vocab-in-context question right. Read the lines surrounding the word *approach* to get the gist of what's going on. In the previous sentences, Mr. Casaubon concludes that his "stream of feeling" is very shallow—basically, he is lacking in passion. Now try your Sentence Completion skills on the next sentence: "sprinkling was the utmost ____ to a plunge which his stream would afford him." A sprinkle is all he can manage with his shallow stream, a poor likeness of a "plunge." **(B)**, *likeness*, is correct. Try substituting the other choices if you like; none makes sense in the context.

2. Mr. Casaubon concludes that his lack of deep feeling for Dorothea derives from

(A) Dorothea's own hidden deficiencies
(B) his advancing age
(C) the gloom and fatigue of studious labor
(D) the distractions of his writing profession
(E) overstated descriptions of romantic passion

Plunging back into Mr. Casaubon's thoughts, we find that he spends quite a bit of energy musing about his lack of passion for Dorothea. We need to forge our way to the very end of the long first paragraph to discern his justification for this lack: "there was clearly no reason to fall back upon but the exaggerations of human tradition." Choice **(E)** paraphrases this nicely, capturing the idea that the fault is not in Mr. Casaubon, but rather in overstated descriptions of what passion should be.

As for the other choices, Mr. Casaubon discusses his thoughts that his lack of passion may be Dorothea's fault, **(A)**, but rejects this theory. **(B)**, **(C)**, and **(D)** are all cited as reasons that Mr. Casaubon should find a wife, but none figure into his lack of passion. Choice **(E)** is correct.

3. According to the passage, which of the following is true about Sir James's reaction to Dorothea's engagement?

    (A) He felt sympathy for Dorothea despite his opposition to her decision.
    (B) He was unhappy but reconciled to the situation.
    (C) He was unsure about the suitability of the proposed union.
    (D) He opposed the engagement but felt daunted by his rival's scholarship.
    (E) His discomfort was lessened after he spoke with Dorothea.

The last two paragraphs deal with Sir James's thoughts about Dorothea's engagement. We learn that Sir James is uneasy, but not as uneasy as he would be if he thought Mr. Casaubon a worthy rival. He's not happy about the engagement, but the end of the second paragraph tells us that he has compassion for her despite his disapproval of the match. This is echoed in choice **(A)**, the correct answer.

We know that Sir James is not reconciled to the situation, **(B)**, and **(C)** isn't strong or descriptive enough of Sir James's feelings. We don't know anything about Sir James' feelings about Mr. Casaubon's scholarship, **(D)**, and there's no mention of his discomfort lessening after speaking with Dorothea, **(E)**.

Paired Passages—The Facts

Paired passages are two passages written by different authors who deal with related issues from different points of view. Your goal in reading these passages is to determine where the authors agree—and where they disagree. We'll take a look at how to do this in a minute.

Paired passages often appear in the 15-minute Verbal section (which is usually either section 6 or 7 of your SAT). However, they occasionally crop up in the earlier verbal sections.

Read the following two passages, and think about how they're similar and how they're different. You should approach them just as you would any other reading passage, with the added component of comparing the two authors as you read.

The following two passages, excerpted from the works of two prominent social observers, were written a little more than one century apart. The first, from Alexis de Tocqueville's Democracy in America, *was first published in 1835, while the second, adapted from Aldous Huxley's* Brave New World Revisited, *was published in 1958.*

Passage 1

When men are no longer united amongst themselves by firm and lasting ties, it is impossible to obtain the cooperation of any great number of them, unless you can persuade every man whose concurrence you require that this private interest obliges him voluntarily to unite his exertions to the exertions of all the rest. This can only be habitually and conveniently effected by means of a newspaper; nothing but a newspaper can drop the same thought into a thousand minds at the same moment. A newspaper is an adviser who does not require to be sought, but who comes of his own accord, and talks to you briefly every day of the common weal, without distracting you from your private affairs.

Newspapers therefore become more necessary in proportion as men become more equal, and individualism more to be feared. To suppose that they only serve to protect freedom would be to diminish their importance: they maintain civilization. I shall not deny that in democratic countries newspapers frequently lead the citizens to launch together in very ill-digested schemes; but if there were no newspapers there would be no common activity. The evil which they produce is therefore much less than that which they cure.

The effect of a newspaper is not only to suggest the same purpose to a great number of persons, but also to furnish means for executing in common the designs which they may have singly conceived. The principal citizens who inhabit an aristocratic country discern each other from afar; and if they wish to unite their forces, they move towards each other, drawing a multitude of men after them. It frequently happens, on the contrary, in democratic countries, that a great number of men who wish or who want to combine cannot accomplish it, because as they are very insignificant and lost amidst the crowd, they cannot see, and know not where to find, one another. A newspaper then takes up the notion or the feeling which had occurred simultaneously, but singly, to each of them. All are then immediately guided towards this beacon; and these wandering minds, which had long sought each other in darkness, at length meet and unite.

Passage 2

The early advocates of universal literacy and a free press envisaged only two possibilities: the propaganda might be true, or it might be false. They did not foresee what in fact has happened, above all in our Western capitalist democracies—the development of a vast mass communications industry, concerned in the main neither with the true nor the false, but with the unreal, the more or less totally irrelevant. In a word, they failed to take into account man's almost infinite appetite for distractions.

In the past people never got a chance of fully satisfying this appetite. They might long for distractions, but the distractions were not provided. For conditions even remotely comparable to those now prevailing we must return to imperial Rome, where the populace was kept in good humor by frequent, gratuitous fights, from recitations of Virgil to all-out boxing, from concerts to military reviews and public executions. But even in Rome there was nothing like the non-stop distractions now provided by newspapers and magazines, by radio, television and the cinema.

Only the vigilant can maintain their liberties, and only those who are constantly and intelligently on the spot can hope to govern themselves effectively by democratic procedures. A society, most of whose members spend a great part of their time, not on the spot, not here and now and in the calculable future, but somewhere else, in the irrelevant other worlds of sport and soap opera, of mythology and metaphysical fantasy, will find it hard to resist the encroachments of these who would manipulate and control it. The dictators of the future will doubtless learn to combine the art and science of manipulation with the non-stop distractions which, in the West, are now threatening to drown in a sea of irrelevance the information and rational argument essential to the maintenance of individual liberty and the survival of democratic institutions.

Passage recap

Whew. That was some dense, tough reading. What did you get out of these passages? The gist of Passage 1 is that newspapers, as a communication device, help to maintain civilization by allowing individuals to work together. Keep in mind that de Tocqueville was writing in 1835, before the dawn of more efficient communication devices.

Huxley, writing more than a hundred years later, is focused on (or perhaps obsessed with) the idea that mass communications are defined by their ability to provide distractions. Huxley is concerned that modern society is in danger of losing individual rights and the power of democracy because of its lack of vigilance against the distractions of various media.

Comparing the two passages, we see that it's not as simple as pro-media versus anti-media. Both writers are concerned with the power of individual rights and the construction and maintenance of viable democratic societies.

Keep this in mind as we look at the questions.

Paired passages: attacking the questions

The questions that accompany paired passages fall into the following categories:

- Questions about Passage 1
- Questions about Passage 2
- Compare and Contrast questions about both passages

Here's our method for attacking paired passages:

Step 1: Read Passage 1 and answer accompanying questions.

Step 2: Read Passage 2 and answer accompanying questions.

Step 3: Answer Compare and Contrast questions.

Try this method as you reread the passages, and then try answering the questions.

> A 1600 test taker first treats Paired passages separately, then compares and contrasts the two passages.

The following two passages, excerpted from the works of two prominent social observers, were written a little more than one century apart. The first, from Alexis de Tocqueville's Democracy in America, was first published in 1835, while the second, adapted from Aldous Huxley's Brave New World Revisited, was published in 1958.

Passage 1

When men are no longer united amongst themselves by firm and lasting ties, it is impossible to obtain the cooperation of any great number of them, unless you can persuade every man whose concurrence you require that this private interest obliges him voluntarily to unite his exertions to the exertions of all the rest. This can only be habitually and conveniently effected by means of a newspaper; nothing but a newspaper can drop the same thought into a thousand minds at the same moment. A newspaper is an adviser who does not require to be sought, but who comes of his own accord, and talks to you briefly every day of the common weal, without distracting you from your private affairs.

Newspapers therefore become more necessary in proportion as men become more equal, and individualism more to be feared. To suppose that they only serve to protect freedom would be to diminish their importance: they maintain civilization. I shall not deny that in democratic countries newspapers frequently lead the citizens to launch together in very ill-digested schemes; but if there were no newspapers there would be no common activity. The evil which they produce is therefore much less than that which they cure.

The effect of a newspaper is not only to suggest the same purpose to a great number of persons, but also to furnish means for executing in common the designs which they may have singly conceived. The principal citizens who inhabit an aristocratic country discern each other from afar; and if they wish to unite their forces, they move towards each other, drawing a multitude of men after them. It frequently happens, on the contrary, in democratic countries, that a great number of men who wish or who want to combine cannot accomplish it, because as they are very insignificant and lost amidst the crowd, they cannot see, and know not where to find, one another. A newspaper then takes up the notion or the feeling which had occurred simultaneously, but singly, to each of them. All are then immediately guided towards this beacon; and these wandering minds, which had long sought each other in darkness, at length meet and unite.

Passage 2

The early advocates of universal literacy and a free press envisaged only two possibilities: the propaganda might be true, or it might be false. They did not foresee what in fact has happened, above all in our Western capitalist democracies—the development of a vast mass communications industry, concerned in the main neither with the true nor the false, but with the unreal, the more or less totally irrelevant. In a word, they failed to take into account man's almost infinite appetite for distractions.

In the past people never got a chance of fully satisfying this appetite. They might long for distractions, but the distractions were not provided. For conditions even remotely comparable to those now prevailing we must return to imperial Rome, where the populace was kept in good humor by frequent, gratuitous fights, from recitations of Virgil to all-out boxing, from concerts to military reviews and public executions. But even in Rome there was nothing like the non-stop distractions now provided by newspapers and magazines, by radio, television and the cinema.

Only the vigilant can maintain their liberties, and only those who are constantly and intelligently on the spot can hope to govern themselves effectively by democratic procedures. A society, most of whose members spend a great part of their time, not on the spot, not here and now and in the calculable future, but somewhere else, in the irrelevant other worlds of sport and soap opera, of mythology and metaphysical fantasy, will find it hard to resist the encroachments of these who would manipulate and control it. The dictators of the future will doubtless learn to combine the art and science of manipulation with the non-stop distractions which, in the West, are now threatening to drown in a sea of irrelevance the information and rational argument essential to the maintenance of individual liberty and the survival of democratic institutions.

1. The author of Passage 1 would most likely agree with all of the following statements EXCEPT

   (A) Newspapers are necessary for the proper functioning of democracy.

   (B) Individualism poses a danger in a democratic society.

   (C) Newspapers can cause the public to act in foolhardy ways.

   (D) Aristocratic nations find it difficult to unite the masses in common activity.

   (E) Newspapers allow like-minded people to seek out and find one another.

This EXCEPT/NOT question allows us to focus on Passage 1. We'll be talking more about this sometimes-tricky question type in the next section, but for now, all you need to know is that you should eliminate choices that agree with the passage.

Choices **(A)**, **(B)**, and **(C)** can all be found in the text of the second paragraph of Passage 1. Each is part of de Tocqueville's argument, so he would certainly agree with these statements. Choice **(E)** is a paraphrase of the author's argument in the third paragraph.

We're left with **(D)**. Because this answer choice discusses aristocratic nations, we should look to see where they are discussed, which is in the second sentence of paragraph 3. There de Tocqueville states that in such countries, principal citizens, i.e., fellow aristocrats, discern each other from afar and draw the multitudes together as they please, which directly contradicts this answer choice. So **(D)** is the correct answer.

2. The author of Passage 2 refers to imperial Rome in order to

   (A) illustrate the types of distractions that enjoy popularity in a nondemocratic society

   (B) suggest that the public distractions of that period pale in comparison to those of today

   (C) cite a source of inspiration for the mass communications industry of the modern era

   (D) note the wide diversity of entertainments that were available to people many centuries ago

   (E) intimate that the public distractions of that era led to the fall of the Roman empire

This question focuses on Passage 2, the Huxley passage, in particular, the second paragraph of this passage. In an attempt to illustrate the number and types of distractions available to modern people, Huxley cites entertainments available in ancient Rome. He then explains that these are barely comparable to "the non-stop distractions now provided…." This is best paraphrased by choice (**B**).

All of the other choices are misrepresentations of the author's intent, as in (**A**) and (**D**), or distortions that go beyond the scope of the argument, as in (**C**) and (**E**).

3. Both authors would most likely agree with which of the following statements?

    (A) Newspapers help people to act together in their common interests.

    (B) The maintenance of democracy requires an informed citizenry.

    (C) Newspapers function most effectively in democratic states.

    (D) A free press guarantees a free and open democracy.

    (E) Newspapers provide a pleasant distraction from private concerns.

This question asks you to test a number of statements against both authors' arguments.

Starting with (**A**), de Tocqueville would certainly agree with this statement, but we can't draw a clear inference on Huxley's views on the subject.

(**B**) is supported by de Tocqueville's entire argument and by the last line of Huxley's passage, so it looks good.

(**C**) isn't supported by either passage, since de Tocqueville doesn't discuss the effectiveness of newspapers in nondemocratic societies, and Huxley doesn't talk in detail about newspapers.

(**D**) is too strong. The word *guarantee* sends the statement beyond the scope of either passage.

(**E**) is a distortion of Huxley's views on distraction, and it's incorrect.

(**B**) is the correct answer.

4. Huxley would most likely respond to the observations made in Passage 1 by pointing out that

    (A) de Tocqueville's faith in newspapers and their usefulness in a democracy was entirely misplaced

    (B) despite de Tocqueville's claims to the contrary, individualism is not more to be feared as men become more equal

    (C) what was useful to the functioning of democracy in de Tocqueville's day no longer applied to Western capitalist democracies

    (D) de Tocqueville could not have predicted that magazines, radio, television, and cinema would come to drown out the useful information provided by newspapers

    (E) de Tocqueville did not live long enough to witness evolution of mass media into its modern form

The first paragraph of Passage 2 almost seems like a response to de Tocqueville's passage. There, Huxley addresses earlier theorists who advocated a free press and states that these thinkers didn't foresee the developments that would accompany the modern mass communications industry. This is best represented in **(E)**, the correct answer. **(A)** is too strong, **(B)** is nowhere discussed in the Huxley passage, and **(C)** is a distortion. So is **(D)**; according to Huxley, newspapers are of a piece with, and just as bad as, magazines, radio, television, and cinema—see lines 50–52.

WHAT MAKES HARD CRITICAL READING QUESTIONS HARD

Hard Critical Reading questions can come in many guises, from inscrutable big picture queries to picayune requests for obscure details. In this section, we'd like to give you some practice with two especially thorny question types: EXCEPT/NOT and inference.

Attacking EXCEPT/NOT Questions

Yes, you saw one of these tricky questions in the paired passage section. EXCEPT and NOT questions are considered among the toughest of all SAT Critical Reading questions. This is because these questions require you to go to the answer choices and find information in the passage that will verify all of the answer choices EXCEPT the correct answer—that is, the one answer that's NOT true. In other words, you're looking for the one answer that's wrong.

Because these questions are so tricky and confusing, the test maker is obliged to tip you off by putting EXCEPT or NOT in caps. Watch out for these words, and you'll avoid careless errors.

Try this example.

In the following, a social scientist reflects on the disparate cultural influences on the Gullah, an island-dwelling people.

Before the recent encroachments of tourism and commercialization, the culture of the Gullah communities on the Sea Islands off the southeast coast of the U.S. retained a unique identity derived partially from the Islands' history as an area reserved for freed slaves after the Civil War. As an almost exclusively black community, the Gullah preserved African traditions concerning family structure and religious practices. At the same time, as a community of ex-slaves, the residents retained several facets of the Southern life they had left behind. This mixture provided a heritage which until recently was strong enough to sustain a vital culture.

As Patricia Jones-Jackson has pointed out, the basic unit of social life on the Sea Islands, as in West Africa, is the extended family. Since many islands are sectioned off into family communities, kinship ties are important to one's acceptance into the social structure. Membership in the extended family also affects property rights. In the traditional Gullah system, family members do not normally buy land from one another, but acquire it by an unwritten contract known as "heir's land." Rules pertaining to marriage seem to be at least as broad in scope. Common-law marriages are considered as legitimate as marriages recorded by contract under law. Indeed, the infrequent occurrence of divorce and separation within the Sea Island communities demonstrates the strong cohesion of Gullah marital and familial institutions.

Unlike the laws and customs relating to family structure, the religious practices of the Sea Islanders, on the surface at least, bespeak a U.S. heritage. Depending on the village, a Baptist or Methodist church acts as an essential social institution. Yet, in contrast to the dualistic body-soul approach to the individual found in Christian teaching, the Gullah believe that a person has an earthly body, a soul that returns upon death to the Divine Kingdom, and a separate spiritual entity that can remain on Earth and influence the lives of those still living. This belief in a "body spirit" is prevalent among West African peoples, according to Jones-Jackson. She also notes the African influences on the interaction between the minister and the congregation: The prayers and sermons "embody a classical, Ciceronian rhetorical style and employ sophistic ornaments capable of divinely inspiring and passionately persuading a congregation to respond with raucous and joyous replies."

Passage recap

Let's do a quick review, which should help us answer the questions that follow.

The topic of the passage is the society of the Gullah, especially their customs. The author wishes to show that Gullah heritage is a mixture of African and U.S. cultures.

Paragraph 1 is an introduction to the Gullah and why their identity is unique. Paragraph 2 covers aspects of Gullah culture that are obviously of African origin. Paragraph 3 describes how religious customs of the Gullah seem to be of U.S. origin but also reveal their African heritage.

1. According to the passage, all of the following aspects of the culture of the Sea Islanders show the influence of African traditions EXCEPT the

    (A) family structure

    (B) conception of the afterlife

    (C) method of acquiring land

    (D) style used in prayers and sermons

    (E) importance of the churches as social institutions

Again, the real key to getting EXCEPT/NOT questions right is reading the question. Once you know what you're trying to eliminate, you're halfway there.

The second tricky part of EXCEPT/NOT questions is that they can take longer to answer than the average question. On a detail question like this one, you often need to go back, read through the text and verify each wrong answer choice so that you can eliminate it. Let's try this now. Just to be clear, we're checking each choice to see if it's an aspect of Sea Island culture that shows an African influence.

> A 1600 test taker often skips a question that looks difficult, going back to it only after answering all the other questions in the set.

The first sentence of paragraph 2 offers the extended family as an example of West African influence on Gullah social life, so **(A)** is out.

In paragraph 3, we're told that the Gullah conception of the "body spirit" is similar to a West African belief, **(B)**.

As for **(C)**, we're told in paragraph 2 that membership in the extended family, itself an African element, affects property rights.

(D) is mentioned as an African influence by Jones-Jackson in the third paragraph.

This leaves us with **(E)**. In the third paragraph, the author cites the role of Baptist and Methodist churches as "essential social institutions." Inferably, the social role of the churches in an American, not an African, element of the culture. **(E)** is correct.

> A 1600 test taker doesn't make careless mistakes on EXCEPT/NOT questions.

Attacking Inference Questions

You've already had some practice with inference questions, and you probably have a pretty good idea of how to manage inferences. However, you'll need to stay on your toes as you work your way through inference questions on tough passages. Let's review some basic principles.

Inferences are conclusions you reach that are hinted at, but not directly stated in the passage. They often require you to "read between the lines"—although sometimes a questions will ask you to "infer" something that is directly stated (although with different wording than the correct answer choice) in the passage.

Inference tips

- Always look for evidence in the passage to support an inference.
- Don't go too far. SAT inferences tend to be straightforward and consistent with the overall idea of the passage.

> A 1600 test taker always chooses an inference that is supported by evidence in the passage.

Here are two inference questions for you to try.

In the following, a social scientist reflects on the disparate cultural influences on the Gullah, an island-dwelling people.

Before the recent encroachments of tourism and commercialization, the culture of the Gullah communities on the Sea Islands off the southeast coast of the U.S. retained a unique identity derived partially from the Islands' history as an area reserved for freed slaves after the Civil War. As an almost exclusively black community, the Gullah preserved African traditions concerning family structure and religious practices. At the same time, as a community of ex-slaves, the residents retained several facets of the Southern life they had left behind. This mixture provided a heritage which until recently was strong enough to sustain a vital culture.

As Patricia Jones-Jackson has pointed out, the basic unit of social life on the Sea Islands, as in West Africa, is the extended family. Since many islands are sectioned off into family communities, kinship ties are important to one's acceptance into the social structure. Membership in the extended family also affects property rights. In the traditional Gullah system, family members do not normally buy land from one another, but acquire it by an unwritten contract known as "heir's land." Rules pertaining to marriage seem to be at least as broad in scope. Common-law marriages are considered as legitimate as marriages recorded by contract under law. Indeed, the infrequent occurrence of divorce and separation within the Sea Island communities demonstrates the strong cohesion of Gullah marital and familial institutions.

Unlike the laws and customs relating to family structure, the religious practices of the Sea Islanders, on the surface at least, bespeak a U.S. heritage. Depending on the village, a Baptist or Methodist church acts as an essential social institution. Yet, in contrast to the dualistic body-soul approach to the individual found in Christian teaching, the Gullah believe that a person has an earthly body, a soul that returns upon death to the Divine Kingdom, and a separate spiritual entity that can remain on Earth and influence the lives of those still living. This belief in a "body spirit" is prevalent among West African peoples, according to Jones-Jackson. She also notes the African influences on the interaction between the minister and the congregation: The prayers and sermons "embody a classical, Ciceronian rhetorical style and employ sophistic ornaments capable of divinely inspiring and passionately persuading a congregation to respond with raucous and joyous replies."

1. It can be inferred that the institution of "heir's land" allows the transfer of property under the terms of

   (A) a formal grant by the government

   (B) a marriage settlement between families

   (C) an oral agreement among family members

   (D) a written deed of ownership

   (E) an alteration of communal rights

To get a handle on this inference question you should begin by scanning the paragraph for information on "heir's land," which can be found in the middle of the second paragraph. That's where you'll find the evidence to support your inference.

The author states that "heir's land" is a way for family members to acquire land through an "unwritten contract," without paying for it. Any contract is by its nature an agreement, and since this kind of agreement is not on paper, it follows that it is orally communicated, **(C)**. This is a straightforward, consistent inference that stays within the scope of the passage.

(A) is outside the scope. There's no reference to government grants with regard to "heir's land." **(B)** distorts the passage by linking "heir's land," which operates within families, to marriage settlements that take place between families. The fact that "heir's land" is defined as an unwritten contract eliminates **(D)**. Finally, no alterations in communal rights are mentioned, disposing of **(E)**.

2. On the basis of information supplied by the passage, which of the following would most likely resemble a social experience of a Sea Islander?

   (A) dividing property in a divorce settlement under court supervision

   (B) being required to sell one's home because it lies in the path of a new highway

   (C) growing up in a communal household composed of unrelated adults

   (D) learning how to play a traditional song on a centuries-old instrument

   (E) being given employment by a relative on the basis of one's standing in the family

This is a tough inference question that asks you to apply knowledge in the passage. Let's begin by looking for a social experience that parallels one described, probably in more general terms, in the passage. The second paragraph notes the importance of family ties and illustrates this by discussing how family members can acquire land through these ties. This is similar to acquiring a job, or any other benefit, through family connections. Note that you don't need to find evidence that the Sea Islanders get jobs this way. The point is that **(E)** is logically similar to an experience of the Sea Islanders, and this choice is a reasonable inference.

(A) is out because of the reference to court supervision. There's no direct mention of courts and other government institutions in the passage. **(B)** is certainly not like anything in traditional Gullah life; it might be like an experience that has occurred since the "encroachments of tourism and commercialization," except that we're never told what these encroachments have been. **(C)** relates to the importance of family units, but it's the extended family that's important to the Gullah, while **(C)** involves unrelated adults. **(D)** comes out of left field, and can't be substantiated.

TOUGH CRITICAL READING: STRATEGY RECAP

Great Advice for Any Passage

How to attack SAT Critical Reading strategically

Step 1: When you first encounter the passage, read enough of it to figure out the author's "Big Idea" and get a general sense of how the passage is organized.

Step 2: Read the question. If a question seems hard, go back to it after you've answered the other questions in the set.

Step 3: As necessary, go back into the passage to locate the answer to a specific question.

Step 4: Put the answer in your own words; the correct answer will most often be a paraphrase of what's stated in the passage.

Step 5: Attack the answer choices, and choose the one that comes closest to the answer you found.

Five principles for Critical Reading

Principle 1: Focus on the author.
Principle 2: Don't sweat the details.
Principle 3: Read the first third closely.
Principle 4: Note paragraph topics and make a roadmap.
Principle 5: Stop to sum up.

Extra-Great Advice for Tough Passages

If the passage is long and/or the subject matter is difficult to get through, read the **first third** of the passage carefully, then read the **first sentence of each subsequent paragraph** and the **last sentence of the passage**. As with all passages, focus on the Big Picture, not the details. Apply the following reading principles:

- Read with the author in mind: Ask yourself, "What is the author trying to convey? Why is the passage structured the way it is?"

- Even in the first third, focus on the big idea(s), not the supporting details.

- If you're still unsure about the main idea from the first third of the passage, pay close attention to the last sentence of the passage; this is where many authors tie together the loose ends and clarify the main idea of the passage.

How to Read Tough Narrative Passages

As you read a narrative passage, you should ask yourself three questions:

Who are the character(s) and how does the author describe them?

What do the characters want?

What are the characters doing?

Can you think of adjectives to describe each character?

What do the characters think of each other, or themselves?

Do they like each other? Hate each other?

Why does each character make a particular decision or take a particular course of action?

What do these decisions or actions tell you about a character?

What's the "point" of the story?

What are the "turning points" in the passage?

Is there a "moral" to the story?

How to Handle Paired Passages:

Step 1: Read Passage 1 and answer accompanying questions.

Step 2: Read Passage 2 and answer accompanying questions.

Step 3: Answer Compare and Contrast questions.

The Question Types Revisited

Big Picture questions ask about the main idea or primary purpose of the passage. You should be able to answer these questions based on your initial reading of the passage. You should concentrate your efforts on attacking and eliminating wrong answer choices. These include answer choices that are too specific, dealing with only one part of the passage; answer choices that are too broad, going beyond the scope of the passage; or answer choices that are too strongly worded, containing language that's too extreme to properly describe the passage.

Detail questions ask about a specific part of the passage. On these questions, you may have to go back into the passage to research the answer. The correct answer to a detail question will almost always be a **paraphrase** of information found in the passage. Wrong answers to detail questions, on the other hand, will usually do one of the following: they don't answer the question—i.e., they refer to a different part of the passage than that which the question addresses; they use language that's too extreme; they contradict or go beyond the scope of the passage, making claims that are not supported by the passage.

Vocabulary-in-Context questions ask you about the usage of a single word. You won't need to define the word, but you'll need to infer the meaning of the word from context. You can treat these questions as if they were Sentence Completion questions and employ the following method:

Step 1: Read the sentence, looking for clues.
Step 2: Predict a word that could replace the vocabulary word.
Step 3: Check the answer choices for a word that matches.
Step 4: Plug your selection into the sentence to make sure it makes sense.

Inference questions ask you to draw conclusions that are hinted at, but not directly stated, in the passage. They often require you to "read between the lines."

Always look for evidence in the passage to support an inference, and don't go too far. SAT inferences tend to be straightforward and consistent with the overall idea of the passage.

EXCEPT/NOT questions require you to go to the answer choices and find information in the passage that will verify all of the answer choices EXCEPT the correct answer, the one answer that's NOT true. In other words, you're trying to find the one answer that's wrong.

Now that you've has a taste of the tough passages and questions and how to deal with them, you can try your hand at some more tough practice passages in the next chapter.

CHAPTER THREE

Critical Reading Practice Set and Explanations

Answer the questions below based on the information in the accompanying passages.

Passage 1

Questions 1–6 are based on the following passage.

The following passage, which examines a debate on possible linkages between the American Populist movement and Joseph McCarthy's anti-communist crusade of the 1950s, has been excerpted from a political science journal.

Historians have long known that there were two sides to the Populist movement of the 1890s: a progressive side, embodying the protests of farmers against big business, and a darker side, marked by a distrust of Easterners, immigrants, and intellectuals. In the 1950s, one school of U.S. social thinkers constructed a parallel between this dark side of Populism and the contemporary anti-communist crusade spearheaded by Wisconsin Senator Joseph McCarthy, which attacked liberalism, Eastern intellectuals, and civil liberties in general. To Seymour Martin Lipset, McCarthyism represented "the sour dregs of Populism"; to Edward Shils, McCarthyism, like Populism, exemplified "the ambiguous American impulse toward 'direct democracy.'"

Noting that McCarthyism and Populism had both found their strongest support in the agrarian Midwest, Lipset argued that voters who backed agrarian protest movements during earlier economic crises had supported McCarthy in the post–World War II period of prosperity. "It would be interesting to know," Lipset wrote, "what percentage of those who supported the isolationist but progressive Bob La Follette in Wisconsin now backs McCarthy." But, in the eyes of these writers, the appeal of McCarthyism extended beyond the agrarian base of Populism to include urban groups such as industrial workers. Lipset claimed that "the lower classes, especially the workers," had backed McCarthy. In a more sweeping fashion, Lewis Feuer claimed that "it was the American lower classes…who gave their overwhelming support to the attacks in recent years on civil liberties."

Writing a few years later, political scientist Michael Paul Rogin challenged these superficially plausible notions, contending that they merely embodied the writers' own assumptions about the supposed intolerance of lower class groups, rather than a valid interpretation of McCarthyism. Rogin critically examined their assertions by the simple method of testing them against the evidence. He tested Lipset's claims about the continuity of McCarthyism and earlier agrarian protest movements by breaking down statewide voting statistics on a county-by-county and precinct-by-precinct basis. He found that Wisconsin counties that had voted strongly for Progressives before World War II did not support McCarthy; McCarthy's support was concentrated in his home region and in ethnic German areas that had been traditionally conservative. The old Progressive vote had in fact gone to McCarthy's opponents, the Democrats.

To test Lipset's generalizations about McCarthy's support among lower-class groups, Rogin attempted to determine whether industrial workers had, in fact, backed McCarthy. Correlating income and employment statistics with voting records, Rogin found that the greater the employment in industry in a given Wisconsin county, the lower was McCarthy's share of the vote. Rogin concluded that the thesis of "McCarthyism as Populism" should be judged "not as the product of science but as a...venture into conservative political theory."

1. The author would probably assert that Populism and McCarthyism
   - (A) were basically similar
   - (B) were completely opposite in character
   - (C) were responses to, respectively, agrarian and industrial conditions
   - (D) were essentially dissimilar movements that shared some common features
   - (E) each had both a progressive and a darker side

2. It can be inferred that Rogin's most serious criticism of Lipset, Feuer, and Shils's methodology would probably be that they
   - (A) reached incorrect conclusions about McCarthy
   - (B) equated support for McCarthyism with anti-intellectualism
   - (C) placed too much emphasis on the dual character of Populism
   - (D) failed to examine the evidence that could support or weaken their conclusions
   - (E) offered a theory that could not easily be tested

3. Rogin studied the class character of Wisconsin voters in order to
   - I. challenge the idea that less affluent socioeconomic groups supported McCarthy
   - II. explain the underlying causes of the links between Populism and McCarthyism
   - III. account for important changes in voting patterns during the twentieth century
   - (A) I only
   - (B) III only
   - (C) I and II only
   - (D) I and III only
   - (E) I, II, and III

4. It can be inferred that both Lipset and Rogin made which of the following assumptions about voter support for McCarthy?
   (A) The voting patterns of industrial workers are representative of lower-class political preferences.
   (B) Industrial workers usually vote for conservative political candidates.
   (C) Supporters of McCarthy were almost exclusively of lower class origin.
   (D) Lower class voters generally tend to vote in favor of civil rights measures.
   (E) Voters in Midwestern counties are typical of American voters elsewhere.

5. According to the passage, Rogin concluded that the writings of Lipset, Shils, and Feuer
   (A) intentionally distorted historical evidence
   (B) were flawed by political presuppositions
   (C) lent support to attacks on civil liberties
   (D) took an overly statistical approach to historical evidence
   (E) were marked by an anti-intellectual bias

6. The author is primarily concerned with
   (A) comparing positions in a political debate
   (B) advocating the use of statistical methods in historical research
   (C) examining the similarities between two political movements
   (D) explaining why historical conclusions should be revised according to later revelations
   (E) discoveries describing an instance of flawed historical analysis

Explanations: Passage 1

The topic of this passage is McCarthyism, and specifically whether it drew support from the Populist movement. The author's main point is that although some would argue that McCarthyism had a following among those who supported Populism, later research does not support this thesis. Paragraph I presents the idea that McCarthyism represents an offshoot of Populism. Paragraph II describes the theories of Lipset and Feuer, who claim that McCarthyism drew its support from Populism's base in the agrarian Midwest and extended it to industrial workers. Paragraph III describes the case against this theory; according to Rogin, counties in Wisconsin that voted for Progressives did not vote for McCarthy. Paragraph IV details Rogin's case against the ideas presented in the second paragraph—statistics show that industrialized workers did not in fact vote for McCarthy. The passage concludes by supporting the case against a linkage of McCarthyism with Populism.

1. D

This question covers the broad outline of the passage, so treat it as a big picture question and look to your purpose and main idea. Choice **(D)** best describes the author's attitude toward McCarthyism and Populism—although they were superficially similar, they were essentially dissimilar.

Answer **(A)** contradicts the passage; it actually states the case against the author's views.

Answer **(B)** is too harsh. The first paragraph does draw some parallels between both movements.

Answer **(C)** is partly right, but partly wrong. Populism was, partially at least, a response to the conditions of farmers, but nowhere is it suggested that McCarthyism was a response to industrial conditions. The passage suggests quite the contrary: As described in the last paragraph, Rogin showed that McCarthyism had little support from workers employed in industry.

Answer **(E)** is out, as it's never suggested that McCarthyism has a progressive side. Only Populism is described (in the first sentence) as having both of these, a progressive and a darker side.

2. D

The substance of Rogin's criticism of Lipset, Feuer, and Shils is explained in the last two paragraphs. The second sentence of the third paragraph says what Rogin did: He "critically examined their assertions by the simple method of testing them against the evidence." This really tells you all you need to know to pick the right choice, **(D)**. If you missed this, both of these last two paragraphs are spent describing how Rogin showed that grass roots voting patterns in both rural Wisconsin counties and more industrial Wisconsin counties failed to support the claims made by Lipset, Feuer, and Shils about who really did and didn't support McCarthy. What Rogin and the author are clearly suggesting is that Lipset, Feuer, and Shils failed to do their homework properly.

(A) doesn't work, because Rogin never really quarrels with any descriptions of McCarthy. The quarrel is with the misrepresentation of lower-class voters and the real nature of Populism.

Answer **(B)** doesn't work, since the passage never describes Rogin as disagreeing with the idea that McCarthyism is linked to anti-intellectualism.

(C) is wrong since it seems that Lipset, Feuer, and Shils seemingly placed too little emphasis on the dual nature of Populism. They failed to perceive the continuity of the progressive aspects of Populism among voters in Wisconsin.

And answer **(E)** is contradicted: Rogin was able to submit the conclusions of the three writers to a test—a devastating one—by taking a close look at the voting patterns in Wisconsin counties.

3. A

The stem is asking why Rogin studied the class character of Wisconsin voting patterns. Primarily, he did this to check to see if the voting patterns supported or contradicted the arguments of Lipset and Feuer. They argued that lower-class farmers and industrial workers provided crucial voter support for both Populism and McCarthyism, and Rogin performed his study of voting patterns in order to challenge their conclusions, by showing that lower-class farmers and workers in fact did not give their votes to McCarthy. Statement I reflects this.

Statement II is wrong since Rogin was out to disprove the alleged links between Populism and McCarthyism, not explain them.

Statement III is way beyond the scope of the passage.

4. A

In the last half of the second paragraph the passage indicates that Lipset argued that lower class support of McCarthy included urban industrial workers. The last paragraph describes the study in which Rogin found that voters in counties with high industrial employment tended to vote against McCarthy. Rogin used this study to support his counterassertion that McCarthy in fact did not enjoy extensive support among the lower classes. Thus, an assumption made by both men is that voters among industrial workers can be classified as lower class voters.

This makes **(B)** a nonfactor as Rogin's overall thesis is to argue that lower-class voters voted more progressively than Lipset, Feuer, and Shils admit.

(C) clearly isn't an assumption of Rogin's, who suggests something quite different: McCarthy lacked extensive support among lower classes.

(D) is beyond the scope of the passage. There's not enough information to conclude that either scholar assumed this.

(E) has no support, since neither Lipset nor Rogin is described in this passage as arguing that Midwestern voters are representative of more general political patterns among American voters.

5. B

This is a detail question, and since it begins with "according to the passage," it will be a paraphrase of something that appears within it. Correct choice **(B)** paraphrases the first sentence of the third paragraph and the concluding sentence of the passage. Rogin's overall charge against Lipset, Feuer, and Shils is that they not only reach faulty conclusions but are politically biased against the lower-classes from the very beginning. It's this latter charge that's summed up in **(B)**.

Answer **(A)** goes too far. Rogin never charges deliberate falsification of evidence by the three men.

(C) is out. Never does Rogin imply that the men's viewpoints will support attacks on civil liberties.

(D) puts things backwards. It's Rogin who makes scrupulous use of statistical analysis. This is what Lipset, Feuer, and Shils failed to do.

Finally, answer **(E)** is out since Rogin never suggests that the writings of Lipset, Feuer, and Shils were essentially anti-intellectual. Rogin might say that they are intellectually or professionally incompetent, since he believes their research methods lack credibility, but this choice distorts this idea.

6. E

For this big picture question, go to your purpose and main idea. The author's main purpose is to describe the criticism of the views on McCarthyism expressed in the second paragraph. The author states that these conclusions were not based on real evidence, and suggests that they were shaped by preconceived prejudices. These are flaws in historical methodology, **(E)**.

(A) uses the wrong verb. The author is not comparing the views; rather, he is supporting one particular view, that of Rogin.

(B) goes for a detail—Rogin's research methods, and **(C)** distorts the author's point of view that the two movements were fundamentally dissimilar.

(D) is out because, although the author would agree with it, it does not address the main point of the passage.

Passage 2

Questions 7–15 are based on the following passage.

The following passage is excerpted from a major scientific journal.

The transformer is an essential component of modern electric power systems. Simply put, it can convert electricity with a low current and a high voltage into electricity with a high current and low voltage (and vice versa) with almost no loss of energy. The conversion is important because electric power is transmitted most efficiently at high voltages but is best generated and used at low voltages. Were it not for transformers, the distance separating generators from consumers would have to be minimized, many households and industries would require their own power stations, and electricity would be a much less practical form of energy.

In addition to its role in electric power systems, the transformer is an integral component of many things that run on electricity. Desk lamps, battery chargers, toy trains, and television sets all rely on transformers to cut or boost voltage. In all its multiplicity of applications, the transformer can range from tiny assemblies the size of a pea to behemoths weighing 500 tons or more. The principles that govern the function of electrical transformers are the same regardless of form or application.

The English physicist Michael Faraday discovered the basic action of the transformer during his pioneering investigations of electricity in 1831. Some fifty years later, the advent of a practical transformer, containing all the essential elements of the modern instrument, revolutionized the infant electric lighting industry. By the turn of the century, alternating-current power systems had been universally adopted and the transformer had assumed a key role in electrical transmission and distribution.

Yet the transformer's tale does not end in 1900. Today's transformers can handle 500 times the power and 15 times the voltage of their turn-of-the-century ancestors; the weight per unit of power has dropped by a factor of ten and efficiency typically exceeds 99 percent. These advances reflect the marriage of theoretical inquiry and engineering that first elucidated and then exploited the phenomena governing transformer action.

Faraday's investigations were inspired by the Danish physicist Hans Christian Oersted, who had shown in 1820 that an electric current flowing through a conducting material creates a magnetic field around the conductor. At the time, Oersted's discovery was considered remarkable, since electricity and magnetism were thought to be separate and unrelated forces. If an electric current could generate a magnetic field, it seemed likely that a magnetic field could give rise to an electric current.

In 1831, Faraday demonstrated that in order for a magnetic field to induce a current in a conductor, the field must be changing. Faraday caused the strength of the field to fluctuate by making and breaking the electric circuit generating the field; the same effect can be achieved with a current whose direction alternates in time. This fascinating interaction of electricity and magnetism came to be known as electromagnetic induction.

7. According to the passage, the first practical transformer was developed in

   (A) 1820
   (B) 1831
   (C) 1860
   (D) 1881
   (E) 1900

8. The passage suggests that advances in the efficiency of the transformer are

   (A) based solely on Faraday's discovery of electromagnetic induction
   (B) due to a combination of engineering and theoretical curiosity
   (C) continuing to occur at an ever accelerated pace
   (D) most likely at a peak that cannot be surpassed
   (E) found in transformers that weigh 500 tons or more

9. According to the passage, Oersted's discovery regarding the production of a magnetic field is considered remarkable because

   (A) the transformer had not yet been universally adopted
   (B) Faraday had already demonstrated that this was impossible
   (C) scientists believed that there was no relationship between electricity and magnetism
   (D) it contradicted the established principles of electromagnetism
   (E) it proved that a magnetic field could generate electricity

10. In line 28, *assumed* most nearly means

   (A) presupposed
   (B) understood
   (C) feigned
   (D) taken
   (E) borrowed

11. Which of the following is NOT true of transformers today as compared to the first transformers?

   (A) They comprise the same basic components.
   (B) They are lighter in weight.
   (C) They are many times more powerful.
   (D) They operate at a much lower voltage.
   (E) They are almost completely efficient.

12. According to the passage, Oersted's discovery proved that

   (A) magnetism and electricity are unrelated forces
   (B) a magnetic field can induce an electric current
   (C) all materials that conduct electricity are magnetic
   (D) electricity can be transported over long distances
   (E) an electric current can create a magnetic field

13. According to the passage, one function of the transformer is to

   (A) convert electricity into the high voltages most useful for transmission
   (B) create the magnetic fields used in industry
   (C) minimize the distance between generators and consumers
   (D) protect electric power systems from energy loss
   (E) transform electrical energy into a magnetic field

14. Which of the following statements is best supported by the passage?

    (A) Faraday was the first to show how an electric current can induce a magnetic field.

    (B) Oersted was the first to utilize transformers in a practical application, by using them to power electric lights.

    (C) Faraday invented the first practical transformer.

    (D) Oersted coined the term "electromagnetic induction."

    (E) Faraday demonstrated that when a magnetic field is changing, it can produce an electric current in a conducting material.

15. According to the passage, electricity would be a much less practical form of energy if there were no transformers because

    (A) generating electricity would become much more expensive

    (B) there would be no dependable source of electric power

    (C) generators would have to be built close to the consumers they supply

    (D) industries and households would have to be supplied with the same power

    (E) household appliances would have to operate with a low voltage

Explanations: Passage 2

This passage describes the origin and use of the AC transformer. In paragraphs I and II, the author introduces the transformer and tells the reader about some of its far-reaching applications. Paragraph III introduces the reader to the first discoveries that led to the invention of a practical transformer. The fourth paragraph returns to the present day to explain how these early discoveries came to be the modern power grid. Paragraphs V and VI give a short history of the discovery of electromagnetic induction.

7. D

The first question is a detail question, asking you to consider information directly from the passage. Easy enough. The passage says that Faraday "discovered the basic action of the transformer" in 1831 (lines 21–23). But note that it was not until 50 years later that a practical transformer was developed (lines 23–26). This means that the first practical transformer was developed in 1881.

8. B

Our first inference question of the bunch. Go to paragraph IV to research the answer. The paragraph lists several advances in the transformer in lines 29–33. This list is followed by the statement that the "advances reflect the marriage of theoretical inquiry and engineering that first elucidated and then exploited the phenomena governing transformer action" (lines 33–35). This makes **(B)** the best answer.

(A) is unrelated to the question being asked, and its wording is too extreme in any case. **(C)** and **(E)**, whereas possibly true, are not necessarily implied in the passage. And answer **(D)** is unsubstantiated.

9. C

A simple one. The answer to this detail question is directly stated in the passage. "At the time, Oersted's discovery was considered remarkable, since electricity and magnetism were thought to be separate and unrelated forces" (lines 39–41). **(C)** is a nice paraphrase of this sentence. **(A)** is probably true, but it has nothing to do with why Oersted's discovery was considered remarkable. **(B)** cannot be true because Faraday did his work much later than Oersted, and based his own work on that of Oersted. Answer **(D)** cannot be the correct choice because it directly contradicts the information in the passage, and **(E)** is a distortion: Faraday demonstrated how a magnetic field could generate current.

10. D

Here's a vocabulary-in-context question for you to solve. Based on the sentence in which it is found, and on the sentences just before and after it, *assumed* can best be interpreted as *taken*, or answer **(D)**. Try to see it as a game of fill-in. Which of the choices would best replace the word in question given its context, i.e., "______ a key role"? Choices **(A)**, **(B)**, **(C)**, and **(E)** simply don't make sense given the gist of the paragraph.

11. D

In this EXCEPT/NOT type question, you as a 1600 test taker must remember that you are looking for the answer that is NOT correct. Referring directly to the passage for the answer, **(A)** can be found; it's a paraphrase of lines 24–25, which state that the first practical transformer "contain[ed] all the essential elements of the modern instrument. "Likewise, **(B)** and **(C)** can both be located in the passage, in the discussion of the improvements in the transformer over the years (lines 29–33), and **(E)** is confirmed in lines 32–33: "efficiency typically exceeds 99 percent." The passage also confirms that **(D)** is NOT true: transformers today are said to be able to "handle...15 times the voltage" (lines 30–31) of earlier transformers, so **(D)** is the correct answer.

12. E

Another detail question to dig up the answer to. Let's head back to the paragraph about the discovery by Oersted and look at lines 37–39. He "had shown in 1820 that an electric current flowing through a conducting material creates a magnetic field around the conductor," which is what **(E)** states. **(A)** contradicts direct information in the passage. **(B)** describes Faraday's later experiment, not that of Oersted, and **(C)** is too extreme, not to mention that it is not supported by information in the passage. **(D)**, finally, is true of transformers, but is not stated as a direct result of Oersted's work.

13. A

Ah, the detail questions keep coming! Here, the first paragraph provides the information about the transformer that we need. A transformer, it says, "can convert electricity with a low current and a high voltage into electricity with a high current and low voltage" (lines 2–4). The passage goes on to state that this "conversion is important because electric power is transmitted most efficiently at high voltages" (lines 5–7). This information supports **(A)** as the best answer. Answer **(C)** contradicts the passage, which says that without transformers, the distance between generators and consumers would have to be minimized, and **(B)**, **(D)**, and **(E)**, true or not, are not addressed by the passage and therefore can be eliminated.

14. E

Now you're asked to take a step back and draw an inference, but as you know, on the SAT many so-called inferences are simply paraphrases of information found in the passage. The answer to this question can be found in the first sentence of the last paragraph. "Faraday demonstrated that in order for a magnetic field to induce a current in a conductor the field must be changing" (lines 44–46). **(E)** is clearly the best answer. Of the wrong answers, **(B)**, **(C)**, and **(D)** are not true statements, as Oersted had nothing to do with the direct application of his findings and Faraday did not invent the practical transformer. Only **(A)** is left, and it is also a misstatement; it's true about Oersted, not Faraday. Therefore, **(E)** is our best choice.

15. C

The answer to this detail question lies in the last sentence of the first paragraph. Here, we are provided with keys to this question. "Were it not for transformers, the distance separating generators from consumers would have to be minimized" (lines 7–9). In other words, without transformers, generators would need to be built near consumers. Thus, **(C)** is our best answer choice. **(A)**, whereas conceivable, is not addressed by the passage. **(B)** and **(E)** are both too speculative to be correct. There is no proof from what you've read to know for sure. **(D)**, meanwhile, is an inference that seems to have no bearing on the information you've just read, so it's clearly not correct.

Passage 3

Questions 16–27 are based on the following passage.

The following excerpt, taken from a novel first published in 1965, describes the narrator's time spent at Magdalen College—part of England's Oxford University system—during the period shortly after WWII, and his first experiences upon graduation.

I went to Oxford in 1948. In my second year at Magdalen, soon after a long vacation during which I hardly saw my parents, my father had to fly out to India. He took my mother with him. Their plane crashed, a high-octane pyre, in a thunderstorm some forty miles east of Karachi. After the first shock I felt an almost immediate sense of relief, of freedom. My only other close relation, my mother's brother, farmed in Rhodesia, so I had no family to trammel what I regarded as my real self. I may have been weak on filial charity, but I was strong on the discipline in vogue.

At least, along with a group of fellow odd men out at Magdalen, I thought I was strong in the discipline. We formed a small club called Les Hommes Révoltés, drank very dry sherry, and (as a protest against those shabby duffle-coated last years of the 'forties) wore dark-grey suits and black ties for our meetings; we argued about essences and existences and called a certain kind of inconsequential behaviour 'existentialist'. Less enlightened people would have called it capricious or just plain selfish; but we didn't realize that the heroes, or anti-heroes, of the French existentialist novels we read were not supposed to be realistic. We tried to imitate them, mistaking metaphorical descriptions of complex modes of feeling for straightforward prescriptions of behaviour. We duly felt the right anguishes. Most of us, true to the eternal dandyism of Oxford, simply wanted to look different. In our club, we did.

I acquired expensive habits and affected manners. I got a third-class degree and a first-class illusion: that I was a poet. But nothing could have been less poetic than my pseudo-aristocratic, seeing-through-all boredom with life in general and with making a living in particular. I was too green to know that all cynicism masks a failure to cope—an impotence, in short; and that to despise all effort is the greatest effort of all. But I did absorb a small dose of one permanently useful thing, Oxford's greatest gift to civilized life: Socratic honesty. It showed me, very intermittently, that it is not enough to revolt against one's past. One day I was outrageously bitter among some friends about the Army; back in my own rooms later it suddenly struck me that just because I said with impunity things that would have apoplexed my dead father, I was still no less under his influence. The truth was that I was not a cynic by nature; only by revolt. I had got away from what I hated, but I hadn't found where I loved, and so I pretended there was nowhere to love.

Handsomely equipped to fail, I went out into the world. My father hadn't kept Financial Prudence among his armoury of essential words; he ran a ridiculously large account at Ladbroke's and his mess bills always reached staggering proportions, because he liked to be popular and in place of charm had to dispense alcohol. What remained of his money when the lawyers and tax men had had their cuts yielded not nearly enough for me to live on. But every kind of job I looked at—the Foreign Service, the Civil, the Colonial, the banks, commerce, advertising—was transpierceable at a glance. I went to several interviews and since I didn't feel obliged to show the eager enthusiasm our world expects from the young executive, I was successful at none.

16. It can be inferred the "discipline in vogue" mentioned in line 9 most nearly refers to

(A) Socratic honesty
(B) radical inquiry
(C) emotional coldness
(D) aristocratic yearning
(E) poetic sensitivity

17. The group of "fellow odd men" mentioned in line 10 are described as being

(A) bookish and sincere
(B) ambitious and philosophical
(C) unconventional and enlightened
(D) ostentatious and shallow
(E) worldly and knowing

18. According to the passage, the narrator and his friends revolted against all of the following EXCEPT

(A) post-war attire
(B) career ambition
(C) parents
(D) academia
(E) the military

19. The author uses the phrase *[L]ess enlightened people* (line 16) to convey a sense of

(A) disapproval
(B) irony
(C) sympathy
(D) remorse
(E) nostalgia

20. According to the passage, French existentialist novels are meant to be read in which of the following ways?

(A) as instructional texts
(B) as fantasies
(C) as allegories
(D) as tragedies
(E) as heroic epics

21. The narrator claims to have acquired all of the following while at Oxford EXCEPT

(A) a costly lifestyle
(B) a cynical worldview
(C) a capacity for self-awareness
(D) a sense of being gifted
(E) a foundation for success

22. In line 24, *affected* most nearly means

(A) influenced
(B) concerned
(C) pretentious
(D) changed
(E) infectious

23. It can be inferred from the passage that the narrator's bitterness towards the army

(A) was not founded in deeply felt beliefs
(B) surprised even his friends in Les Hommes Révoltés
(C) would not have been expressed if his father were not dead
(D) revealed a deep and abiding cynicism
(E) led him to realize that he was not a poet

24. The passage does NOT suggest that which of the following is true about the narrator's father?

(A) He and his son were not close.
(B) He enjoyed entertaining others.
(C) He held favorable attitudes towards the military.
(D) He was a misanthrope by nature.
(E) He had a strong effect on his son's beliefs.

25. In line 47, *tranpierceable* most nearly means

(A) easy to penetrate
(B) easy to attempt
(C) easy to understand
(D) easy to achieve
(E) easy to dismiss

26. According to the passage, the narrator and his father shared which of the following traits?
    (A) prodigality
    (B) cynicism
    (C) unconventionality
    (D) bonhomie
    (E) self-doubt

27. This passage serves mainly to
    (A) describe a dominant post-war sensibility
    (B) depict a difficult period of immaturity
    (C) condemn an emotionally callow youth
    (D) portray a bohemian element at Oxford
    (E) explain one person's failure to find a livelihood

Explanations: Passage 3

This narrative passage is an insightful look at one young man's struggles with growing up and his immature reaction to the outside world. Paragraph I quickly tells the reader about the narrator's background. Paragraph II speaks of the narrator's chosen life of misplaced radicalism and his camaraderie with other like-minded, would-be "existentialists." In paragraph III, the narrator begins to make statements of remorse and confronts his cynical and vacuous behavior. Paragraph IV details the young man's rough exodus from school and into the real world.

16. B

So you start here with a classic detail question asking you to go back and dig up a contextual meaning from a specific line or two. No problem. The phrase in question, "discipline in vogue" (line 9), refers, in the author's unsentimental and sarcastic tone, to his youthful and angry radical tendencies, described in the next paragraph. Thus, answer **(B)** is the best inference to make. While he may have also been emotionally chilly, **(C)** is not referenced by these words. Answers **(A)**, **(D)**, and **(E)** are all mentioned later in the piece, but not in conjunction with the phrase you have been asked about.

17. D

Back-to-back line-reference questions make life a little easier, as you know what to look for and where to look for it. The "fellow odd men" and the author, as mentioned in line 10, fancy themselves as existentialist anti-heroes. But the narrator's tone throughout this descriptive passage is far from flattering. So any of the answers that seem to imply his description is positive can be dismissed. Answers **(A)**, **(B)**, and **(E)**, however true in theory, are not the intended description of the narrator and his "fellow odd men." And however unconventional they may have seemed, by the author's own admission, they were enlightened only in their own opinion, eliminating **(C)**. Only **(D)** gives us a harsh, and accurate, summary description of the narrator's "ostentatious and shallow" group at Oxford.

18. D

Time to test your skills on an EXCEPT/NOT type of question. Always remember that these require you to find the correct answer choice, which, technically speaking, is the one incorrect response: The test maker understands that 1600 test takers need a good challenge. In this case, the question asks you to decide which of the five choices the narrator and his compatriots did NOT revolt against. As radicals, they made it their business to oppose all those things they saw as ordinary or expected. In lines 12–13, the narrator speaks of how they protested "those shabby duffle-coated last years of the 'forties." Thus, answer **(A)** is out. It's clear from the speaker's discussion of his boredom with "making a living" (line 27) that career plans were not high on his list of priorities, so **(B)** is a no go as well. Finding his revolutionary sentiments towards his father in this piece is easy enough, so clearly **(C)** is not the choice. One can infer from his bitter discussion with friends about the army (line 33) that their attitude toward the military was one of disdain, so cancel answer **(E)**. Only **(D)**, academia, is something that the young wannabe intellectuals didn't protest.

19. B

Go back and check out line 16 for the phrase in this line-reference question. "Less enlightened people" here isn't meant to be taken literally. It's clear from the narrator's tone that his feelings about himself and his friends in retrospect are certainly not positive. Saying that this phrase conveys a sense of disapproval, choice **(A)**, is misleading because the phrase is intended sarcastically. Similarly, the speaker is certainly not sympathetic or nostalgic for his former self, so **(C)** and **(E)** can also be eliminated. Finally, while he may be remorseful about his actions and attitudes at the time, the narrator is not addressing that emotion in this phrase. The narrator means the phrase as a reflection of the poor attitudes he and his comrades showed—in contrast to "less enlightened people"—in those days. The phrase is a good example of irony, or **(B)**.

20. C

Be careful with detail questions like these. One of the young narrator's radical pastimes is trying to live the life of a character in the French existentialist novels, stories in which metaphor and symbolism play a major role. Certainly, therefore, answer **(A)** is incorrect, as he expressly states that the boys were mistaken in trying to take the books literally. While the books are metaphorically driven, they are not fantasy **(B)**; nor are they classic works of tragedy **(D)** or heroism **(E)**. The passage does state in lines 17–21 that the stories were not intended realistically, but rather metaphorically—i.e., they were meant to be read as allegories **(C)**.

21. E

Here's another EXCEPT question, so let's research the passage and see what we can eliminate. In this passage, the narrator makes many claims about what he learned or did not learn in terms of knowledge and experience. He notes in line 24 that he had acquired "expensive habits" **(A)**, and in line 25 he says that he acquired a "first-class illusion: that I was a poet," which gets rid of **(D)**, a sense of being gifted. In addition, he expresses in line 36 that he had a "cynicism" **(B)**. In the discussion of Socratic honesty (lines 30–32), it's noted that the narrator did acquire one useful thing—a capacity for self-awareness **(C)**. The only one of the choices that is not found in the passage is any sense that he acquired a "foundation for success." In fact, the final paragraph implies that the idea of success was nearly impossible given his attitude. Since this is a question that asks for the one that doesn't belong, the correct choice is **(E)**.

22. C

Finally, a vocabulary-in-context question! OK, so whether or not you share our enthusiasm for vocabulary, here's a good example of one type of question you're bound to see in the CR section of the SAT. In line 18, the narrator says he acquired "affected" manners. From the passage, you can cull that due to his shallow attitude and self-serving motivations, it's clear that any idea of the young man being **(B)**, *concerned*, or **(D)**, *changed*, is questionable at best. Here, the speaker is referring to his effete mannerisms. Answers **(A)**, *influenced*, and **(E)**, *infectious*, don't apply to this specific quote. Only **(C)**, *pretentious*, fits the bill. And it fits quite well, by all accounts.

23. A

This inference question asks you to consider a very specific part of the passage in which the narrator refers to his heated discussion of the army (lines 32–33). You can see that he says he was "outrageously bitter." But look closer and you'll see that he admits a few lines later he "was not a cynic by nature; only by revolt," hinting that he has since realized that his beliefs were as much a response to his surroundings and his rebellion against his father as to any sort of deep and profound convictions. So bearing these statements in mind, one can see that **(A)** makes the most sense. Answer **(B)** is unlikely, because his friends appeared to be cut from much the same cloth. **(C)**, whereas conceivable, was not discussed in the passage and therefore is too speculative to be a correct answer here. **(D)** is directly refuted by the statement that his cynicism was not "by nature" and **(E)** is totally unrelated to the question.

24. D

Another EXCEPT/NOT question for you. We can infer a lot about the father of the narrator regarding his personality and his relationship with his angry son both before and after his death. From the opening paragraph, it is abundantly clear that the narrator, whether because of his age or despite it, had a strained relationship with his family. It's mentioned that he "hardly saw" his family, and later that he was revolting against "what I hated" (line 37). From these statements, it's safe to say that the father and son were not close emotionally and that they had vastly different views on the world. Thus, you can dismiss **(A)** and **(C)** as incorrect answers, if only because the narrator speaks directly to the contrary. As for **(B)**, see line 42 where the narrator notes that his father "liked to be popular" and spent a great deal of time and money entertaining his friends and supposed comrades. Finally, there is no doubt from the narrator's discussion of the contentious relationship between himself and his father (both when alive and deceased) that the father had a strong affect on his son's belief system. Because the question is asking you to find the one answer that doesn't belong, the only answer remaining is **(D)**. Nowhere in the passage is it discussed that the father is a misanthrope. If anything, he sounded like a fairly jovial sort.

25. E

Here's another vocabulary-in-context question. Read carefully the final lines of the passage to find the best possible meaning for the word *transpierceable*. When you see the word "pierce" as part of the larger word, your first instinct might be to guess that it refers to a penetrating act. But look at the context again: If something is considered "transpierceable at a glance" (line 47), it's safe to say that the implication is of a sudden or fleeting moment. Thus, *easy to understand* **(C)** and *easy to penetrate* **(A)** are not really what you're looking for. **(D)** is easy to eliminate if you read the final lines of the passage as well. The last words are "successful at none"; this hardly conveys a sense that any success came easily to the narrator. Of the other choices remaining, only **(E)** makes sense; *transpierceable* here refers to a series of choices that were easy for the flippant and naïve young narrator to dismiss.

26. A

Here's a great example of a typical big picture question. The test makers ask you to glean from the various parts of the text what traits are shared by the two main characters. Examining all the evidence in this case isn't enough. What happens if you aren't sure whether you understand the meaning of all the answer choices given? No worries. Start by eliminating the answers that you do know. From the text, which by now you must know nearly by heart, you can safely say that the father and the narrator shared little in the way of obvious outward personality traits. If the father had bonhomie, or good cheer, the son had extreme cynicism, and never the two shall meet. Thus, answers **(B)** and **(D)** pretty much cancel each other out. As to whether the young man and his father shared a sense of the unconventional, one can infer from the passage that the father found refuge in the sort of ordinary existence that his son sought to eschew. So it's fairly safe to say that **(C)** isn't a shared trait either. Finally, there is no mention made of the father's sense of self-doubt, and since the question asks you to consider the answers in light of the passage you've read, you can eliminate **(E)**. Thus, your best choice seems to lie in answer **(A)**, *prodigality*, meaning reckless extravagance. The father's lack of "Financial Prudence" (lines 39–43) and the son's "expensive habits" (line 24) both fit this definition.

27. B

Now here's a classic big picture question. The final question in this section asks you to consider the overall purpose of the passage. A tough task for many, but not for 1600 test takers! Take a step back and consider the tone, content, and meaning, also taking into account the work you've done analyzing the passage in the questions preceding this one. While the passage certainly heads in any of several directions, note that the question asks you to name which purpose the passage seems to "mainly" serve. So answer choices such as a "post-war sensibility" **(A)** or a "bohemian element" **(D)**, while aspects of the passage, do not really satisfy the needs of the question. Similarly, **(E)** seems too narrow a focus, as the passage's discussion of the narrator's difficulties in finding work only come in towards the end. That leaves you with two choices. Of the two, **(C)** comes off as too harsh and extreme. There is little in the way of true condemnation here. Only **(B)** really approaches all aspects of the passage, especially given the hardships that the young man faces once he is distanced from his family. The narrator is asking the reader to understand his youthful indiscretions as just that, youthful.

Passage 4 (Paired Passage)

Questions 28–40 are based on the following passages.

The following passages present two views of the genius of Leonardo da Vinci. Passage 1 emphasizes Leonardo's fundamentally artistic sensibility. Passage 2 offers a defense of his technological achievements.

Passage 1

What a marvelous and celestial creature was Leonardo da Vinci. As a scientist and engineer, his gifts were unparalleled. But his accomplishment in these capacities was hindered by the fact that he was, before all else, an artist. As one conversant with the perfection of art, and knowing the futility of trying to bring such perfection to the realm of practical application, Leonardo tended toward variability and inconstancy in his endeavors. His practice of moving compulsively from one project to the next, never bringing any of them to completion, stood in the way of his making any truly useful technical advances.

When Leonardo was asked to create a memorial for one of his patrons, he designed a bronze horse of such vast proportions that it proved utterly impractical—even impossible—to produce. Some historians maintain that Leonardo never had any intention of finishing this work in the first place. But it is more likely that he simply became so intoxicated by his grand artistic conception that he lost sight of the fact that the monument actually had to be cast. Similarly, when Leonardo was commissioned to paint the *Last Supper*, he left the head of Christ unfinished, feeling incapable of investing it with a sufficiently divine demeanor. Yet, as a work of art rather than science or engineering, it is still worthy of our greatest veneration, for Leonardo succeeded brilliantly in capturing the acute anxiety of the Apostles at the most dramatic moment of the Passion narrative.

Such mental restlessness, however, proved more problematic when applied to scientific matters. When he turned his mind to the natural world, Leonardo would begin by inquiring into the properties of herbs and end up observing the motions of the heavens. In his technical studies and scientific experiments, he would generate an endless stream of models and drawings, designing complex and unbuildable machines to raise great weights, bore through mountains, or even empty harbors.

It's this enormous intellectual fertility that has suggested to many that Leonardo can and should be regarded as one of the originators of modern science. But Leonardo was not himself a true scientist. "Science" is not the hundred-odd principles or *pensieri** that have been pulled out of his Codici. "Science is comprehensive and methodical thought." Granted, Leonardo always became fascinated by the intricacies of specific technical challenges. He possessed the artist's interest in detail, which explains his compulsion with observation and problem-solving. But such things alone do not constitute science, which requires the working out of a systematic body of knowledge—something Leonardo displayed little interest in doing.

**pensieri*: thoughts (Italian)

Passage 2

As varied as Leonardo's interests were, analysis of his writings points to technology as his main concern. There is hardly a field of applied mechanics that Leonardo's searching mind did not touch upon in his notebooks. Yet some of his biographers have actually expressed regret that such a man, endowed with divine artistic genius, would "waste" precious years of his life on such a "lowly" pursuit as engineering.

To appreciate Leonardo's contribution to technology, one need only examine his analysis of the main problem of technology—the harnessing of energy to perform useful work. In Leonardo's time, the main burden of human industry still rested on the muscles of humans and animals. But little attention was given to analyzing this primitive muscle power so that it could be brought to bear most effectively on the required tasks. Against this background, Leonardo's approach to work was revolutionary. When he searched for the most efficient ways of using human muscle power, the force of every limb was analyzed and measured.

Consider Leonardo's painstaking approach to the construction of canals. After extensive analysis of the requirements for building a particular canal by hand, he concluded that the only reasonable solution was to mechanize the whole operation. Then he considered and ultimately discarded numerous schemes to clear excavated material by wheeled vehicles. It was not that Leonardo underestimated wheeled vehicles. But he realized that a cart is useful only on level ground; on steep terrain the material's weight would nullify the effort of the animal.

Having systematically rejected several solutions in this way, Leonardo began to examine the feasibility of excavation techniques incorporating a system of cranes. Power was again his main concern. To activate a crane, the only transportable motor available at the time would have been a treadmill, a machine that converts muscle power into rotary motion. This is not to suggest that Leonardo invented the external treadmill. However, it was Leonardo who first used the principle of the treadmill rationally and in accordance with sound engineering principles.

Because Leonardo's insights were sometimes so far beyond the standards of his time, their importance to the development of modern engineering is often underestimated. Many scholars, in fact, still regard his work merely as the isolated accomplishments of a remarkably prophetic dreamer, refusing to concede that Leonardo was one of our earliest and most significant engineers.

28. The author of Passage 1 suggests that Leonardo failed to bring many of his engineering projects to completion because
    (A) he knew that he could not achieve the perfection that he found in his art
    (B) his designs were limited by the energy sources that were then available for such projects
    (C) he felt incapable of imparting a sufficiently divine demeanor to such endeavors
    (D) he preferred devoting his genius to works of art rather than science
    (E) he became engrossed in the intricacies of specific technical challenges

29. According to the author of Passage 1, Leonardo's ability to make meaningful contributions to science was hindered by all of the following EXCEPT
    (A) an artistic sensibility
    (B) an intellectual restlessness
    (C) a propensity to come up with impractical solutions
    (D) a compulsion to observe situations and solve problems
    (E) an unsystematic method of inquiry

30. The author of Passage 1 mentions Leonardo's work on the *Last Supper* in order to
    (A) point out that he left many works of art unfinished
    (B) argue that his failure to finish projects was forgivable in the realm of art
    (C) observe his humility when approaching representations of the divine
    (D) contrast his approach to artistic projects with his approach to scientific projects
    (E) reveal his intimate understanding of the perfection of art

31. The author's tone in describing Leonardo's mental processes when "he turned his mind to the natural world" in Passage 1 (lines 25–26) is
    (A) indifferent
    (B) awed
    (C) critical
    (D) disillusioned
    (E) ironic

32. In line 32, *suggested* most nearly means
    (A) recommended
    (B) mentioned
    (C) indicated
    (D) insinuated
    (E) resembled

33. It can be inferred that the author of Passage 1 believes that Leonardo's *pensieri*
    (A) represent an incomplete attempt to advance modern science
    (B) epitomize his tendency to drift randomly from topic to topic
    (C) lack empirical data to back up their conclusions
    (D) signify the crowning achievement of his Codici
    (E) fail to present a systematic body of thought

34. The author of Passage 2 mentions some of Leonardo's biographers (lines 46–49) in order to
    (A) call into question Leonardo's artistic genius
    (B) acknowledge a downside to Leonardo's engineering pursuits
    (C) illustrate the lack of appreciation for Leonardo's engineering contributions
    (D) underscore the prodigal nature of Leonardo's gifts
    (E) demonstrate a bias against the engineering profession among biographers

35. According to the author of Passage 2, Leonardo ultimately abandoned plans to use wheeled vehicles in the construction of canals because

(A) the excavated material had to be cleared mechanically
(B) the vehicles were prone to breaking down on steep terrain
(C) muscle power would prove inadequate to the task at hand
(D) animals would be unable to pull the vehicles at the worksite
(E) wheeled vehicles were less impressive than treadmills

36. The author of Passage 2 would agree with all of the following statements EXCEPT

(A) Leonardo's engineering accomplishments remain undervalued by many scholars
(B) Leonardo's inquiries led to the invention of the external treadmill
(C) Leonardo's writings show him to be more interested in technology than in art
(D) Leonardo was the first person to apply sound engineering principles to the harnessing of muscle power
(E) Leonardo's engineering achievements were at least as notable as his artistic achievements

37. In line 81, *isolated* most nearly means

(A) disconnected
(B) inaccessible
(C) remote
(D) lonely
(E) unique

38. The author of Passage 1 would probably regard the painstaking analysis of canal-building described in Passage 2 as an example of Leonardo's

(A) revolutionary approach to work
(B) ability to complete ambitious engineering projects
(C) artistic fascination with details
(D) predisposition to lose interest in specific problems
(E) penchant for designing unbuildable machines

39. The authors of Passage 1 and Passage 2 would probably agree with which of the following statements?

(A) Leonardo cannot properly be considered a scientist.
(B) Leonardo's intellectual restlessness hampered his ability to complete projects.
(C) Leonardo made significant contributions to the field of applied mechanics.
(D) Leonardo possessed a great natural genius for engineering.
(E) Leonardo's greatest accomplishments were in the realm of art.

40. The author of Passage 2 would most likely dispute the author of Passage 1's assessment of Leonardo's scientific contributions by pointing out that

(A) Leonardo's inquiries spanned practically every field of applied mechanics
(B) Leonardo considered and ultimately discarded many designs in his attempt to mechanize the building of canals
(C) many biographers fail to grasp Leonardo's accomplishments in the field of engineering
(D) many of Leonardo's insights were too advanced to be realized in his era
(E) Leonardo's approach to the construction of canals demonstrated sound scientific methodology

Explanations: Paired Passage 4

Passage 1

The author here examines the difference between Leonardo da Vinci's brilliance as an artist and his deficiencies as a serious scientist. Paragraph I begins by examining the author's perception that Leonardo's artistic sensibilities led him to expect a perfection that he could not bring to science or engineering and that this led to an inconsistency in focus. Paragraph II provides examples of Leonardo's penchant for the impractical solution and how he understood the difference between his art and his engineering. Paragraph III details Leonardo's fertile, if unfocused attention to detail, while paragraph IV summarizes and concludes with a statement that it was Leonardo's unsystematic approach to science that made him an artist with scientific interests rather than a true scientist.

Passage 2

This passage focuses on Leonardo da Vinci's prowess as an engineer and mechanical wizard. Paragraph I quickly rebuffs the idea that some biographers seem to have that Leonardo wasted his talent dabbling in science. Paragraph II conveys the author's feeling that Leonardo's greatest accomplishment may have been his realizations about power and muscle. Paragraphs III and IV offer detailed examples of Leonardo's unique approach to problem solving and engineering. Paragraph V summarizes the author's view that Leonardo's engineering feats are misunderstood precisely because they are so revolutionary.

28. A

This first question asks you to consider the author's intent in regards to Leonardo's engineering projects in passage 1. The best way to attack this question is to return to the paragraphs that discuss Leonardo and engineering. The test makers will, in the paired passages sets, try to get you to confuse the two passages. Answer **(B)** is a good example of this, as the subject of energy sources is addressed in passage 2, not passage 1. **(C)**, regarding "divine demeanor," is a reference to a specific and unrelated part of passage 1 and can therefore be dismissed as a possible answer. There is no proof given in either passage that **(D)** is a viable answer. While Leonardo certainly felt compelled to pursue his art, and while both authors acknowledge his preeminence among his peers in the fields of science and engineering, there is no discussion that he preferred doing his art. Similarly, **(E)** may seem feasible. But looking at lines 4–6 of the first paragraph, we see that the author notes that Leonardo perhaps did not bring the same perfectionism to his engineering tasks because he, "as one conversant with the perfection of art, and knowing the futility of trying to bring such perfection to the realm of practical application," did not feel the need to devote himself in the same way to completion, and therefore, to perfection. You can see that answer **(A)** nicely sums this up for you.

29. D

Here's the first EXCEPT/NOT question in this set of questions. To find the correct answer here, look back at the specifics of passage 1, most notably any section in which the author discusses Leonardo's failures in scientific inquiry. In paragraph I, lines 2–4, he states that Leonardo was "hindered by the fact that he was . . . an artist," answer **(A)**. In line 24, the author says it was Leonardo's "mental restlessness" that proved "problematic," summing up answer **(B)**. The bronze statue example given in paragraph 2 is a solid example of the author's sentiments regarding Leonardo's penchant for impractical solutions, **(C)**. Answer **(E)** can be seen in the very end of the passage, where Leonardo is noted for his unwillingness to use a "systematic body of knowledge," something this author feels true scientific discovery requires. So you're left with only answer **(D)**, which the author discusses in lines 38–40; "a compulsion with observation and problem-solving" is not a hindrance to a scientist. Thus, given that you're looking for the one which does NOT belong, **(D)** is here the correct response.

30. B

A good chance to test your mettle on a detail question. Go back to the section of passage 1 regarding Leonardo and the *Last Supper*, namely the second half of paragraph 2. At this point, the author has already discussed Leonardo's failure to see his scientific tasks through to their conclusion. Here the point is that Leonardo's inability to finish the head of Jesus in the painting was forgivable because the rest of the piece was "still worthy" (line 21) of praise as a work of art. Answer **(A)** is from the wrong part of the passage. Whether Leonardo did or did not leave other works of art unfinished isn't the issue. Discussion of Leonardo's feelings on the divinity of his artistic subjects, answer **(C)**, is discussed in the passage, but here it isn't the reason that the author chooses to bring up the subject of the *Last Supper*. Beware details that may be applicable but are not necessarily linked to the question at hand. **(D)** is a nebulous answer that is certainly at play but cannot be found in the discussion here in Paragraph II, and **(E)** isn't a major part of this discussion at all, either. Only choice **(B)** correctly answers the question.

31. C

This "tone" question offers you an interesting mix of detail and inference. On the one hand, you are given a specific line to analyze. On the other, you are asked to infer the author's *tone*. Taken in context, you can figure out that the author doesn't mean the phrase in question, "he turned his mind to the natural world" (lines 25–26) in an ironic way. Nor is his tone throughout the piece in any way indifferent, awed, or disillusioned. Clearly, he or she has a definite goal in writing this line and the passage in general. Looking back at what you've read and answered about this passage, what can you say about the author's intent and tone? Its easy to see that the author is fairly critical of Leonardo's effectiveness as a scientist, observer of nature, and engineer. Thus, **(C)** seems the likeliest interpretation.

32. C

Ah, a vocabulary-in-context question to decipher. Don't you just love these? You probably know what the word *suggested* means already, even in its various forms. So looking closely at the way it's used here, you should be able to quickly figure this one out. Lines 32–34 says that it's Leonardo's intellectual genius that "has suggested to many that [he] can and should be regarded as one of the originators of modern science." You could try to predict a replacement word, or you could perform a simple fill-in-the-blank with the prospective answers. Neither answer **(A)**, *recommended*, nor **(B)**, *mentioned*, work. The same goes for **(D)**, *insinuated*. None of these really captures the fact that many *do* consider Leonardo as one of the forefathers of modern science. **(E)**, *resembled*, simply makes no sense in this context. Here, the author means the word *suggested* to mean *indicated*, **(C)**.

33. E

Inference time! You are asked to infer the author's impressions of Leonardo's principles of science, the *pensieri* he included in his Codici. The writer implies that Leonardo's words have been "pulled out" of his writing. So he doesn't believe Leonardo meant to use the *pensieri* as proof of his scientific faculties. Only others have done this. Answer **(A)** implies that Leonardo had some doing in creating his reputation as a scientist. Answer **(B)** is a recapitulation of an argument that permeates this essay, but one which in this case does not apply to the Codici. Both **(C)** and **(D)** represent ideas that the passage does not discuss. The only mention of the Codici is in reference to Leonardo's scientific knowledge and there is no discussion of the contents of the *pensieri*. The only thing that you do know about the author's feelings on the *pensieri* is that he or she believes they are falsely held up as proof of Leonardo's scientific acumen. It is the author's view that Leonardo did not display a systematic approach to science. Answer **(E)** neatly sums up this argument.

34. C

The first question related to passage 2 asks you to consider the author's intentions in mentioning outside sources. Read over the passage's opening paragraph again. Clues to the author's intent are everywhere. There is no implication that the author questions Leonardo's artistic prowess, answer **(A)**. Nor is there any validity to the claim in **(B)** that the author wishes to acknowledge Leonardo had a problem with his engineering feats. On the contrary, it is the author's aim to show that it is a too widely held belief that Leonardo's engineering contributions were second to his artistic ones. While Leonardo may have had prodigal talents, this answer makes no sense in regards to this particular passage. **(E)** is simply too harsh in its wording, as the author has no particular beef with the biographers, and certainly not enough to accuse them of bias. Answer **(C)** is the most accurate, especially if you take into account the writer's use of the words *waste* and *lowly* to describe, sarcastically, the biographer's perceptions.

35. D

This detail question requires you to take a look at paragraph III of passage 2. Leonardo's ability to design machinery was not for pure fancy, this author seems to imply. It was utilitarian. On steep terrain, the weight and bulk of the earth that needed to be excavated and transported would "nullify the effort of the animal" that was trying to haul it away. **(D)** is the correct answer and is easily found in reexamining the text. Answer **(A)** is too simplistic, because the excavated material had only to be moved mechanically to increase productivity. While answers **(B)** and **(C)** may have been true to some extent, they are not here mentioned by the author as reasons for why Leonardo abandoned the use of wheeled carts. Answer **(E)** can be dismissed entirely as it has no bearing on the passage you've just read.

36. B

This EXCEPT/NOT question wants you to find the one statement that the author of passage 2 would not agree with. Quickly check for some direct statements in the passage that give you proof of what the author *does* think about these statements. He states in lines 80–81 that "many scholars" still believe that Leonardo's scientific exploits were "isolated" incidents of achievement. Answer **(A)** is, therefore, easily dismissed. In lines 74–75, the author notes that Leonardo did not invent the external treadmill. This statement certainly seems to directly refute answer **(B)**. Quickly looking at the remaining answer choices, answer **(C)** is proven true by the opening few lines of the passage while **(D)** and **(E)** are nearly word for word statements found in the text; **(D)** in line 57 when his work with sound engineering principles is called "revolutionary," and **(E)** in the final line of the passage. Since you want to find what the author does *not* agree with, **(B)** is the best and only answer.

37. A

To solve this vocabulary-in-context question, let's head back to the final paragraph, where the word in question rests. From the sentence from which *isolated* is taken, you can tell that the author is using it in reference not to his or her own opinion, but to show that there are "many scholars" that believe that Leonardo's scientific accomplishments were not connected to the greater development of modern engineering, but rather the *isolated* musings of an artistic genius. You might even have predicted that a good replacement word would mean "not connected" —as in the correct answer choice *disconnected*, **(A)**. In any case, you should be able to weed out a few which don't fit this tone and intent. Answer **(B)**, *inaccessible*, and answer **(E)**, *unique*, don't really fit with this close reading. Meanwhile, **(C)**, *remote*, is off kilter; despite whatever feelings the "scholars" have about why Leonardo did what he did, they don't seem to feel his work was *remote*, or for that matter, *lonely* **(D)**. Therefore, choice **(A)** is your only choice.

38. E

Ah, finally a chance to test your abilities of interpretation across the two passages. Bet you couldn't wait for that one! You'll ace it if you take a really quick look at the paragraph in question and then think back to all the analysis you did in answering all the questions about passage 1. The paragraph in question refers to Leonardo's problem solving in excavating the canals; a problem he solved by creating a design for a mechanical solution. But the author of passage 1 pointed towards Leonardo's penchant for creating complex designs to solve what could be seen as much simpler problems. The author's fairly critical tone regarding Leonardo's engineering feats would probably make the first answer choice wrong. No way would passage 1's author agree with **(A)** or **(B)**, if only because it was the author's contention that Leonardo's designs maximized effort and that he rarely completed such projects. Similarly, answer **(C)** has a fairly positive slant, and thus can be disregarded in favor of a more critical response. Of the remaining two choices, **(D)** can't be corroborated, given the amount of time Leonardo spent on this particular project. Answer **(E)** is most consistent in tone and focus to passage 1, and is therefore correct.

39. D

This big picture inference question also pits passage 1's author against the author of passage 2. This time, the goal is to figure consensus. Take a look at each answer and think about what each author had to say and, more importantly, how he or she said it. Answer **(A)**, for example, fits the focus of passage 1, but most definitely not passage 2. Same thing with answer **(B)**. **(C)**, on the other hand, accords with what author 2 has to say (see lines 44–46), but runs contrary to author 1's central thesis. **(E)** again fits author 1's thesis, but not that of author 2. Only **(D)** really cuts across both authors' seemingly disparate arguments. Author 1 concedes Leonardo's natural genius as an engineer in his second sentence ("As a scientist and engineer, his gifts were unparalleled"), and author 2 states the same in the concluding sentence ("...Leonardo was one of our earliest and most significant engineers").

40. E

Given the tone and content of passage 2—which by now you are no doubt very comfortable with—you should be able to make a strong case for Leonardo's scientific achievements, and address any objections from the author of passage 1. **(A)** regards applied mechanics, a field into which passage 1's author does not delve specifically. **(B)** does not adequately refute passage 1's basic tenet, which is that Leonardo spread himself too thin when solving engineering problems. Answers **(C)** and **(D)**, even if directly stated in passage 2, don't really counter passage 1's assessment of Leonardo's work. Only **(E)** deals directly with author 1's claim that Leonardo da Vinci did not possess sound methodology when executing scientific and engineering work. To the author of passage 2, Leonardo's work on the canal problem is a shining example of his sound approach to engineering.

section two

SENTENCE COMPLETIONS

CHAPTER FOUR

The Sentence Completion Challenge

- Practice the Four-Step Method for Sentence Completions.
- Learn the four categories of Sentence Completion questions.
- Find out what makes hard Sentence Completions hard.

If you're reading this book, most Sentence Completions are probably easy for you. In fact, you may not even have to think about how to fill in the blank; the answer is just there, staring you in the face, and all of the other choices seem absurd. That's great news, and it means that you'll have no problem getting a good score. But wait . . . you want a great score, right? Flying through the easy short verbal questions is important, but it's not going to get you a 1600. In order to ace the hard questions, you'll need to backtrack a little bit and figure out what's going on in your brain when you answer the easy ones. Knowing which strategies work for you on the easy questions is the quickest path to nailing the tough ones.

Let's slow things down for a minute and think about how you find the answer to an easy Sentence Completion.

Blatantly Easy Sentence Completion:

Despite getting a good night's sleep, Dennis was extremely - - - - at work the next day.

Okay, so you read that sentence, then automatically filled in the blank. Right now you're flipping to the Grid-Ins section of the book, your intelligence gravely insulted. Come back! This really won't take long.

Inside your brain

"*Despite* (ding ding ding! That's a clue that something contradictory is about to happen) *getting a good night's sleep* (lucky son-of-a-gun—wish I got a good night's sleep), *Dennis was extremely . . .* (what? *tired*? *lethargic*? *perky*? No, not *perky*, because of the word *despite*—*tired* sounds good) *at work the next day*."

If your thought process was anything like this, you're on your way to that 1600. In a few split seconds, you read the sentence for clues (Step 1) and predicted an answer (Step 2).

> A 1600 test taker makes a prediction for the blank based on clues in the sentence.

On the SAT, every Sentence Completion must contain clues that lead directly to the correct answer. Finding those clues will get you points. Once you've spotted the clues in the sentence, the next step is to predict what word would fit in the blank. As you saw in the sentence above, your mind usually does this automatically. Our minds don't like to see incomplete sentences, so we rush to stick words into blanks—it's human nature. With practice, you'll learn to trust your predictions and make the right choices.

However, unlike those Grid-Ins that you're so eager to get to, Sentence Completions have answer choices for you to deal with. Let's finish this question.

Blatantly Easy Sentence Completion:

Despite getting a good night's sleep, Dennis was extremely - - - - at work the next day.

(A) energetic
(B) fatigued
(C) motivated
(D) quixotic
(E) fractured

Inside your brain

"Okay, which word means *tired*? *Fatigued* is good. Nothing else means *tired*. *Despite getting a good night's sleep, Dennis was extremely fatigued at work the next day*. Works for me. Choice (**B**) it is."

You just completed Steps 3 and 4: You scanned the answer choices for a match and read your selected answer choice back into the sentence.

This may seem elementary, but if you use these steps on every Sentence Completion, every time, you'll avoid careless errors on the easy questions and you'll have a solid foundation for tackling the tough ones.

Step 1: Read the sentence for clues.
Step 2: Predict an answer.
Step 3: Scan the answer choices for a match.
Step 4: Read your selected answer choice back into the sentence.

WHAT MAKES HARD SENTENCE COMPLETIONS HARD

Just what is it that makes a tough question tough? There are four major categories of hard Sentence Completions. In this section, we'll introduce you to each potential problem area and talk you through four tough questions.

Long Sentences

Some tough Sentence Completions will have you wondering whether you've accidentally turned the page and plunged into the Critical Reading section. These monsters look more like short passages than long sentences, and those gaping holes in the middle don't help.

Let's look at a long, tough Sentence Completion and see how we can break it down.

1. The Wankel Rotary Engine was an engineering marvel that substantially reduced automobile emissions, but because it was less fuel-efficient than the standard piston-cylinder engine, it was - - - - in the early 1970s when - - - - pollution gave way to panic over fuel shortages.

    (A) needed . . disillusionment with
    (B) conceived . . awareness of
    (C) modified . . opinion on
    (D) abandoned . . preoccupation with
    (E) discarded . . interest in

Whew. Between the capital letters, the hyphenated words, and the sheer length of the darned thing, this sentence is quite a mouthful. You'll certainly run into long sentences like this one toward the end of your Sentence Completions.

> A 1600 test taker tackles the easier blank first on two-blank Sentence Completions.

Your first task, as with easy questions, is to read the sentence, looking for clues. Let's go phrase by phrase.

> The Wankel Rotary Engine was an engineering marvel that substantially reduced automobile emissions . . .

Try putting this into your own words.

In your brain

"The engine was a marvel that reduced pollution."

And now the next section:

> ... but because it was less fuel-efficient than the standard piston-cylinder engine ...

Here you're given a crucial clue: *but because. But* tells you that the second part of the sentence will contrast with the first, and *because* tells you that an explanation is coming. In this section, we learn that the engine was less fuel-efficient than the standard engine. Put together, we know so far that the engine reduced pollution, but it wasn't fuel-efficient.

... it was - - - - in the early 1970s when - - - - pollution gave way to panic over fuel shortages.

Now we've got two blanks staring at us. Something happened in the early '70s when something about pollution gave way to fuel shortage panic.

A good prephrasing would be: the engine was *rejected or changed* in the 1970s, when *concern with* pollution gave way to panic over fuel shortages.

STRATEGY TIP

For any two-blank sentence, you should do the easier blank first. You can eliminate wrong choices, leaving less work for you to do with the harder blank.

Now we can turn to the choices.

(A) needed . . disillusionment with
(B) conceived . . attention to
(C) modified . . opinion on
(D) abandoned . . preoccupation with
(E) discarded . . interest in

The first blank may seem the easier of the two to tackle, so we'll start there. **(C)**, **(D)** and **(E)** all look good. Moving to the second blank, **(C)** doesn't look so great. *Opinion on*, the second phrase in **(C)**, is probably wrong, since *opinion* doesn't carry the strong feeling that would induce "panic." In **(D)**, if a *preoccupation with* pollution gave way to panic over fuel shortages, it would explain why the engine was no longer valued. This looks like the best answer, but let's check **(E)** to be sure. The second word in **(E)** doesn't fit well in the context. A mere loss of *interest in* pollution wouldn't explain why this marvelous engine was abandoned. **(D)** is our best choice.

STRATEGY HIGHLIGHT: LONG SENTENCES

That was a long, sticky sentence, but we handled it the same way that we handled the blatantly easy sentence, by reading the sentence, looking for clues, prephrasing, and finding the right answer. We also supplemented the basic approach with *Paraphrasing*, a technique that we'll discuss in more detail in the next chapter.

Hard Vocabulary

You may come across one or two Sentence Completions that are Greek to you. Either the sentence or the choices will contain words that are completely unfamiliar to you, and you'll wonder how you can possibly complete a sentence that you don't even understand.

Here's an example that's chock-full of tough words.

While the price of - - - - has often been a high one, never before, it seems, has the press been so intent on - - - - the lives of celebrities.

(A) turpitude . . expunging
(B) notoriety . . surveying
(C) infamy . . determining
(D) idiosyncrasy . . espousing
(E) testimonial . . purging

This is the type of sentence that might look like a nice relief at the end of a long Sentence Completions section. It's short, it's clear, and the longest word is *celebrities*, a word everyone knows. But then you sneak a look at the choices and . . . wham! It must be a hard question after all, because you have no idea what half the words in the choices mean.

What should you do? Forget that you even looked at the choices, and proceed as you would for an easy question.

A 1600 test taker uses prephrasing to help with tough answer choices.

The "lives of celebrities" are the topic here, and the first word that probably leaps to mind for the first blank is *fame*. "The price of fame?" you may be thinking. "What a cliché. If I used that phrase in an essay, my English teacher would kick me out of class." That's probably true, but on SAT Sentence Completions, clichés can be trustworthy tools to help you make predictions.

Moving to the second blank, we can guess that it will be something like "writing about" or "exposing" the lives of celebrities. After all, that's what the press does.

So we get the sentence, we've got a strong prephrase, and it's time to tackle the choices.

(A) *Turpitude*? Does the phrase "moral turpitude" sounds familiar? You may get a serious negative feeling about this word, since it doesn't sound too pleasant. Not sure? How about the second word, *expunging*? You know that the prefix *ex* means "out"; this word probably doesn't mean anything like our prediction "writing about." Let's move on.

(B) *Notoriety*. If you don't know this word, think of "notorious." Yup, that has something to do with fame. It's a keeper for now.

(C) *Infamy*. The word has *fame* right in it, so we may be on the right track.

(D) *Idiosyncrasy*. Even if you don't know exactly how to define this word, you may know that it has a general meaning of being odd or offbeat. It doesn't click with *fame*.

(E) *Testimonial*. You might think of a "testimonial dinner" as something that a famous person might have, but *testimonial* doesn't mean fame.

STRATEGY HIGHLIGHT: HARD VOCABULARY

Being able to understand a sentence and make good predictions will help you when you find tough vocabulary in the answer choices. In the explanation for this question, we talked a little bit about using *Word Charge* to help you with difficult vocabulary. We'll talk more about this strategy in the next chapter.

A 1600 test taker tries to get a fix on unfamiliar words by looking for familiar word roots and prefixes, or thinking about where he could have possibly heard the word before.

We're down to **(B)** and **(C)**. *Surveying* sounds good, and matches our prediction of "writing about." As for **(C)**, does the press *determine* the lives of celebrities? No, that can't be right. **(B)** is correct.

Subtle Structural Clues

As you learned in the introduction to this chapter, clues are your friends. They are the fingerprints, the scraps of cloth left behind in the getaway car, that will help you solve the Mystery of the Empty Blank. However, some tough sentence completions will have subtle or ambiguous clues that may baffle you or even lead you down the path to an incorrect deduction.

Take a look at this example.

> Influenced by the years he spent growing up in a household filled with strife, the author often sought out acquaintances who demonstrated - - - - for argument and showed a veritable - - - - consensus.
>
> (A) a penchant . . reverence for
> (B) an animosity . . veneration of
> (C) a distaste . . disrelish for
> (D) an aptitude . . zeal for
> (E) a disdain . . contempt of

There are no ifs, ands, or buts in this sentence. (Okay, there's one *and*.) No clear, helpful structural clues jump out at us. On top of it all, there are a few tough words to deal with in the sentence.

STRATEGY HIGHLIGHT: SUBTLE STRUCTURAL CLUES

As we worked through this tough Sentence Completion, we discovered that even the most subtle structural clues can help to decode a sentence. We Paraphrased in order to make the sentence clearer. We also used Word Charge to help with the answer choices. You'll learn more about both of these strategies in the next chapter.

First, let's see what we can do to make the sentence clearer. The author grew up in a household filled with strife, or conflict. This influenced him to seek friends who felt some way about *argument* and did something with *consensus*. You might guess that growing up in a strife-filled house would make him desire peaceful friends, but, on the other hand, he might want friends who reminded him of his childhood.

The best clue you have in this sentence is that little word *and*. The *and* tells you that the two blanks will have opposite word charges. Why? Because *argument* and *consensus* are opposites, and the author's friends would either demonstrate a liking for argument and a dislike of consensus, or a dislike of argument and a liking for consensus.

That's as far as we can go with the sentence, so let's attack the answer choices.

In **(A)**, we find two positive words. A *penchant* is a liking for something. **(B)** has *animosity*, a negative word, coupled with veneration, a positive word. So far, so good. Let's check the other choices. **(C)** is easy to eliminate, since these two *dis* words are both negative. In **(D)**, *aptitude* and *zeal* are both positive, and in **(E)**, *disdain* and *contempt* are both negative. **(B)** is the only one that fits our prediction, and it's correct.

> A 1600 test taker knows how to recognize and use subtle structural clues to decode tough sentences.

Unpredictable Two-Blankers

So far, we've looked at three tough two-blank sentences. In general, however, two-blank sentences aren't harder than one-blankers. In fact, many two-blank sentences fall into the easy category, because you have twice as many opportunities to zero in on the correct answer.

Two-blank sentences can seem tough, however, when you can't make a good prediction for either of the blanks. When this happens, as we saw in the previous example, you need to examine the relationship between the blanks.

Here's an example:

> Considering the - - - - era in which the novel was written, its tone and theme are remarkably - - - - .
>
> (A) enlightened . . disenchanted
> (B) scholarly . . undramatic
> (C) superstitious . . medieval
> (D) permissive . . puritanical
> (E) undistinguished . . commonplace

Sometimes Sentence Completions can feel like MadLibs™. In this sentence, it seems that you could just fill in (adjective)/(adjective) and the sentence would take on any meaning you wanted. Prephrasing won't do us much good here, so what can we do?

Following our standard method, let's look for clues. Two words are especially important here: *considering* at the beginning of the sentence and *remarkably* before the second blank. Thinking about how these words are typically used, we can determine that the two blank words will be opposites of each other.

With that in mind, we can go to the choices. **(A)** and **(B)** won't work because there's no specific relationship, opposite or otherwise, between *enlightened* and *disenchanted*, nor between *scholarly* and *undramatic*. **(C)** and **(E)** are out because in both of them, the words are closely related, not opposites of one another. **(D)** looks good: *permissive* and *puritanical* are direct opposites, making **(D)** our answer.

STRATEGY HIGHLIGHT: UNPREDICTABLE TWO-BLANKERS

This question showed us that, while prephrasing is a great tool, it doesn't work on every question. When you run across a tough two-blanker, it helps to get as much information as you can about how the blanks are related before you move to the answer choices. To answer this question, we used the strategy *Working Backwards*, which you'll learn more about in the next chapter.

A 1600 test taker tries to determine the relationship between the blanks—i.e., whether the missing words are closely related or more like opposites—when it's impossible to make an good prediction for either blank.

CHAPTER FIVE

Strategies for Tough Sentence Completions

- Focus on the strategies of Using the Clues, Paraphrasing, Word Charge, and Working Backward.
- Practice the strategies on the tough questions.
- Tackle long sentences, hard vocabulary, subtle sentence structure, and two-blank Sentence Completions.

Sure, the tough Sentence Completions that we looked at in the last chapter didn't seem so bad when we went through them step by step. But unfortunately we won't be there with you on test day, so you're going to need some strategies to take with you. The following strategies tend to work very well for high-scoring students on hard questions. Learn them well, and they will be there to bail you out on the very hardest Sentence Completions.

In this chapter, you'll see more examples of our four categories of hard questions. Watch out for them, and read the explanations carefully.

USING THE CLUES: ADVANCED DETECTIVE WORK

As a top scorer, you probably use clues without thinking very much about it. Like Sherlock Holmes, you walk into your room and know that your little brother has been there by the trail of cookie crumbs leading to the computer.

We mentioned clues in the previous chapter, but now it's time to learn how to really put structural clues to work for you on the toughest questions. As you learned in the last chapter, clues on tough SAT sentence completions can be subtle, but they're often the best tools you've got for cracking the case.

Here's an example of a medium-difficulty Sentence Completion. Find the clues, and solve the case.

> A 1600 test taker recognizes that harder questions tend to have subtle clues that require careful reading.

1. Because she has often been regarded as an author of entertaining light fiction, critics were struck by the - - - - of her latest novel.

   (A) somberness
   (B) jocularity
   (C) popularity
   (D) brevity
   (E) implausibility

Why Is It Hard? Subtle Structural Clues

Key Strategy: Using the Clues

Here's a classic example of tricky clues on a not-so-hard question. You're sweeping along, filling in bubbles at a record pace. You see the obvious clue *because*. You read the rest of the clause, "she has often been regarded as an author of entertaining light fiction." You skip to the choices, pick **(B)**, *jocularity*, the first choice that seems to go with "entertaining light fiction," and you move on. And you get the question wrong.

Yes, *because* is an important clue, but the fact that critics were "struck" by the tone of the author's latest novel indicates that the missing word contrasts with the phrase, *entertaining light fiction*. A good prediction for the missing word would be *seriousness*. Only **(A)**, *somberness*, matches that prediction.

Let's try a tougher one.

2. An ancient and mythopoeic neurological disorder, epilepsy is - - - - in part by the sensation of intense and altered consciousness doctors call an "aura," which - - - - the epileptic seconds before his seizure.

   (A) neutralized . . overcomes
   (B) characterized . . grips
   (C) obviated . . afflicts
   (D) enhanced . . debilitates
   (E) diagnosed . . proselytizes

Why Is It Hard? Subtle Structural Clues, Tough Vocabulary

Key Strategy: Using the Clues

Okay, first of all, stop scanning your brain-dictionary for *mythopoeic*. It means "giving rise to myths," but its meaning isn't very important. In fact, you can ignore the entire first clause and focus on the blanks.

Doctors have connected this "aura" with epilepsy in some way. By taking apart this clause, we see that the word must show this connection: epilepsy is discovered or diagnosed or accompanied by the aura. Looking at the second blank, we see that the aura has some effect on the epileptic before the seizure.

There are no stop, go, or yield signs in this sentence, yet we managed to squeeze some clues out of the dense text. Now try your prediction against the choices.

As always, you should start with the easier blank. The second blank is probably the easier place to start, but all the choices look good except for choice **(E)**, proselytizes. Moving to the first blank, only **(B)**, *characterized*, fits our prediction and is correct.

Paraphrasing

Paraphrasing is one of the most important tools you can use to attack tough Sentence Completions. Putting difficult text into your own words probably comes easy to you. In fact, you probably do it without even realizing it. Still, practicing your paraphrasing skills now will help your speed and accuracy on test day.

> A 1600 test taker practices paraphrasing skills to help decode difficult text.

Read through the sentences below and come up with a paraphrase of your own.

> In addition to the large monetary resources allocated to the project, - - - - manpower assets were made available to its director.
>
> Cinema's focus on the cruelty and decadence of rulers such as Nero and Caligula has led to the popular image of a Roman Emperor as being the very personification of - - - - .

Here's what we came up with:

> *In addition to a lot of money, <u>a lot of</u> men were made available to the project.*
>
> *Cinema focuses on really bad rulers, so people think that the typical Roman Emperor was <u>really bad</u>.*

Pretty easy? Let's put this strategy into practice answering a question.

3. The Victorian novel, notable for its detailed examination of the psychology of its characters, reached its - - - - with the works of George Eliot, which are unmatched in their ability to delineate characters who harmonize devotion to everyday duties with the full development of inner lives.

   (A) dissolution
   (B) advent
   (C) conclusion
   (D) apex
   (E) intention

Why Is It Hard? Long Sentence, Tough Vocabulary

Key Strategy: Paraphrasing

Paraphrasing this bloated sentence is mostly a matter of getting rid of excess verbiage. The meat of the sentence could be written as follows:

> "The Victorian novel reached its - - - - with the works of George Eliot, which are unmatched in their ability to delineate characters."

Once you've pruned the sentence, it becomes clear that the missing word means something like height or pinnacle. **(D)**, *apex*, matches this prediction beautifully.

WORD CHARGE

If you're a top scorer, you probably read all the time: newspapers, magazines, novels, nonfiction books. Odds are that you can't come up with a dictionary definition for every single word that you read on a page. However, as a good reader, you've taught yourself how to get the gist of what you're reading. You instinctively make inferences about whether a word is positive or negative based on your knowledge of roots, prefixes, and suffixes, and the context in which you've seen the word.

This skill will serve you well on tough Sentence Completions. Often, all you really need to get the correct answer is this sense of the positive or negative "charge" of a word.

Let's take a look at a few examples:

Circle the word *positive* or *negative* under each sentence to indicate the word charge of the blank.

1. His face was - - - - , his features pulled downward by the weight of heavy thoughts.

   Positive Negative

2. Though the morbid legends attached to the tower gave it a - - - - aspect at first, the impression is soon softened by the sight of children playing inside.

   Positive Negative

3. The politician's speech was - - - -, exaggerating the latest crime statistics in order to incite angry reactions from frustrated voters.

   Positive Negative

How did you do? In each of these cases, we would look for a negatively charged answer choice, and eliminate any neutral or positively charged answers.

In sentence 1, "pulled downward" and "heavy thoughts" indicate that a negatively charged word would appear in the blank.

In sentence 2, "morbid" and the contrast with "children playing inside" indicate that a negatively charged word would appear in the blank.

In sentence 3, "exaggerating the latest crime statistics" to "incite angry reactions" is not a positive thing for a politician to do. You would anticipate a negative word to fill this blank.

> A 1600 test taker uses her sense of a word's "charge" when the word's definition is not clear.

Let's see how Word Charge can help you cope with tough Sentence Completions.

4. Before she took dance classes, Julia was ---- on the dance floor; now she executes difficult maneuvers with ---- that impresses even experienced partners.

   (A) ecstatic . . an aplomb
   (B) awkward . . a naivete
   (C) incompetent . . an ungainliness
   (D) timorous . . a polish
   (E) assured . . an agility

Why Is It Hard? Tough Vocabulary

Key Strategy: Word Charge

In this sentence, it's clear that Julia's performance on the dance floor was greatly improved by dance classes, so much so that now she "impresses even experienced partners." Thus we can expect that the first blank will be a negative word and the second blank will be a positive word.

If you start with the first blank, you can eliminate **(A)** *ecstatic* and **(E)** *assured,* because these words are too positive to contrast with her later performance. If you then go to the second blank, you can eliminate **(B)** *a naivete*, and **(C)** *an ungainliness*, because you're looking for a positive phrase. Thus, by the process of elimination the answer has to be **(D)**. If you read this selection back into the sentence, it does indeed make sense.

WORKING BACKWARDS

As a good test taker, you probably use the process of elimination as a matter of course. If you can't predict the answer to a question, your gut instinct is to move to the choices and get rid of that ones that won't work. In this section, we can help you enhance your elimination skills and give you practice so you can cross off wrong choices quickly and accurately.

Working Backwards allows you to synthesize everything that you know about Sentence Completions and put that knowledge to work for you on the toughest questions.

> A 1600 test taker knows how to eliminate wrong choices on tough questions.

Try working backwards on this question.

5. Anarchists contend that government is by definition the repression of natural human desire, and their - - - - rivals concur; it is over the - - - - of this definition that the two groups battle.

   (A) sympathetic . . phraseology
   (B) perennial . . semantics
   (C) ideological . . implications
   (D) fascistic . . expression
   (E) fiercest . . etiology

Why Is It Hard? Tough Vocabulary, Unpredictable Two-Blanker

Key Strategy: Working Backwards

For the first blank, which is the easier one, we need a word to describe rivals. The second blank is tougher: we need to read for context. Since the two clauses are joined by a semicolon, the two ideas will support each other or continue a similar thought. The second clause will tell us how the two rival groups differ.

It's time to work backwards. Start at the top, and try out each choice. Since the first blank describes rivals, you can eliminate **(A)** since rivals aren't sympathetic. The second blank helps you eliminate **(B)**: *semantics* means "the meaning of words." If the rivals agreed on the definition, they couldn't disagree on the meaning of the words in the definition. **(C)** looks good: ideological rivals would disagree on the philosophy of whatever it is that they disagree about. It would make sense that these rivals would differ in opinion about something important like the implications of the definition.

Part of working backwards is trying every choice, just in case. In **(D)**, the second word, *expression*, means "the way something is stated." It seems unlikely that the rivals would agree on the definition, but not on how it's stated. **(E)** is out because *etiology* is the study of causes, and it doesn't make sense that they would disagree about the causes of the definition. Don't be tempted by a Sentence Completion answer choice just because it contains tough, unfamiliar vocabulary if there's another answer choice that makes sense.

TOUGH SENTENCE COMPLETION: STRATEGY RECAP

Great Advice for Any Sentence Completion

How to attack SAT Sentence Completions strategically

Step 1: **Read the sentence for clues.**

Every sentence completion sentence contains clues that make only one of the five answer choices correct. With practice, these clues should become more and more apparent.

Step 2: **Predict an answer.**

Sometimes you will be able to come up with a clear, strong prediction. Other times, you will have only a sense of the "charge" of the correct answer. Regardless, it pays off to take a shot at a prediction prior to looking at the answer choices.

Step 3: **Scan the answer choices for a match.**

Depending on the strength of your prediction, this step can go quickly or slowly—the better your prediction, the quicker you'll be able to locate your match.

Step 4: **Read your selection back into the sentence.**

To confirm your choice and avoid careless errors, read your choice back into the sentence. Trust your ear at this point. If it sounds right, pick it. If it sounds wrong, check the other choices again.

How to Attack Two-Blank Sentence Completions

The approach is basically the same, with some slight modifications:

Step 1: Read the sentence for clues.
Step 2: Decide which blank is easier to predict.
Step 3: Predict an answer.
Step 4: Scan the answer choices and eliminate those that don't match the prediction.
Step 5: Read the remaining answer choices back into the sentence. Keep the one that works with both blanks.

Note: We added the extra step of deciding which blank is easier to work with. By focusing on one blank at a time, and eliminating answer choices based on that blank, your job becomes much easier.

What Makes Tough Sentence Completions Tough, and What to Do about It

1. ***Long sentence***

- Paraphrase the sentence
- Ignore the filler
- Use the clues

2. ***Tough vocabulary***

- Use word charge and word roots
- Look for clues
- Work backwards

3. ***Subtle structural clues***

- Read closely
- Paraphrase the sentence
- Use the clues

4. ***Unpredictable two-blanker***

- Focus on the relationship between the blanks
- Use word charge
- Work backwards

Now that you're armed with all the strategies you need to crack the really hard Sentence Completions, try your hand at the practice set in the next chapter to hone your skills.

CHAPTER SIX

Sentence Completion Practice Set and Explanations

Select the lettered word or set of words that best completes the sentence.

Example:

Today's small, portable computers contrast markedly with the earliest electronic computers, which were - - - -.

(A) effective
(B) invented
(C) useful
(D) destructive
(E) enormous

Ⓐ Ⓑ Ⓒ Ⓓ ●

1. The critic was happy to report that the artist had finally attained a maturity of style utterly - - - - his early amateurish pieces.

   (A) descriptive of
   (B) superseded by
   (C) absent from
   (D) celebrated in
   (E) featured in

2. Unlike the - - - - pieces she composed in her youth, her later works were jarring and - - - -.

   (A) immature . . illicit
   (B) placid . . immense
   (C) melodious . . discordant
   (D) saccharine . . prosaic
   (E) dissonant . . cacophonous

3. After the animal behaviorist Karl Lorenz established that many facets of animal behavior are - - - -, psychologists sought to build on his research by defining the influence that hereditary factors have on the development of the human personality.

   (A) unconstrained
   (B) innate
   (C) destructive
   (D) meritorious
   (E) accomplished

4. Though a hummingbird weighs less than one ounce, all species of hummingbird are - - - - eaters, maintaining very high body temperatures and - - - - many times their weight in food each day.

   (A) voracious . . consuming
   (B) fastidious . . discarding
   (C) hasty . . locating
   (D) prolific . . producing
   (E) delicate . . storing

5. The - - - - demise of the protagonist in the final scene of the movie - - - - all possibility of a sequel.

(A) catastrophic . . beguiled
(B) lamentable . . obviated
(C) beneficent . . raised
(D) ironic . . exacerbated
(E) temporary . . precluded

6. The majority of the city's police officers have nothing but - - - - things to say about their new chief, a novel situation for that chronically disgruntled organization.

(A) tepid
(B) querulous
(C) truculent
(D) stentorian
(E) laudatory

7. Usually the press secretary's replies are terse, if not downright - - - -, but this afternoon his responses to our questions were remarkably comprehensive, almost - - - -.

(A) rude . . concise
(B) curt . . verbose
(C) long-winded . . effusive
(D) enigmatic . . taciturn
(E) lucid . . helpful

8. To the - - - - of those who in bygone years tiptoed their way past poinsettia displays for fear of causing leaves to fall, breeders have developed more - - - - versions of the flower.

(A) consternation . . amorphous
(B) dismay . . fragrant
(C) surprise . . alluring
(D) disappointment . . diversified
(E) relief . . durable

9. Artists of the pop art movement emphasized contemporary social values—the vulgar, the flashy, the transitory—in a - - - - from the traditional - - - - with which art had been treated.

(A) departure . . reverence
(B) severance . . whimsy
(C) reemergence . . respect
(D) break . . tolerance
(E) loss . . equality

10. Though scientific discoveries are often disproved shortly after they've been accepted as fact, scientists still seem to leap to hasty conclusions, - - - - that the - - - - nature of what can be called "fact" has not eroded their confidence.

(A) proving . . undeniable
(B) demonstrating . . transitory
(C) showing . . predictable
(D) denying . . distinctive
(E) admitting . . volatile

11. Any large-scale study of another culture will likely result in stereotype by composite in the sense that it will - - - - the highly variable characteristics of individuals into a more generalized norm.

(A) adumbrate
(B) extrapolate
(C) qualify
(D) abbreviate
(E) consolidate

12. High ratings for a television show offer little indication as to its quality, as audiences have become so accustomed to - - - - and so - - - - to television that they will watch practically whatever is on, regardless of its merit.

(A) inadequacy . . averse
(B) mediocrity . . inured
(C) drama . . endeared
(D) entertainment . . habituated
(E) inferiority . . opposed

13. The inflated tone with which some art historians narrate exhibitions would make one think that to attain a legitimate appreciation of art, one is required not only to devote years to its study, but also to possess the ability to offer - - - - interpretations of artistic pieces.

(A) subversive
(B) grandiloquent
(C) intractable
(D) clairvoyant
(E) immutable

14. Paradoxically, Collinsworth's remonstrations against the banality of most detective novels attest to his - - - - the genre.

(A) comprehension of
(B) antipathy toward
(C) ignorance of
(D) devotion to
(E) derision of

15. It would be - - - - to try to - - - - a relationship between mathematics and music, since it is already widely accepted that music is based in mathematical relationships between sounds.

(A) apropos . . extrapolate
(B) superfluous . . establish
(C) intemperate . . posit
(D) redundant . . refute
(E) inappropriate . . fathom

16. In order to achieve her goals, a diplomat must not be too ready to - - - -; success in negotiation depends on the ability to - - - - certain positions while maintaining a firm stance on the goals considered most essential.

(A) compromise . . abide by
(B) challenge. . appease
(C) yield . . resist
(D) persevere . . surrender
(E) conciliate . . concede

17. Some English scholars believe that students tend to have greater difficulty understanding Shakespeare than they do other authors because his works become - - - - on the printed page; it is in their performance that their meaning - - - -.

(A) opaque . . emerges
(B) obtuse . . dispels
(C) muddled . . tapers
(D) evident . . emanates
(E) overwrought . . ensues

18. To some scholars, Freud's fame for popularizing the scientific study of the mind is at least partially undeserved, for he built directly upon the work of psychologists such as Charcot and Janet without - - - - their contributions to his theories.

(A) enlisting
(B) acknowledging
(C) disparaging
(D) differentiating
(E) exploring

19. The resident, in an attempt to prove his stamina, never - - - - to assist in the most detailed and lengthy procedures at the end of a 36-hour shift, in spite of the - - - - potential for error from subsisting on such a minimal amount of sleep.

(A) scrupled . . elevated
(B) failed . . diminished
(C) presumed . . heightened
(D) declined . . immutable
(E) deigned . . negligible

Explanations

1. C

Why Is It Hard? Tough Vocabulary

Key Strategies: Using the Clues, Paraphrase

You can begin by paraphrasing this sentence: The critic was happy that the artist's new work was more mature than his earlier work. A contrast is being drawn between the early, amateurish pieces and the new, mature style. We need a choice that demonstrates this contrast. Choices **(A)**, **(D)**, and **(E)** all imply that the maturity of style was part of the early pieces, which we know to be incorrect. **(B)**, *superseded by*, doesn't make sense. Choice **(C)**, *absent from*, works perfectly.

2. C

Why Is It Hard? Tough Vocabulary

Key Strategies: Word Charge, Working Backwards

It's easier to predict the second blank, because the missing word has to be similar in meaning to "jarring." Working backwards, you can eliminate **(A)**, **(B)**, and **(D)**. If you didn't know the meaning of *discordant*, you could have guessed that *dis-*, a negative prefix, makes this a negative word. *Cacophonous* is another negative word, so **(C)** and **(E)** are in the running.

Turning to the first blank, you'll notice the clue *unlike*, which indicates that the musician's earlier works contrasted with her later works. You can predict that the first blank will mean something like "pleasant sounding." **(C)**'s *melodious* matches this prediction, and is correct.

3. B

Why Is It Hard? Long Sentence, Tough Vocabulary

Key Strategy: Using the Clues

Clues don't always jump right out at you, but sometimes one word can make all the difference. *Hereditary*, or inherited, is a direct parallel with the word in the blank, and only **(B)**, *innate*, has the same meaning.

4. A

Why Is It Hard? Long Sentence, Tough Vocabulary

Key Strategies: Using the Clues, Working Backwards

It's all about eating habits in this question. Don't be put off by the length of the sentence or the few tough words in the answer choices. Begin by using the clue word *though*: it tells you that the hummingbird's tiny weight is at a contrast to its eating habits. You can start with the first blank and eliminate **(B)**, **(C)**, and **(E)**. A fastidious, hasty, or delicate eater wouldn't be at contrast to a low weight. *Voracious*, **(A)**, and *prolific*, **(D)**, both work fairly well, so let's go to the second blank. **(A)** works, since *consuming* means eating, and **(D)** is out since we don't know anything about hummingbirds producing their food.

5. B

Why Is It Hard? Tough Vocabulary, Unpredictable Two-Blanker

Key Strategies: Word Charge, Working Backwards

It's difficult to make good predictions for these blanks. However, we can get an idea of the gist of the sentence and the word charge that the blanks should have. Start with the second blank. The protagonist, or main character, dies in the last scene of the movie (*demise* means death). That means that a sequel would be impossible, so our second blank word must be negative. Looking back to the first blank, we can guess that the protagonist's demise was probably a negative thing.

Let's look at the choices, starting with the first blank. Only **(A)** and **(B)** have very negative words, *catastrophic* and *lamentable*. But if you turn to the second blank, *beguiled* in **(A)** means "tricked," which doesn't work in this context. **(B)**, *obviated*, or removed, works, and it's the answer.

6. E

Why Is It Hard? Subtle Structural Clues

Key Strategies: Using the Clues, Word Charge

The second part of the sentence refers to the police as a "disgruntled organization," which sounds very negative. However, there's one word that changes everything: *novel.* This little clue tells us that the blank word must be positive. **(E)**, *laudatory*, means praiseworthy, and it's correct. If the answer choices were unfamiliar to you, you could have used Word Charge to help eliminate negative words.

7. B

Why Is It Hard? Long Sentence, Tough Vocabulary

Key Strategies: Word Charge, Use the Clues

At first glance, this seems like a tough sentence. Give it a good read, however, and you'll see that there are two excellent clues staring right at you. The first blank is an extreme version of *terse*, or short, and the second blank is an extreme of *comprehensive*. Looking down the choices, you'll see that only **(A)**, *rude*, and **(B)**, *curt*, work for the first blank. *Concise*, **(A)**, is the opposite of comprehensive, and was probably put there to trick you. **(B)**, *verbose*, or wordy, is correct.

8. E

Why Is It Hard? Long Sentence, Tough Vocabulary

Key Strategies: Paraphrase, Working Backwards

The word choice and structure of this sentence make it seem very formal and stuffy. However, it's quite easy to decode if you start with a simple paraphrase. People who used to be very careful around poinsettias feel a certain way now that breeders have changed the plants in some way. Since the plants were fragile in the past, we can assume that they are now more hardy. Only **(E)**, *durable*, fits the bill for the second blank, and it makes sense that the plant shoppers would feel relief that the plants don't fall apart when they walk by anymore.

9. A

Why Is It Hard? Unpredictable Two-Blanker, Tough Vocabulary

Key Strategy: Using the Clues, Working Backwards

The key to this question is the sense of contrast between the vulgar values of the pop art movement and the traditional something with which art used to be treated. Start with the second blank, and you can eliminate **(B)**, *whimsy*, right off. It means "fancifulness" and it doesn't fit the sentence. **(E)**, *equality*, just doesn't make sense, so get rid of it. There's nothing in the sentence about the pop movement being intolerant, so eliminate **(D)**, *tolerance*, because it doesn't provide the necessary contrast. Now look at the first blank. **(C)** doesn't work because *reemergence* is the opposite of what you're looking for, which is a word that indicates a contrast. Only **(A)**, *departure*, works in the first blank, and *reverence* is perfect for the second.

10. B

Why Is It Hard? Long Sentence, Unpredictable Two-Blanker

Key Strategies: Paraphrase, Working Backwards

Paraphrasing this long sentence will help you cut to its essentials. Here we learn that even though discoveries are disproved quickly, scientists still jump to conclusions. What does that indicate about the scientists? It must not bother them that what is supposed to be "fact" is indeed likely to change. After all, they continue leaping to hasty conclusions even though it is common that their discoveries are disproved.

It may be hard to prephrase this one, so let's work backwards. **(A)** can be eliminated because the second word, *undeniable*, is inconsistent with the notion that the facts are changing, and that what we know about them now may not be accepted later. **(B)** looks good, so let's hold on to it for now. **(C)** is out because *predictable* is the opposite of what the sentence is saying about scientific knowledge. **(D)** is illogical in the context. The scientists are still jumping to conclusions, so their confidence must not have been eroded. **(E)** is incorrect because it's not logical to say that the scientists are admitting that they are wrong to jump to conclusions. **(B)** fits best, and is correct.

11. E

Why Is It Hard? Long Sentence, Tough Vocabulary

KeyStrategies: Paraphrase, Working Backwards, Word Roots

We would call this a definition sentence. The phrase *stereotype by composite* is being defined in the second half of the sentence. Your clue to this fact is the phrase *in the sense that. Stereotype by composite* implies the creation of an image that doesn't quite accurately represent any given individual, but rather draws on the most common characteristics, so the missing word is probably something like *combine.*

(**A**), *adumbrate* (to give a sketchy outline of), is not the same thing as to combine. Don't be tempted by an answer choice just because it's a tough vocabulary word. (**B**), *extrapolate*, means to estimate on the basis of known facts, and taking information *outside* the given culture will not help in creating a picture *within* it. (**C**), *qualify*, means modify or limit, and this sentence is not about limiting, but rather, combining. You are now left with two options, and maybe you don't know that *consolidate* means to combine or unite, the correct answer, while to *abbreviate* is to shorten. You can guess, though, knowing the prefix *con-* means "with" or "together." You would imagine that a verb based on bringing things together would probably fit the bill, and it clearly does.

12. B

Why Is It Hard? Long Sentence, Tough Vocabulary

Key Strategies: Paraphrase, One Blank at a Time

You have two straight-ahead structural clues in this sentence, *as* and *and*. It's a safe bet that the missing words will further the concept that high ratings do not tell you how high a television show's quality is. People have probably become accustomed to *low quality television*, so the answer for the first blank should convey that concept. The second blank is best approached by examining the end of the sentence. If people will watch *practically whatever is on*, they are not discriminating, and hence, *used* to television. The second word should connote this idea.

Regarding the first blank, people could be accustomed to *inadequacy*, *mediocrity*, or *inferiority*, but *drama* and *entertainment* don't convey the sense of diminished quality, so (**C**) and (**D**) can be eliminated. Regarding the second blank, people who will watch *practically whatever is on* are unlikely to be (**A**), *averse* (hostile toward), or (**E**), *opposed* to television. (**B**), however, works for both blanks. Even if you didn't know that *inured* meant "accustomed to," you could have gotten to the correct answer by process of elimination.

13. B

Why Is It Hard? Long Sentence, Tough Vocabulary

Key Strategies: Using the Clues, Word Roots

Your content clue in this sentence is *inflated tone*, so you can cut through all filler in the sentence and look for a word that describes an ability that would result in an *inflated tone*, such as *bombastic. Grandiloquent*, (**B**), matches our prediction. If you don't know the definition, you could break the word apart: *grand* = big, *loq* = talk.

Of the wrong answer choices, *subversive* means corrupting; *intractable* means unyielding; *clairvoyant* means psychic; and *immutable* means unchanging, none of which matches our prediction.

14. D

Why Is It Hard? Tough Vocabulary

Key Strategies: Paraphrase, Word Charge, Working Backwards

Your clue word in this sentence is *paradoxically*, which means *seemingly in contradiction*. Thus, Collinsworth objected to the fact that most detective novels were trite or commonplace not because he disliked such novels in general, but because he *liked* them.

Going to the answer choices, *comprehension of* is too neutral; *antipathy toward* is too negative (*antipathy* is severe dislike); *ignorance of* is at best neutral; likewise *derision of* is the wrong charge (*derision* means scorn or ridicule). So all of these choices can be eliminated for being of the wrong charge. *Devotion to* works well, as it shows that Collinsworth had a real dedication to the detective genre.

15. B

Why Is It Hard? Unpredictable Two-Blanker, Tough Vocabulary

Key Strategies: Paraphrase, Working Backwards

The structural clue *since* lets you know that the sentence will continue in one direction throughout. The two words need a specific relationship, and this is the best way to approach the answer choices. Since the relationship between music and math is *widely accepted*, it will either be *logical* to *exploit* a relationship between them, *unnecessary to posit* one, or *useless* to *discredit* one. The best way to approach the answer choices is to work backwards and ask yourself if each pair makes sense, given that the relationship between math and music is already accepted.

Is it *apropos* (appropriate and opportune) to *extrapolate* (infer from known information) a relationship? No, that has already been done, and the relationship established, so **(A)** is out. Is it *superfluous* (more than is needed) to *establish* a relationship? Yes, that is true, since the relationship has already been established. **(B)** looks good, but let's check out the other answer choices. Would it be *intemperate* (excessive) to *posit* (assume the existence of) a relationship? No, it would in fact be quite fitting. Would it be *redundant* to *refute* such a relationship? That makes no sense, since the relationship is beyond refute. Would it be *inappropriate* to *fathom* (comprehend) a relationship? No, it would be highly appropriate, since the relationship is widely known. **(B)** is correct.

16. E

Why Is It Hard? Tough Vocabulary, Subtle Structural Clues

Key Strategies: Paraphrase, One Blank at a Time

The semicolon is a clue that the second part of the sentence will describe what a diplomat must not be too ready to do. The other structure clue is the word *while*, which indicates that a diplomat must maintain two different postures, so if she holds a firm stance on essential goals, she must also be able to *give in* at other times. Thus a good prediction for the second blank is *yield*. So let's begin eliminating based on the second blank: Only **(D)**, *surrender*, and **(E)**, *concede*, match our prediction.

Now check out the first word. A diplomat must not be too ready to *persevere* **(D)**? That doesn't accord with the last part of the sentence, which states that she must maintain a firm stance, so **(D)** is out. How about **(E)**? A diplomat must not be too ready to *conciliate* (meaning placate, as in *conciliatory*)? That does make sense with the rest of the sentence, so **(E)** is correct.

17. A

Why Is It Hard? Long Sentence, Tough Vocabulary; Subtle Structural Clues

Key Strategies: Paraphrase, Working Backwards

You have two structure clues in this sentence, the word *because* and the use of a semicolon. Each indicates that the sentence will continue in one direction throughout. If students have *difficulty* understanding Shakespeare in English classes, you can assume that his works become *harder to understand* on the printed page, which is how students would be experiencing them. Meanwhile, in performance their meaning would *come forth*. So even though the sentence continues in one direction, the two words will contrast with each other, one meaning *harder to see* and the other meaning *easier to see.*

Regarding the first blank: Neither *evident* nor *overwrought* means *difficult to understand*, so rule out **(D)** and **(E)**. Regarding the second blank: Neither *dispels* nor *tapers* contrasts with the first word in each set, making **(B)** and **(C)** incorrect. Try reading **(A)** into the sentence. To be *opaque* is to be difficult to understand, while *emerges* means *comes forth*, so **(A)** is correct.

18. B

Why Is It Hard? Long Sentence

Key Strategies: Paraphrase

The word *for* is acting as a structural clue in this sentence. The missing word will continue the notion that, to some extent, Freud's fame is *undeserved.* The second half of the sentence addresses *why* his fame may be undeserved. He built directly on the work of other people without doing something to do with their *contributions to his theories.* A safe guess would be that he did not *credit* their contributions.

Enlisting (engaging the support of) is the opposite of what he did—Freud used their theories extensively, so eliminate **(A)**. **(B)**, *acknowledging,* means crediting or admitting, so that would work here. But let's be sure. **(C)** *disparaging* (belittling) is negative in tone, which does not work in this sentence. **(D)**, *differentiating*, clearly does not work, as it means to discriminate or see as different. Finally, **(E)**, *exploring* (searching, investigating systematically), makes no sense either, as he must have explored their work to use it. The correct answer is thus **(B)**.

19. A

Why Is It Hard? Long Sentence; Tough Vocabulary

Key Strategies: Paraphrase; Working Backwards

The words *in spite of* are clues in this sentence. In addition, the negatives in this sentence flip the meaning in important ways. The first half of the sentence discusses the resident's actions at work, while the second half reminds us that performing difficult procedures on little sleep can *do something* to one's potential for error. It seems obvious that the second word will be something like *increased.* So let's begin eliminating there. Only **(A)**, *elevated*, and **(C)**, *heightened*, match our prediction for the second blank.

Given the contrast, and the fact that the resident was attempting to prove his stamina, we can expect that he continued to offer his help in difficult procedures, even if doing so could result in a greater chance of making mistakes. Given the negative *never*, if he always offered his help, he never *hesitated* to offer his help. Now let's check out the answer choices. Your two remaining options are *scrupled* and *presumed.* Even if you didn't know that *scrupled* means to show reluctance on grounds of conscience, you should *know* that *presumed* doesn't make sense here, and so the correct answer is **(A)**.

section three

ANALOGIES

CHAPTER SEVEN

The Analogies Challenge

- Learn the Three-Step Kaplan Method for tackling Analogies
- Identify weak and strong Analogy bridges
- Find out how to deal with Tough Vocabulary, Tempting Wrong Answers, and Traps

Instinctive test takers usually fly through Analogies, snapping up points left and right without mumbling the words "blank is to blank as blank is to blank" even once. If you're one of these test takers, you may find that the last few questions are like hitting a brick wall, fast. The mental magic that works on easy Analogies doesn't always work on the hard ones, especially if you don't know some of the tough vocabulary words.

Let's break down how your mind works when you attack simple analogies, then see how we can apply the same skills to tougher questions.

Blatantly Easy Analogy Stem Pairs

APPLE : FRUIT

KITTEN : CAT

SLUGGISH : FAST

Inside your brain

"Okay, what does apple have to do with fruit? An APPLE is a type of FRUIT. Moving on . . . A kitten, by definition, is a cute little cat. Wait, I can do better than that. A KITTEN is a baby CAT or a young CAT. Yeah, that's more precise. And something sluggish is slow, so SLUGGISH means not FAST."

When you evaluate an Analogy, you ask the question: What's the relationship between the paired words? The key to Analogy questions lies in forming a sentence that shows the relationship between the word pairs. We call this sentence a bridge.

Try out your bridge skills on this question.

Blatantly Easy Analogy Question

WRITER : NOVELIST ::

(A) scientist : astronomer
(B) teacher : student
(C) physician : patient
(D) poet : researcher
(E) worker : debutante

Inside your brain

"Writer and novelist. Hmm . . . it's easier to turn this one around: A NOVELIST is a type of WRITER. That's a good bridge. Let's look at the choices one by one. An *astronomer* is a type of *scientist*. That's true. Must be right. I guess I'd better check the other choices, though. A *student* is a type of *teacher*. It's possible, but definitely not necessary. A *patient* is a type of *physician*. Well, a physician could be a patient, but no, this doesn't work. A *researcher* is a type of *poet*. Nope. A *debutante* is a type of *worker*. No way. **(A)** must be correct."

A 1600 test taker builds a strong bridge the first time, so she doesn't need to waste time refining the bridge.

Here's a recap of the thought process you just went through. Whenever you answer an SAT Analogy question, you should follow these steps:

Step 1: Make a **strong** bridge between the stem words.

Step 2: Go through **all** the answer choices and plug them into this bridge. Eliminate any pair that makes no sense when plugged into this bridge.

In some cases, you'll need one more step:

Step 3: In the (rare) event that more than one answer choice works, **refine** your bridge by making it more specific, and try it again on the remaining answer choices.

STRONG AND WEAK BRIDGES

Like any good civil engineer, you evaluated the strength of your bridges as you built them. This skill should be a natural part of your bridge-building technique. Here's why:

- The correct answer always has the same strong bridge as the words in the stem pair.
- The incorrect answer choices will either have weak bridges or different bridges from the words in the stem pair.

As we tackle some harder Analogies, keep this in mind:

STRONG BRIDGES: The word pairs are linked by strong and certain terms, such as **is**, **does**, **lacks**, **are always**, and **can never.**

WEAK BRIDGES: The word pairs are linked by uncertain terms such as **can**, **sometimes**, **usually**, and **may or may not**.

STRATEGY TIP:

One way to know you have a strong bridge is to apply the "by definition" test. Try sticking "by definition" into your bridge. If the bridge still makes sense, you know you have a strong bridge.

WHAT MAKES HARD ANALOGIES HARD

What makes a tough question tough? There are three major categories of hard Analogies. In this section, we'll introduce you to each potential problem area and talk you through some tough questions.

Tough Vocabulary

MYMBILLIC : COMBNORCTION

Don't worry. These words don't really exist, although some stem words towards the end of a set of Analogies might seem about as indecipherable. When this happens, you can still earn points by using the answer choices, and, where necessary, making strategic guesses.

1. PATHETIC : RUTH ::
   (A) cryptic : puzzlement
   (B) arrogant : humility
   (C) criminal : contempt
   (D) beautiful : sorrow
   (E) glib : loathing

2. ARCANUM : SECRECY ::
   (A) agreement : confidentiality
   (B) guffaw : anger
   (C) grudge : generosity
   (D) slumber : imagination
   (E) genius : intelligence

These two questions have something in common. Each has a tough word in the stem that may have thrown you off for a moment. *Ruth*? *Arcanum*?

> A 1600 test taker uses his knowledge of word roots, combined with common sense, to decode hard vocabulary words.

When you have a question with a word you don't know in the stem, take a two-pronged approach:

1. **Decode the word.** Use your knowledge of roots, prefixes, and suffixes and your common sense to guess what the word might mean.

2. **Eliminate choices.** In most Analogies, you can eliminate a few choices because they're inherently flawed.

Let's look at question 1. What is *ruth*, besides the last name of a famous baseball player? If you know the word *ruthless*, you can guess that *ruth* means "mercy" or "sympathy," since a ruthless person lacks those qualities. If you made this guess, you can make a strong bridge: Something PATHETIC causes people to feel RUTH. You're in business. Go directly to the choices.

What if you didn't make the leap from *ruth* to *ruthless*? You still have a good chance of nailing this hard Analogy. Evaluate the strength of the bridges in the choices.

(A) Something *cryptic* causes people to feel *puzzlement*. Gee, that sounds familiar.
(B) Someone who is *arrogant* lacks *humility*. That's a good strong bridge.
(C) Can you make a strong bridge for *criminal* and *contempt*? Not really.
(D) Can you make a strong bridge for *beautiful* and *sorrow*? Nope.
(E) Can you make a strong bridge for *glib* and *loathing*? I don't think so.

Only **(A)** and **(B)** have strong bridges. Even if you were clueless about *ruth*, you'd now be down to two choices, which greatly improves your odds.

But you can go even further by working backwards with the bridges you built. Try them out on the stem pair. "Something *pathetic* causes people to feel *ruth*." Okay. "Someone who is *pathetic* lacks *ruth*." If the first sentence sounds better to you, you should pick **(A)**, which is, in fact, the correct answer.

Let's look at question 2. Can you decode the word *arcanum*? Say it to yourself. It kind of sounds like *arcane*, doesn't it? Something that is *arcane* is secret. Maybe an *arcanum* is a secret thing, making your bridge: an ARCANUM is characterized by SECRECY. That's a nice, strong bridge.

STRATEGY HIGHLIGHT

In both of these Analogies, we used the strategy of *Working Backwards*, which you'll learn more about in the next chapter. We also reminded you that you should use your general knowledge to make educated guesses about the meaning of tough words.

A 1600 test taker works backwards on tough questions, eliminating choices that can't be right.

If you didn't catch the arcane definition of this word, you could go right to the choices and start eliminating.

(A) An *agreement* may or may not involve *confidentiality*, so you can eliminate this weak bridge.

(B) A *guffaw* is a type of laugh, and laughing doesn't have a direct relationship with *anger*.

(C) A *grudge* is a feeling of resentment. It doesn't have anything to do with *generosity*. Eliminate this choice.

(D) A *slumber* has no clear relationship to *imagination*, so you can eliminate this choice.

(E) A *genius* is characterized by *intelligence*. That's a great bridge that happens to match the one we built, and it's correct.

Tempting Wrong Answers

Sometimes you'll be tempted. You'll see an answer choice that is jumping up and down on the page yelling "Pick me! Pick me!" You know something must be wrong because there's that other choice sitting there calmly, a smile on its face, secure in the knowledge that it's correct. You need to learn how to turn down the volume on those tempting choices. High scorers are particularly susceptible to flashy wrong choices because these tempters often contain tough words. Check out these examples and try to find the tempting wrong answers. While you're at it, find the right answers too.

A 1600 test taker knows how to resist temptation and consider each choice carefully.

3. PUNISHMENT : REPRIEVE ::

    (A) guilt : confession
    (B) disease : remission
    (C) security : insurance
    (D) freedom : manumission
    (E) legislation : veto

4. SUPERCILIOUSNESS : ARROGANT ::

    (A) parity : concerned
    (B) rest : elderly
    (C) pulchritude : homely
    (D) knowledge : omniscient
    (E) somnolence : sleepy

Question 3 isn't too tough, since you probably know most of the vocabulary words. A release from PUNISHMENT is called a REPRIEVE. Check out the choices.

(A) A *confession* may or may not be a release from *guilt.*

(B) A *remission* is a release from *disease.* That sounds pretty good.

(C) An *insurance* is a release from *security.* No, that sounds totally wrong.

(D) A *manumission* is a release from *freedom.* That could be....

Uh oh. I don't know what *manumission* means. What if it's better than **(B)**? It's got that fancy word in it. Maybe it's right. And "freedom" kind of goes with "punishment." This sounds good. I'd better pick it.

No. You have a good choice, **(B)**. It's a better bet to go with a choice that you know works than one that you don't. And, in fact, *manumission* means "the granting of freedom," which makes this choice the opposite of what we need.

(E) A *veto* is not a release from *legislation*, though a veto can be used to block a law.

(B) is your best choice for this tricky Analogy.

Let's look at question 4.

Someone who is characterized by SUPERCILIOUSNESS is ARROGANT. This is a fairly tricky stem pair: If you had trouble with the vocabulary, peek back to the last section for decoding and elimination help. If you're with us, read on.

(A) Someone who is characterized by *parity*, or equality, is *concerned*? That doesn't make sense.

(B) Someone who is characterized by *rest* is *elderly*? No. The elderly may rest more than younger people do, but that doesn't fit our bridge.

(C) *Pulchritude* means "beauty" (yes, it is an awfully ugly word to have such a definition). *Homely* means "plain," so these two words are near opposites, and not a match for our bridge.

(D) Someone who is characterized by *knowledge* is *omniscient*? Pick me, pick me? Hold on for a second.

(E) Someone who is characterized by *somnolence*, or sleepiness, is *sleepy*. Bingo. This choice must be right.

But what about the "Pick Me!" choice? Well, simply having *knowledge* doesn't make someone *omniscient*. Having knowledge makes you knowing, but not all-knowing, which is the definition of omniscience. **(D)** was tempting, but wrong. That's why you have to try out all the answer choices. Stick with **(E)**.

STRATEGY HIGHLIGHT

You used what you've learned about strong and weak bridges to answer these questions. You also used the strategy of *Working Backwards* and learned about trusting your gut when confronted with tempting wrong answers.

Traps

If you were going to write a hard Analogy question, how would you make it hard? You'd probably put in some "trick" answers to try to fool high scorers into making careless mistakes. The Analogy section is full of traps, and we'll show you how to avoid several different types of pitfalls that can occur in any question, even an easy one. Here's an example.

5. ASSAILANT : ATTACK ::
   (A) perpetrator : identify
   (B) criminal : charge
   (C) adversary : support
   (D) interlocutor : converse
   (E) protagonist : halt

Look at **(A)** and **(B)**. Don't they seem to just go with the stem pair? "The assailant attacked at 0900 hours...." "Identify the perpetrator from this line of suspects." "Charge this criminal with murder!" They're not only words that you'd hear on cop shows, they're also cliché phrases. A careless test taker (and yes, you high scorers can be the worst offenders in this category) might see one of these choices, and make a quick guess, based on the topic they share with the stem pair (we call this *Same Subject Temptation*) or the clichéd nature of the choice. Remember how we told you in Sentence Completions that clichés can help you find the answer? Not so in Analogies.

Let's answer the question. To ATTACK is the defining action of an ASSAILANT. You can form the simple bridge, an ASSAILANT ATTACKS.

We should already be very suspicious of **(A)** and **(B)** because of the Same Subject Temptation and Cliché issues, but let's take a look.

Does a *perpetrator identify*? No, a perpetrator is the person who commits a crime, and so the perpetrator is usually identified.

Does a *criminal charge*? No, a criminal is charged with a crime.

STRATEGY HIGHLIGHT

We introduced you to the Same Subject Temptation and Cliché traps in this question. In the next chapter you'll be introduced to other trap types and learn more about how to avoid traps in Analogy questions.

Moving on to **(C)**, does an *adversary support*? No, in fact, an *adversary*, or enemy, opposes or undermines.

Does an *interlocutor converse*? Yes, an interlocutor is someone who, by definition, is conversing.

Does a *protagonist halt*? A protagonist, or main character, may or may not halt.

Note that even if you didn't know what *interlocutor* meant, you could have eliminated the other choices because none had the same bridge as the stem pair.

(D) is correct.

A 1600 test taker recognizes traps and avoids them.

CHAPTER EIGHT

Strategies for Tough Analogies

- Learn the most important strategies for acing Analogies
- Study the six Classic Bridges
- Apply the Three Step Method for working backwards on tough Analogies
- Identify and avoid the six most common traps

In the last chapter we talked you through those hard Analogy types step by step. If things are moving a little too slowly for you, we promise to pick up the pace in this chapter. We're going to show you the most important strategies for getting any Analogy question right so you can scoop up every possible point on test day. Learn and practice these strategies, and your Analogy skills on the toughest questions will improve dramatically.

In this chapter, you'll see more examples of our three categories of hard questions. Watch out for them, and read the explanations carefully.

KNOW YOUR BRIDGES: THE CLASSICS

Certain bridge types show up over and over again on the SAT. We call them "Classics" because of their timeless, elegant quality. Also, they can help you kick butt.

Learning the Classic Bridges is all about increasing your speed. It can help you on easy, medium, and difficult questions. Classic Bridges also make you feel like an insider on test day. *Sure, I'm cool. I know that bridge. It's the bridge of* function. *I rule.*

Let's look at six of the most common bridges.

Lack: Someone/Something _____ *lacks* _____ or A _____ *lacks* _____.
Examples: MISER : GENEROSITY or BRAGGART : MODESTY

Characteristic: A _____ *is always* _____ or A _____ *is never* _____.
Examples: CLICHÉ : TRITE or DESERTER : LOYAL

Extreme: Something/Someone ____ *is extremely* ____
Examples: DISCONSOLATE : SAD or DERISIVE : CRITICAL

Function: A _____ *is used to* _____.
Examples: AIRPLANE : TRANSPORT or SCALPEL : CUT

Type: A ______ *is a type of* _____.
Examples: PATELLA : BONE or HIBISCUS : FLOWER

Part/Whole: A _____ *is part of a* _____.
Examples: SHIP : FLEET or THORN : ROSE

A 1600 test taker uses her knowledge of Classic Bridges to save time on test day.

Give this question a try, keeping your eye out for Classic Bridges.

FATIGUE : ENERGY ::

(A) sleep : restfulness
(B) jealousy : envy
(C) narcissism : mirror
(D) patience : time
(E) health : illness

Why Is It Hard? Traps

Key Strategy: Classic Bridges

Start, as always, by building a bridge between the stem words. In this case, the bridge is prefabricated, and it's a classic, the bridge of lack. FATIGUE is characterized by a lack of ENERGY. You can go to the choices.

(A) should set off very loud alarm bells in your head. *Sleep* and *restfulness* are directly related to fatigue and energy, and you need to watch out for Same Subject temptation. *Sleep* is not characterized by a lack of *rest*, so this choice can't be right.

Jealousy is not characterized by a lack of *envy*. *Narcissism* is not characterized by a lack of a *mirror*. *Patience* is not characterized by a lack of *time*.

Choice **(E)** looks great: *health* is characterized by a lack of *illness*. This pair and the stem pair both have the classic bridge of lack. **(E)** is correct.

WORKING BACKWARDS

When analogies get tough, the tough work backwards. Frequently you can make a good guess without even knowing the meanings of the words in the stem pair.

Smart test-takers use the fact that the stem and the correct answer will always have the same strong bridge to get the right answer, even when the stem pair stumps them.

Let's work backwards. For starters, you know all the **weak bridges** in the answer choices can't be right. You can also eliminate any two choices with **identical bridges**. Last, you can get rid of any answer choice with a **bridge that can't work with the stem pair**.

Here's what we mean.

Step 1: Eliminate all the answer choices that have weak bridges.

XXXXX : XXXXX ::

(A) angry : violent
(B) diligent : lazy
(C) outrageous : improper
(D) studious : perceptive
(E) circumspect : careful

We've hidden the stem pair, so there will be no cheating. Let's run down the choices, searching for weak bridges.

Someone who is *angry* might be *violent*. That "might be" tells us that this is a weak bridge. Eliminate **(A)**.

Someone *diligent* is never *lazy*. That's a nice strong bridge (in fact, it's a Classic). Hang on to **(B)**.

Something *outrageous* is very *improper*. Here's another strong Classic bridge. **(C)** is good.

Someone *studious* might be *perceptive*. That's a weak bridge, and **(D)** can be eliminated.

Someone *circumspect* is very *careful*. That's a strong, Classic, familiar-sounding bridge. Hang on to **(E)**.

We're left with **(B)**, **(C)**, and **(E)**.

Moving on, let's try **Step 2:** Eliminate any two choices with identical bridges.

Remember how familiar **(E)**'s bridge sounded? That's because **(C)** and **(E)** have identical bridges. They can't both be right, so they must both be wrong, leaving **(B)** as the correct answer.

Just to be thorough, let's reveal the stem pair.

HALCYON : TURBULENT ::

(A) angry : uncontrolled
(B) diligent : lazy
(C) outrageous : improper
(D) studious : perceptive
(E) circumspect : careful

Why Is It Hard? Tough Vocabulary

Key Strategy: Working Backwards

HALCYON means "calm or peaceful." Something HALCYON is never TURBULENT, so **(B)** is a perfect fit. Someone *diligent* is never *lazy*.

We didn't need to use Step 3 for that question, so let's try it out on another example:

Step 3: Eliminate any choice that can't work with the stem pair.

FORD : RIVER

(A) slope : hill
(B) path : hiker
(C) pass : mountains
(D) stalactite : cave
(E) peak : crest

Why Is It Hard? Confusing Stem Bridge

Key Strategy: Working Backwards

FORD™ is a common enough type of car. Here, though, that can't be its meaning. Unless you're an Eagle Scout, you may not be familiar with the definition of FORD, although you should be able to tell that it's being used as a noun here. If you can't build a bridge, go to the choices.

> **(A)** What's the relationship between *hill* and *slope*? A hill has a slope, sort of. This is a pretty weak bridge.
>
> **(B)** A *hiker* walks on a *path*. That's not too bad. Could the stem pair have this bridge? A RIVER walks on a FORD? I don't think so. **(B)** is an example of a choice that can't work with the stem pair.
>
> **(C)** A *pass* is a possible crossing place for *mountains*. Could a FORD be a possible crossing place for a RIVER? I don't see why not. If you didn't know the meaning of *pass* when used as a noun in conjunction with mountains, you could have skipped this choice for now.

(D) A *stalactite* is a hanging protrusion from the roof of a *cave*. Could a FORD be a hanging protrusion from the roof of a RIVER? That doesn't seem likely. If you didn't know the meaning of *stalactite*, you could have skipped this choice for now.

(E) A *crest* is the same as a *peak*. Both are the top of something, like a mountain. This isn't a very strong bridge. In fact, it's a bridge of exact synonyms, which cannot be right, as you'll learn about in the next section.

We're left with **(C)** and possibly **(D)**. In fact, a FORD is a possible crossing place in a RIVER, so **(C)** is correct.

Let's recap what we've learned here. You can eliminate choices that have weak bridges, choices that have identical bridges, and choices that can't work with the stem pair. As you work through the questions in the practice set in the next chapter, watch out for these wrong answer choice types, especially when you have a hard time with the stem pair.

AVOIDING TRAPS

In the last section, you met some of the wrong answer types that you can expect to see on tough SAT Analogies. Getting comfortable with the typical tempting but wrong answers you'll encounter will help you knock these trap answers out quickly. Here are some examples.

A 1600 test taker is familiar with common traps that appear on the SAT.

Unrelated words

Sometime wrong answers are wrong simply because there is no relationship between the words in the choice. These are the easiest to spot and eliminate.

Examples: obsolete : superficial; antagonist : satiate

Same subject trap

We encountered these false friends in the last section. Same subject traps can be tricky. They include a word or words that belong to the same general subject area as a word or words in the stem pair. On closer analysis, these answer choices have totally different bridges from the stem pair.

Example: If your stem pair were MARITIME : SEA, same subject traps might include words such as *boat*, *ship*, or *ocean*. Same subject traps appear most often on difficult analogies. Be wary of answer choices that contain words that are related to the same subject as the question stem on later analogy questions.

"Both are" bridge

"Both are" bridges are word pairs in which there is no clear relationship between the words, but instead the two words both belong to a larger group or category.

Examples: earring : necklace; cat : dog. Both an *earring* and a *necklace* are pieces of jewelry. Both a *cat* and a *dog* are pets. Neither of these bridges is strong, and they can quickly be eliminated.

Exact synonyms or antonyms bridge

Examples: verbose : loquacious ; happy : glad ; brilliant : idiotic ; succeed : fail

You might think that all of the above word pairs have very strong bridges, and you might even have a point, but not on the SAT. Correct SAT bridges will never be of exact synonyms or exact antonyms, so if you see these relationships among the answer choices, you can eliminate accordingly. Just be careful when you apply this strategy that you actually are dealing with exact synonyms or exact antonyms. For instance, two words may seem like synonyms—such as affectionate : doting—when in fact they are connected by a classic Extreme bridge: A *doting* person is excessively *affectionate.*

Context/cliché trap

The words in the pair are not linked by a strong bridge, but they sound good together only because they often appear together in common phrases or cliches.

Examples: roast : beef; mitigating : circumstance; happy : camper. In these cases, although the pair of words sound familiar, they do not actually form a strong bridge, and you should steer clear of them.

Wrong bridge

The bridge in the answer choice is strong; it simply is a different bridge from the stem pair.

Example: If the stem pair were RIB : BONE, and **(B)** was simpleton : intelligence, even though **(B)** has a strong bridge, it still would not be correct, since a rib is a type of bone, while a simpleton lacks intelligence.

Reversed bridge

The bridge is strong, but the order is reversed from the bridge in the stem pair.

Example: If the stem pair were FEMUR : BONE we would be looking for a choice that satisfies the "_____ is a type of _____" bridge. A tempting wrong answer of this type would reverse the bridge like this: mollusk : clam, or flower : hibiscus. A *clam* is a type of *mollusk*, and a *hibiscus* is a type of *flower*, but these bridges go in the wrong direction.

TOUGH ANALOGIES: STRATEGY RECAP

How to Attack SAT Analogies Strategically

What to do when you know both stem words

Step 1: **Build a strong bridge between the stem words.**
Keep the sentence short and to the point. Use one word to define the other. Be on the lookout for "Classic" bridges.

Step 2: **Plug in the answer choices.**
Go through all the answer choices and plug them into your bridge. Eliminate any pair of words which make no sense when plugged into this bridge.

Step 3: **Adjust your bridge if you need to.**
In the event that more than one answer choice works, refine your bridge by making it more specific. Try out your new bridge on the remaining answer choices.

What to do when you don't know both stem words

Step 1: **Eliminate all answer choices with weak bridges.**
Any answer choice with a weak bridge cannot be the correct answer.

Step 2: **Eliminate answer choices with identical bridges.**
If you're really sure that two or more answer choices share the exact same bridge, you can be confident that none of those choices will be correct.

Step 3: **Eliminate answer choices with bridges that can't fit the stem.**
In other words, find strong bridges for each of the remaining answer choices, and try out each of these bridges on the stem pair. Eliminate those that don't make sense, and pick the one that sounds the best.

Tempting Wrong-Answer Traps to Avoid

- Same subject traps
- Cliché traps
- "Both are" bridges
- Reversed bridges
- Wrong bridges
- Exact synonyms or exact antonyms

Armed with all these strategies, you should be able to crack the tough Analogies in the practice set that follows this chapter.

CHAPTER NINE

Analogies Practice Set and Explanations

Choose the lettered pair of words that is related in the same way as the pair in capital letters.

Example:

FLAKE : SNOW ::

(A) storm : hail
(B) drop : rain
(C) field : wheat
(D) stack : hay
(E) cloud : fog

Ⓐ ● Ⓒ Ⓓ Ⓔ

1. OMINOUS : DISASTER ::
   (A) auspicious : success
   (B) dangerous : alert
   (C) difficult : task
   (D) corrected : error
   (E) terrifying : legend

2. EDIFICE : BUILDING ::
   (A) shack : bungalow
   (B) tome : book
   (C) magazine : newspaper
   (D) couch : bench
   (E) jewelry : necklace

3. INEFFABLE : EXPRESS ::
   (A) interminable : delay
   (B) inscrutable : see
   (C) intangible : touch
   (D) insouciant : charm
   (E) infallible : alter

4. COAGULATE : CLOT ::
   (A) prosecute : sentence
   (B) inject : needle
   (C) obstruct : blockade
   (D) freeze : ice
   (E) dwindle : hoard

5. DROSS : METAL ::
   (A) sawdust : wood
   (B) coke : steel
   (C) sludge : wine
   (D) ozone : atmosphere
   (E) fossil : dinosaur

6. MENDACIOUS : VERACITY ::
   (A) nosy : inquisitiveness
   (B) irreproachable : isolation
   (C) amoral : fidelity
   (D) tardy : punctuality
   (E) dubious : question

7. CUR : BASE ::
   (A) victor : defeated
   (B) octogenarian : wise
   (C) genius : twisted
   (D) villain : evil
   (E) athlete : heavy

8. PENITENT : REGRET ::
   (A) imperceptible : detect
   (B) zealous : doubt
   (C) exuberant : socialize
   (D) critical : rue
   (E) querulous : quibble

9. ABDICATE : THRONE ::
   (A) rule : nation
   (B) revolt : government
   (C) defeat : candidate
   (D) impeach : politician
   (E) resign : office

10. CASTIGATE : WRONGDOING ::
   (A) congratulate : success
   (B) amputate : crime
   (C) annotate : consultation
   (D) deface : falsehood
   (E) fulminate : habit

11. CANT : SPEECH ::
   (A) dogma : belief
   (B) flattery : praise
   (C) skill : faculty
   (D) dance : minuet
   (E) diatribe : essay

12. APOSTATE : BELIEF ::
   (A) patriot : tolerance
   (B) libertine : debauchery
   (C) gadfly : resentment
   (D) ascetic : comfort
   (E) hedonist : indulgence

13. EXCULPATE : BLAME ::
   (A) abash : shame
   (B) forswear : violence
   (C) decipher : code
   (D) compensate : crime
   (E) forgive : debt

14. UNGUENT : IRRITATION ::
   (A) acid : corrosion
   (B) balm : relief
   (C) bridle : mobility
   (D) sextant : direction
   (E) debate : controversy

15. MAVEN : EXPERTISE ::
   (A) monarch : wisdom
   (B) athlete : determination
   (C) neophyte : honesty
   (D) lummox : grace
   (E) supplicant : humility

16. STAND : TREE ::
   (A) park : bench
   (B) academy : cadet
   (C) wool : yarn
   (D) flotilla : ship
   (E) hospital : patient

17. INCHOATE : FORM ::
   (A) languid : vitality
   (B) diverse : harmony
   (C) spontaneous : judgment
   (D) inept : recognition
   (E) circumscribed : limit

18. PANEGYRIC : CRITICAL ::
   (A) farce : subtle
   (B) biography : analytical
   (C) diatribe : passionate
   (D) satire : humorous
   (E) abstract : concise

19. CARE : FUSS ::
   (A) talk : whisper
   (B) assert : imply
   (C) object : quibble
   (D) demote : dismiss
   (E) interest : engage

Explanations

1. A

Why Is It Hard? Tough Vocabulary

Key Strategy: Working Backwards

Looking at the question stem, you can see that the words are closely related. Something OMINOUS predicts or foreshadows DISASTER.

Does something *auspicious* foreshadow *success*? Yes. In fact, something *auspicious* is considered a good omen, just as something OMINOUS is considered a bad omen.

Does something *dangerous* foreshadow *alert*? No, that doesn't work.

Does something *difficult* foreshadow *task*? No. That doesn't make sense.

Does something *corrected* foreshadow *error*? No again.

Does something *terrifying* foreshadow *legend*? That's the only other choice that sounds possible, but not all legends are terrifying, and they're not foreshadowed.

If you had trouble with vocabulary, or had a hard time making a bridge, you could work backwards from the answer choices. There's no strong bridge for **(B)**, **(C)**, or **(E)**. **(D)** is a strong contrast, which you know can't be right in this case. This reasoning could help you guess the right answer, even if you didn't know the definition of *auspicious*.

2. B

Why Is It Hard? Traps

Key Strategy: Classic Bridges

On the surface, this one doesn't look so hard, as long as you know what EDIFICE means. It's a large, imposing BUILDING. However, on a question like this one, it's easy to fall prey to traps. You should have suspected that **(A)**, with its words *shack* and *bungalow*, was a Same Subject trap. Remember the "both are" trap? A *magazine* and a *newspaper* are both forms of printed media, but you can't build a strong bridge between the two. If you were careless, you may have built the bridge "an EDIFICE is like a BUILDING" and settled on **(D)**, "a *couch* is like a *bench*." When the stem words look like synonyms, you need to find the distinction between them to build your bridge. An EDIFACE is a large BUILDING, just as a *tome* is a large *book*. This is one version of the Classic Extreme Bridge, and this is the correct answer.

3. C

Why Is It Hard? Tough Vocabulary, Traps

Key Strategies: Working Backwards, Avoiding Traps

Something INEFFABLE is impossible to EXPRESS. Likewise, something *intangible* is impossible to *touch*. Something *interminable*, **(A)**, is never-ending. A *delay* may or may not be described that way.

You can eliminate **(B)**, **(D)**, and **(E)** on the basis of the Unrelated Words trap. *Inscrutable* means not easily understood, which doesn't have a clear link to seeing. *Insouciant* means lacking concern, and *infallible* means incapable of error. None of these has any close relation to the word with which it's paired.

4. D

Why Is It Hard? Tempting Wrong Answers

Key Strategy: Avoiding Traps

When a liquid (like blood) COAGULATES, it forms a CLOT. When a liquid *freezes*, it forms *ice*. You may have been tempted by **(C)**. People can *obstruct* something by forming a *blockade*, but those words don't refer to changes that a liquid undergoes. When you find a choice like this, don't try to force it to work—it's just a tempting wrong answer. Let it go, and stick with the one that works best.

5. A

Why Is It Hard? Tough Vocabulary

Key Strategy: Working Backwards

DROSS is a tough word. Even if you know what it means, let's pretend you don't and work backwards from the answer choices.

(A) *Sawdust* is a waste product from working with *wood*. That's a good bridge, so let's hang on to this one. Could DROSS be a waste product of working with METAL? Why not?

(B) Is there a relationship between *coke* and *steel*? Hard to say. In fact, *coke* is a residue of coal, not steel. You can eliminate this one.

(C) *Sludge* doesn't have anything to do with *wine*, so you can eliminate this one.

(D) *Ozone* is part of the *atmosphere*. Not a bad bridge. Could it work for our stem pair? Dross is part of metal? That doesn't seem likely.

(E) A *fossil* can be the remains of a *dinosaur*, but it can be the remains of other organisms as well, so you can eliminate this choice.

(A) is our best sounding choice. In fact, DROSS is a waste product of working with METAL, and it's correct.

6. D

Why Is It Hard? Tough Vocabulary, Traps

Key Strategies: Working Backwards, Classic Bridges

Here's the bridge we built: Someone who is MENDACIOUS, or apt to lie, lacks VERACITY, or truthfulness. But both of the stem words might seem tough. If you can't build a bridge, you can go right to the choices.

In **(A)**, someone who is *nosy* is characterized by *inquisitiveness*. This is an example of a trap wrong answer: It's the opposite of what we're looking for.

Someone *irreproachable*, in **(B)**, is beyond criticism. *Isolation* means "alone." This choice can be eliminated because there's no bridge between these words.

Does someone *amoral*, or lacking morals, lack *fidelity*, or faithfulness? Possibly, but not by definition. Eliminate **(C)**, a wimpy-bridged choice.

In **(D)**, someone who is *tardy* lacks *punctuality*. Keep this choice.

Something *dubious* deserves to be *questioned*. Eliminate this choice.

(D) is the only choice that works, and it's correct.

7. D

Why Is It Hard? Tough Vocabulary

Key Strategies: Working Backwards, Classic Bridges

A CUR, a word often applied to dogs, is bad-tempered and despicable. BASE, when used as an adjective, means low or contemptible. Therefore, our bridge is a CUR is characterized by being BASE. If you had trouble with these words, you can go directly to the choices and use elimination strategies.

In **(A)**, a *victor* is not *defeated*. That's not a bad bridge, though it's the opposite of the bridge we need. If you suspected that the stem words were close in meaning, rather than being more like opposites, as in this case, you could have eliminated this choice.

Is an *octogenarian*, a person in their eighties, characterized by being *wise*? Not necessarily.

Is a *genius* characterized by being *twisted*? Only in certain science fiction movies. You can eliminate this choice.

Is a *villain* characterized by being *evil*? Yes, that's correct. Keep this choice.

Is an *athlete* characterized by being *heavy*. Not necessarily.

(D) is the only choice that fits our bridge. As you see, even if you didn't understand the stem pair, you could have eliminated **(B)**, **(C)**, and **(E)**.

8. E

Why Is It Hard? Tempting Wrong Answers, Tough Vocabulary

Key Strategy: Working Backwards

A PENITENT person tends to REGRET.

Glancing down the choices, **(D)** may have seemed like a tempting answer, since REGRET and *rue* mean the same thing. You may have heard someone say "I rue the day that . . . ." We know that you know that just because you see a synonym in the choices doesn't mean that it has the same bridge as the stem pair. But when you're whipping through a section, your mind can play tricks on you. A *critical* person may or may not *rue*, so you can eliminate this tempting choice.

Starting back at the top, in **(A)**, you can't *detect* something *imperceptible*. **(B)**, *zealous* and *doubt*, and **(C)**, *exuberant* and *socialize*, have weak bridges.

In choice **(E)**, a *querulous* or habitually whining person tends to *complain*, or argue over minor details. This fits our bridge and is correct.

9. E

Why Is It Hard? Tempting Wrong Answers

Key Strategy: Avoiding Traps

This question has Same Subject Temptation written all over it. In fact, the stem pair and all the answer choices have the same subject: government. You can't use the strategy of elimination on those grounds, but you can avoid some of the more tempting wrong answers if you build a very good bridge.

To ABDICATE a THRONE is to give up any claim to it. When a king abdicates, he willingly passes his hereditary right to rule his country to the next in line for the throne. **(E)** is the only choice to match this bridge. When a politician gives up *office*, he or she voluntarily *resigns*.

(A) was easy to eliminate, since *rule* has nothing to do with losing authority.

(B), **(C)**, and **(D)**, however, made things a little more tricky. In each of these situations, though, authority is involuntarily lost or challenged. Once you got the gist of this, it should have been easy to eliminate all of these similar choices.

10. A

Why Is It Hard? Tough Vocabulary

Key Strategy: Working Backwards

CASTIGATE is a tough word that means "criticize." Knowing that, we can build the bridge: people CASTIGATE others for their WRONGDOINGs.

Let's try this bridge on the choices.

People *congratulate* each other for their *successes*. Keep this one.

Do people *amputate* others for their *crimes*? Let's hope not. Eliminate this choice.

Do people *annotate* others for their *consultations*? No, you can eliminate this choice.

Do people *deface* others for their *falsehoods*? No, eliminate this choice.

Do people *fulminate* others for their *habits*? No. Eliminate.

Working backwards, there is no strong bridge between *amputate* and *crime* or between *annotate* and *consultation*. *Deface* means "to disfigure," which doesn't have a strong bridge with *falsehood*. *Fulminate* means "to explode," which doesn't have anything to do with *habits*. All of these choices can be eliminated accordingly.

11. B

Why Is It Hard? Tough Vocabulary

Key Strategy: Working Backwards

Let's say you didn't know the meaning of CANT. In that case it's time to work backwards.

Dogma is a doctrinaire or rigidly held *belief*. Could CANT be doctrinaire or rigidly held SPEECH? You can eliminate this unlikely bridge.

Flattery is insincere *praise*. Could CANT mean insincere SPEECH? That sounds possible.

Skill and *faculty* both mean ability, although *faculty* is more innate than *skill*, which is often learned. In any case, there is no strong bridge here, so you could eliminate this pair.

Finally, a *minuet* is a type of *dance*, but even if you thought that CANT is a type of SPEECH, this bridge is going in the wrong direction.

A *diatribe* is a scathingly critical *essay* (although the word can also refer to speech). Do you think that CANT means scathingly critical SPEECH? If so, you may have to go with your best hunch between **(B)** and **(E)**; however, **(B)** is the correct answer. CANT is an insincere SPEECH, just as *flattery* is insincere *praise*.

12. D

Why Is It Hard? Tough Vocabulary

Key Strategy: Working Backwards

By definition, an APOSTATE (meaning religious defector) rejects or abandons BELIEF, just as an *ascetic* (meaning a holy man who renounces material comforts) rejects or abandons *comfort*.

But once again, you may have not know all the vocabulary, so let's work backwards with the other answer choices.

A *patriot* may or may not have *tolerance*. You could eliminate this weak bridge. A *libertine* (meaning lecher), by definition, practices *debauchery*. Perhaps you think this bridge could work with your stem pair, so keep this for now.

By definition, a *gadfly* (meaning a persistent, irritating critic) is likely to provoke *resentment*. An APOSTATE is likely to provoke BELIEF? You can eliminate this unlikely bridge.

By definition, a *hedonist* (meaning a pleasure seeker) practices *indulgence*. This is the same bridge as **(B)**, so you can eliminate both. Thus, by the process of elimination, the answer has to be **(D)**.

13. E

Why Is It Hard? Tough Vocabulary

Key Strategies: Use Word Roots, Working Backwards

By definition, to EXCULPATE is to clear from BLAME. If you weren't sure of the meaning of EXCUPATE, you could try breaking the word apart: *ex-* means remove or undo, *culpa-*, as in *culprit*, means guilt or blame. Likewise, *forgive* (secondary meaning: to grant relief from payment) is to clear from *debt*. **(E)** is correct.

Of the wrong answers: To *abash*, or embarrass, may or may not involve *shame*. You can eliminate this weak bridge. (Even if you thought there was a bridge here, the *ex-* in EXCULPATE should have told you your words shouldn't be going in the same direction, as they do here.) One may or may not *forswear*, or renounce, *violence*. So **(B)** is also out. To *decipher* is to break or unlock a *code*. This bridge makes no sense with the stem pair. To *compensate* is to make payment, though not necessarily for a *crime*. This weak bridge can be eliminated.

14. C

Why Is It Hard? Tough Vocabulary

Key Strategy: Working Backwards

Here's another case where you may not know one of the stem words. By definition, the function of an UNGUENT (meaning salve or ointment) is to reduce IRRITATION, just as the function of a *bridle* is to reduce *mobility*. **(C)** is the correct answer.

Going to the wrong answers: By definition, an *acid* causes *corrosion*. Do you suspect that an UNGUENT causes IRRITATION? If not, eliminate **(A)**. By definition, the function of a *balm* is to provide *relief*. Likewise, by definition, the function of a *sextant* (a navigational tool) is to provide *direction*. Because both choices have the same bridge, you can eliminate **(B)** and **(D)** on that basis. Finally, a *debate* may or may not settle a *controversy*. Perhaps a better bridge would be: a subject of *controversy* is open to *debate*. In any case, there's no bridge that works with the stem pair, so you can eliminate **(E)** as well.

15. E

Why Is It Hard? Tough Vocabulary

Key Strategies: Classic Bridges, Working Backwards

By definition, a MAVEN, or expert, has EXPERTISE. This is a Classic Bridge. Likewise, a *supplicant*, or humble beggar, by definition has *humility*, making **(E)** the right answer.

Of the wrong answers: A *monarch* may or may not have *wisdom*, an *athlete* may or may not have *determination*, and a *neophyte*, or beginner, may or may not have *honesty*. You could eliminate all of these weak bridges. Finally, a *lummox*, or awkward person, lacks *grace*. This is a strong but wrong bridge.

16. D

Why Is It Hard? Tricky Vocabulary

Key Strategies: Avoiding Traps, Working Backwards

Sometimes tough vocabulary on the SAT comes in the form of familiar words with unfamiliar definitions. Take STAND here. You may not know a definition for stand that involves trees, but by one definition, a STAND is a group of TREES, just as a *flotilla* is a group of *ships*.

Of the wrong answers: A *park* may or may not have *benches*. "Park bench" is a Cliché trap. A *cadet* goes to an *academy*. Could a TREE go to a STAND? Unlikely, at best. *Yarn* is composed of *wool*. Could it be that a TREE is composed of STAND? That makes no sense. Finally, a *hospital* may have *patients*, but it is not a group of *patients*. You can eliminate this unlikely bridge.

17. A

Why Is It Hard? Tough Vocabulary

Key Strategies: Classic Bridges, Working Backwards

By definition, something INCHOATE lacks FORM. Likewise, something *languid* lacks *vitality*, making **(A)** the best answer. Here we have a classic LACK bridge.

Now look at the next three answer choices: Things that are *diverse* may or may not have *harmony*, something *spontaneous* may or may not lack *judgment*, and something *inept* may or may not get *recognition*. These are all weak bridges. Even if you did not know the meaning of INCHOATE you should have been able to eliminate these. Finally, by definition, something *circumscribed* has a *limit*. **(E)** is a strong but wrong bridge, so eliminate.

18. A

Why Is It Hard? Killer Vocabulary

Key Strategy: Working Backwards

By definition, a PANEGYRIC, meaning formal or elaborate praise, is not critical, just as a *farce*, or broad satirical comedy, is not *subtle*.

Of the wrong answers: A *biography* may or may not be *analytical*. You can eliminate this weak bridge. By definition, a *diatribe*, or tirade, is *passionate*. Wrong bridge. A *satire* does not have to be *humorous*. Even if you thought this was a strong bridge, it would still be the wrong bridge. Finally, an *abstract*, or summary, is *concise*. Wrong bridge. If you noticed that **(C)** and **(E)** share the same bridge, you could have eliminated them on that basis.

19. C

Why Is It Hard? Tough Vocabulary

Key Strategy: Working Backwards

By definition, to FUSS is to pay excessive attention to small details, or to CARE excessively. Likewise, to *quibble* is to raise minor objections, or to *object* excessively. This is a version of the classic Extreme bridge.

To *whisper*, by definition, is to *talk* quietly without vocalizing. You might have thought you had an Extreme bridge here, but in any case it goes in the wrong direction—from greater to lesser as opposed to the stem bridge, which goes from lesser to greater.

To *imply*, or hint at, is to *assert*, or state, something indirectly. Neither of these bridges works with the stem pair.

To *demote*, or lower in rank, is not quite the same as to *dismiss*, or fire someone. You could eliminate this weak bridge. To *interest* means to *engage*, or fascinate. The words are synonyms, and exact synonyms will never be a correct bridge on the SAT.

section four

SAT 1600 MATH—THE BASICS

CHAPTER TEN

The SAT Math Challenge

- What to expect from SAT math
- Where the hard SAT math questions are found and what makes them hard
- Tricks for dealing with the two "weird" SAT math question types

If you're already an above-average test taker and if you've ever taken an SAT or PSAT math section, you probably aren't overly fearful of SAT math. After all, the truly scary math that you've had to study in high school—subjects like trigonometry, pre-calculus, and calculus—doesn't even appear on the SAT. This is all set to change in 2005, but fortunately you are graduating at the right time. As a result, you don't even have to enjoy math to do fairly well on the quantitative portion of the SAT. But whether you do or don't enjoy high school math, we bet you could be doing even better.

If math is one of your favorite subjects, you probably find taking practice SAT math sections to be fairly painless, if not downright pleasant. But then when it comes to scoring yourself and seeing how you did, you may also find that you didn't do as well as you thought. Why? Well, it could be you thought that the same skills that reward success on other math tests necessarily translate to success on the SAT. Alas, they do not. On other math tests, solving a problem the way you've been taught to in class is rewarded. On the SAT, solving problems the correct way can often get you into trouble. On other math tests, if you do the work properly but accidentally miss a step you'll still get partial credit. On the SAT you will not.

SAT math isn't very tough, but it can be tricky. Turning a good SAT Math score into a great SAT math score requires learning to avoid "careless" errors—and realizing that these errors are often the result of traps built into the questions. We want to show you a different approach to test taking, one that takes advantage of, rather than falls prey to, the nature of the SAT.

A 1600 test taker learns how to watch out for traps, and thus avoids making "careless" errors.

If, on the other hand, you're a generally good test taker but math isn't one of your favorite subjects, you still can do great on the SAT math sections. We'll show you how to avoid doing more math than is necessary for the SAT. By following our advice and taking advantage of the standardized test format of the SAT, you too can get an excellent math score. But to do that, first you need to understand the nature of the test.

KNOW WHAT TO EXPECT FROM SAT MATH

As you probably know, there are a total of 60 questions in the math portion of the SAT, all of which deal with basic concepts in arithmetic, algebra, and geometry. The questions are divided into two 30-minute sections and one 15-minute section.

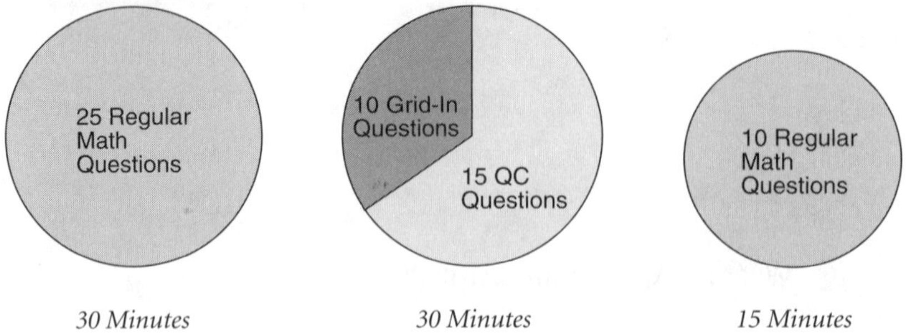

Two of the sections contain "Regular Math" questions. That's what we call those familiar multiple-choice questions with five answer choices. The two "weird" question types are both contained in the other 30-minute section, where you'll get 15 Quantitative Comparison questions, or QCs as we call them, and 10 Grid-In questions.

All the SAT math question sets are arranged to start off with easy questions and gradually increase in difficulty.

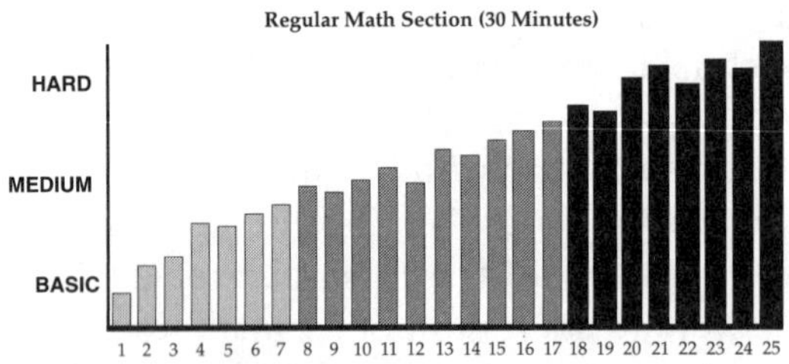

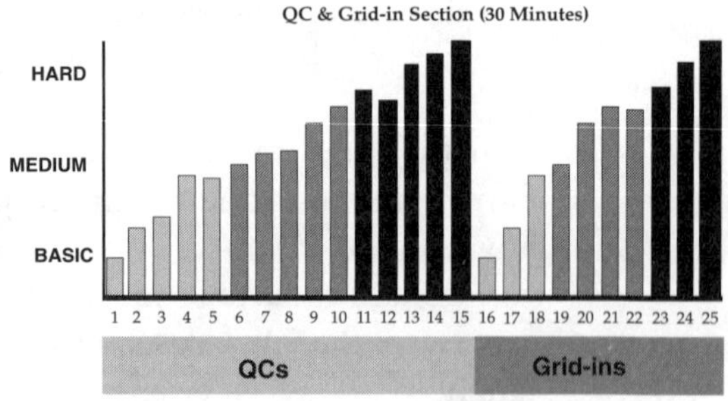

Note: The 10-question Regular Math section is also arranged from easy to difficult.

In the math sections, it's especially important to be aware of where you are in the question set. The later you are in the set, the more traps you're likely to encounter.

A 1600 test taker pays attention to where he is in a math question set. If a late-appearing question seems easy, he knows to double-check the question for traps.

WHAT MAKES AN SAT MATH QUESTION "HARD"?

That's a good question, and there's not just one answer to it. Here are the four most common ways that SAT math questions are deemed hard enough to end up in the latter part of the set.

- They look easy, but contain traps for the unwary.
- They deal with a straightforward concept, but in tricky ways that involve added steps.
- They seem overly abstract, containing variables or unknown values instead of actual numbers.
- They contain math concepts that many high school students don't quite "get."

To show you the difference between an easy SAT math question and a more difficult one, we'll begin by giving you four blatantly easy SAT math questions to do. Then we'll give you four hard questions that somewhat resemble the easy questions, but have been made tricky in one of the four ways described above.

Four Blatantly Easy SAT Math Questions

Consider these a warm-up, and be prepared to feel embarrassed if you get them wrong.

1. One number is 3 times another number and their sum is 60. What is the lesser of the two numbers?

   (A) 12
   (B) 15
   (C) 20
   (D) 40
   (E) 45

2. Which of the following is not a prime number?

   (A) 2
   (B) 19
   (C) 37
   (D) 51
   (E) 67

3. Six years from now, Clyde will be twice as old as his cousin Bonnie will be then. If Clyde is now 16 years old, how many years old is Bonnie?

   (A) 2
   (B) 4
   (C) 5
   (D) 10
   (E) 11

4. A high school band is composed of 13 freshmen, 20 sophomores, 16 juniors, and 15 seniors. What is the probability that a band member chosen from random will be a sophomore?

(A) $\frac{2}{5}$

(B) $\frac{1}{3}$

(C) $\frac{4}{13}$

(D) $\frac{5}{16}$

(E) $\frac{3}{10}$

Explanations: Blatantly Easy Questions

You still want to be somewhat careful when you're answering early questions on the SAT. If you rush through them in your race to get to the tough ones, you can easily get them wrong. Which is criminal on the SAT, since an early, easy question is worth exactly the same as a difficult question.

STRATEGY HIGHLIGHT

Knowing the *rules of divisibility* can help you when dealing with problems involving prime numbers, multiples, or factors. For instance, in question 2 here one should be able to see quickly that 51 is divisible by 3, because its digits—5 and 1—add up to 6, which is a multiple of 3.

1. B

Let's translate the English into Math: $x + 3x = 60$, $4x = 60$, so $x = 15$ and the two numbers are 15 and 45. Thus the lesser number is 15. The correct answer is **(B)**.

2. D

We hope you are comfortable with basic mathematical definitions. 2, 19, 37 and 67 are all prime. $51 = 3 \times 17$, so it is not prime. **(D)** is correct.

3. C

This problem is a bit trickier than the previous two, but it's still easy enough if you read carefully. You're told that Clyde is now 16; thus in six years he will be 22. If he will then be twice as old as Bonnie will be then, that means Bonnie will be 11 years old in six years. Thus she must be $11 - 6 = 5$ years old now, making **(C)** the correct answer.

4. D

To figure out the probability that a band member chosen at random will be a sophomore, you just have to apply the probability formula:

$$\text{Probability} = \frac{\text{\# of favorable outcomes}}{\text{\# of possible outcomes}}\text{, or in this case:}$$

$$\text{Probability} = \frac{\text{\# of sophomores}}{\text{\# of band members}} = \frac{20}{13 + 20 + 16 + 15} = \frac{20}{64} = \frac{5}{16}.$$

Thus, the correct answer is **(D)**.

A 1600 test taker handles the easy math questions quickly, but not so quickly as to possibly get them wrong.

Four Difficult Math Questions

Now here are some similar, but more difficult questions.

5. One number is 5 times another number and their sum is –60. What is the lesser of the two numbers?

   (A) –5
   (B) –10
   (C) –12
   (D) –48
   (E) –50

6. A positive integer n is defined as a "prime interlude" if $n - 1$ and $n + 1$ are both prime numbers. Which of the following is NOT a "prime interlude"?

   (A) 4
   (B) 18
   (C) 30
   (D) 72
   (E) 90

7. Six years from now, Clyde will be twice as old as his Cousin Bonnie will be then. If Clyde is now C years old, how many years old is Bonnie?

   (A) $\frac{C - 12}{2}$
   (B) $C - 12$
   (C) $\frac{C - 6}{2}$
   (D) $C - 6$
   (E) $\frac{C + 6}{2}$

8. A class contains five juniors and five seniors. If one member of the class is assigned at random to present a paper on a certain subject, and another member of the class is randomly assigned to assist him, what is the probability that both will be juniors?

   (A) $\frac{1}{10}$
   (B) $\frac{1}{5}$
   (C) $\frac{2}{9}$
   (D) $\frac{2}{5}$
   (E) $\frac{1}{2}$

Explanations: Difficult Math Questions

5. E

Again let's translate the English into math: $x + 5x = -60$, $6x = -60$, so $x = -10$, and the two numbers are –10 and –50. Thus the lesser number is –50, making **(E)** correct.

This is where most students mess up. They forget that the "lesser" of two negative numbers is the "larger" negative number (since *less* means to the left of on the number line):

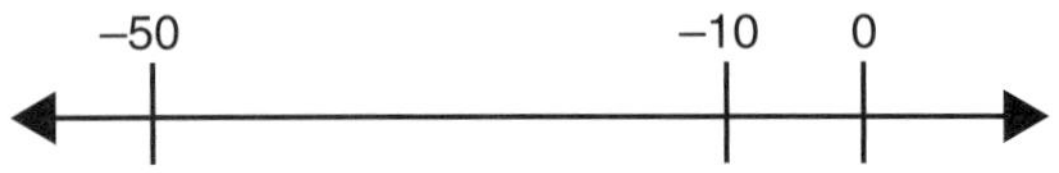

STRATEGY HIGHLIGHT

Knowing that question 5 was supposed to be a tough question, although it didn't seem so bad, should have slowed you down. Being on the alert can keep you from falling for the testmaker's traps.

By the way, numbers on the SAT are usually listed in the answer choices from lowest to highest, but you're not guaranteed of this. Here the numbers were listed from highest to lowest just to trip students up.

6. E

Once you figure out what "prime interlude" means (i.e., the integers immediately before and after your number are both prime), you're ready to tackle the answer choices:

(A) 4	3 and 5 are both prime, so eliminate.
(B) 18	17 and 19 are both prime, so eliminate.
(C) 30	29 and 31 are both prime, so eliminate.
(D) 72	71 and 73 are both prime, so eliminate.
(E) 90	89 and 91 may both seem prime, but $91 = 7 \times 13$.

Thus **(E)** is the answer.

STRATEGY TIP

On questions that ask "Which of the following . . . " and require you to check out the answer choices, you can usually save time by starting with choice (E).

7. C

Here's the "textbook approach" to solving this one. If Clyde is now C years old, then in six years he will be $C + 6$.

If Bonnie is now B years old, in six years she will be $B + 6$.

So in six years, $2(B + 6) = C + 6$, or $2B + 12 = C + 6$.

Solving for B we get:

$2B = C + 6 - 12 = C - 6$

So $B = \dfrac{C-6}{2}$, making **(C)** the correct answer.

STRATEGY TIP

It's very easy to set up an algebra equation wrong, and if you do, the testmaker will often include your mistake among the five answer choices.

If you're not 100 percent confident of your ability to solve this problem algebraically, here's a safer method for handling this question. This is actually the exact same problem as question 3 earlier, but with a variable, C, instead of the number 16 for Clyde's age. So to make this question easier and more concrete, we just need to replace a number, such as 16 (or any number that makes sense), for Clyde's age.

We then get:

7. Six years from now, Clyde will be twice as old as his cousin Bonnie will be then. If Clyde is now 16 years old, how many years old is Bonnie?

(A) $\frac{C-12}{2} = \frac{16-12}{2} = 2$

(B) $C - 12 = 16 - 12 = 4$

(C) $\frac{C-6}{2} = \frac{16-6}{2} = 5$

(D) $C - 6 = 16 - 6 = 10$

(E) $\frac{C+6}{2} = \frac{16+6}{2} = 11$

So once again the correct answer is **(C)**.

A 1600 test taker picks numbers to make abstract questions concrete.

We'll examine this technique of picking numbers in much more depth in the next chapter.

8. C

Finally, this is considered a tough problem simply because most students don't know how to handle "multiple-event" probability questions. To find the probability of two or more independent events happening, first calculate the probability of each separate event, then multiply the probabilities for each of the separate events together. Just be careful when you calculate the probability of each subsequent event; you have to assume that prior events happened successfully. For instance, in this case:

Probability that the first student picked will be a junior $= \frac{\text{\# of juniors}}{\text{\# of students}} = \frac{5}{10} = \frac{1}{2}$

Probability that the 2nd student picked will be a junior $= \frac{\text{\# of juniors remaining}}{\text{\# of students remaining}} = \frac{4}{9}$

Probability that both students will be juniors $= \frac{1}{2} \times \frac{4}{9} = \frac{2}{9}$. The correct answer is **(C)**.

A 1600 test taker knows what math could appear on the SAT and learns all the relevant formulas.

So far we've just looked at Regular Math questions. Now let's take a quick look at the "weird" question types.

Quantitative Comparisons

QCs often throw students at first, but with a little practice they should take much less time to answer than the other math question types. That's because on QCs your job is simply to compare two quantities to determine which, if either, is greater. Not only do you usually not have to calculate the values in the question, but it's often a waste of time. Take a look at the directions, and then we'll try a few questions.

The directions

The directions you'll see will look something like this. Familiarize yourself with them now, if you haven't already.

DIRECTIONS FOR QUANTITATIVE COMPARISON QUESTIONS

Compare the boxed quantity in Column A with the boxed quantity in Column B. Select answer choice

A if Column A is greater;
B if Column B is greater;
C if the columns are equal; or
D if more information is needed to determine the relationship.

An E response will be treated as an omission.

Notes:

1. Some questions include information about one or both quantities. That information is centered and unboxed.
2. A symbol that appears in both Column A and Column B stands for the same thing in both columns.
3. All numbers used are real numbers.

EXAMPLES

	Column A	Column B	Answers
E1	3×4	$3 + 4$	● Ⓑ Ⓒ Ⓓ Ⓔ
	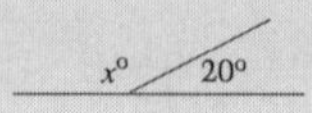		
E2	x	160	Ⓐ Ⓑ ● Ⓓ Ⓔ
	x and y are positive		
E3	$x + 1$	$y - 1$	Ⓐ Ⓑ Ⓒ ● Ⓔ

WARNING: Never pick choice (E) as the answer to a QC.

About D

(A), **(B)**, and **(C)** all represent definite relationships between the quantities in the two columns. **(D)**, however, is the option to pick when the relationship cannot be determined. There are two important things to understand about **(D)**:

- **(D)** is NEVER correct if both columns contain only numbers. Relationships between numbers never vary, but **(D)** states that more than one relationship is possible. **(D)** is only possible when at least one of the columns contains a variable or unknown value.

- **(D)** is ALWAYS correct when it can be shown that more than one relationship can exist between the two columns. One way to prove that more than one relationship can exist is to pick different kinds of numbers for the variables in the question.

Now let's try some questions.

QC Practice

	Column A	Column B
	$x > 0$ $x = 4y$	
9.	$x + y$	xy
10.	$\sqrt{7} + \sqrt{8}$	$\sqrt{15}$
	$\frac{x}{5} = \frac{y}{10}$	
11.	$\frac{x+1}{5}$	$\frac{y+1}{10}$

Explanations: QC Practice

9. D

Here's a good example of how picking numbers on QCs with variables can help you get a fix on the relationship between the columns. Just make sure to pick numbers that conform to the centered information. Here you're told that $x > 0$, so you could pick $x = 4$, which makes $y = 1$ since $x = 4y$. Now you have $4 + 1 = 5$ in Column A, and $4 \times 1 = 4$ in Column B. Column A is greater, so you can eliminate answer **(B)** and **(C)**.

Now to see whether the relationship can change, pick a different number for x, such as $x = 8$, making $y = 2$. You then have $8 + 2 = 10$ in Column A, and $8 \times 2 = 16$ in Column B. Since Column B is now greater, the relationship can change, and **(D)** is the correct answer.

10. A

Before you even try to answer this question, note that the answer here cannot be **(D)**, because there are only numbers in the answer choices. You should also note that this question contains a classic SAT QC trap. When the columns look alike, making **(C)** a tempting choice, look again. Appearances can be deceiving on QCs. You can't simply add or subtract square roots that have different numbers under the radical signs. You can, however, estimate the values:
In Column A, $\sqrt{7} + \sqrt{8} \approx 2^{+} + 3^{-} \approx 5^{+}$. In Column B, $\sqrt{15} < 4$, so Column A is greater. The correct answer is **(A)**.

> A 1600 test taker doesn't fall for lookalikes and other common QC traps.

11. A

Here again, you could pick numbers to get a handle on the relationship between the columns. For instance, you could pick $x = 5$ and $y = 10$. You then have $\frac{6}{5}$ in Column A and $\frac{11}{10}$ in Column B. Column A is larger, so **(B)** and **(C)** cannot be correct.

Now try another set of numbers. When you pick numbers the second time on a QC, you want to try to make the relationship change, so you want to pick different kinds of numbers. Note that the centered information doesn't restrict what x and y can be, so you could make x and y negative. Let's say $x = -10$ and $y = -20$. Now you have $-\frac{9}{5}$ in Column A and $-\frac{19}{10}$ in Column B. The quantity in Column A is still greater. We could keep picking, but Column A will always be greater. Because we picked different types of numbers and the relationship remained the same, we can be confident picking **(A)**.

> A 1600 test taker doesn't assume that the answer is **(D)** just because the columns contain variables.

P.S.: Of course, picking numbers isn't the only way to solve this problem. Another good approach would be to use the centered information and put the quantities in the columns into a form that makes it easier to compare them. For instance, Column A could be rewritten as $\frac{x}{5} + \frac{1}{5}$ and Column B could be rewritten as $\frac{y}{10} + \frac{1}{10}$. The centered information tells you that $\frac{x}{5} = \frac{y}{10}$, and for purposes of comparison you can always disregard equal values in both columns, leaving you with $\frac{1}{5}$ in Column A and $\frac{1}{10}$ in Column B. So the answer must be (**A**).

We'll look more closely at this and other strategies for handling QCs in the next chapter.

GRID-INS

The 10 Grid-In questions on the SAT are designed to be more like the math questions you are used to answering in math class. In school math tests, you usually don't get five answer choices from which to choose the correct answer. Likewise, when you come to a Grid-In in the SAT test booklet, you'll just see a question and you'll have to come up with the answer yourself.

So far, so simple. The tricky thing about Grid-Ins is that you have to fill your answer into this funny looking grid:

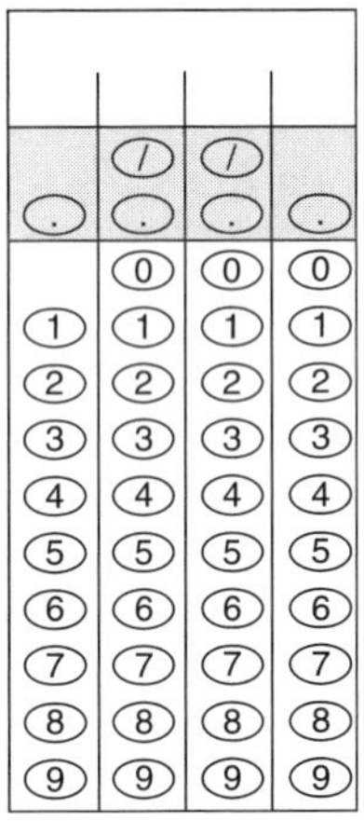

Filling in the Grid

Here's all you need to know about Grid-Ins. First, note that the grid cannot accommodate the following:

- Negative answers
- Answers with variables
- Answers greater than 9,999
- Answers with commas
- Mixed numbers
- Fractions with more than four digits

So if you come up with an answer that cannot be gridded, look again. For instance, if you come up with a mixed number, or a fraction that won't fit, you should be able to convert it into a decimal or a fraction that does fit.

STRATEGY TIP

There may be several acceptable ways to grid in an answer, and there may be several possible correct answers to a Grid-In question. Just look for a safe, correct answer and fill in the grid carefully.

For instance, let's say you came up with an answer of $2\frac{1}{2}$. That's a mixed number, and if you tried to grid it as is, your answer would be misinterpreted as $\frac{21}{2}$. So you could either turn your answer into the fractional equivalent $\frac{5}{2}$, or the decimal equivalent 2.5.

Now let's say you came up with an answer of $\frac{25}{27}$. You can't reduce this fraction any further, and it's too big as is to fit into the grid. You can, however, easily turn it into its decimal equivalent by pulling out your calculator. $25 \div 27 = .925925925$, etc.

A 1600 test taker is more likely to use a calculator on Grid-Ins than on any other math question type.

Note that when you get an answer in decimal form, you have to grid your answer as fully as possible, but you don't have to bother to round up. For instance, here either .925 or .926 would be acceptable, but .92 or .93 would not. Because of this need to fill in numbers as fully as possible, we have some general recommendations.

Always start your answer in the first column box. Do this even if your answer has only one or two figures. Technically, you can start in any column, but by following this rule you'll avoid mistakes. If you always start with the first column, your answers will always fit. Since there is no oval for 0 in the first column, grid an answer of 0 in any other column. Also, since you don't have to round up on decimal answers, why bother?

Now you can try some Grid-In problems on your own.

Grid-In Practice

12. The expression $\frac{7x + 11}{5} - \frac{2x - 2}{5}$ is how much more than x?

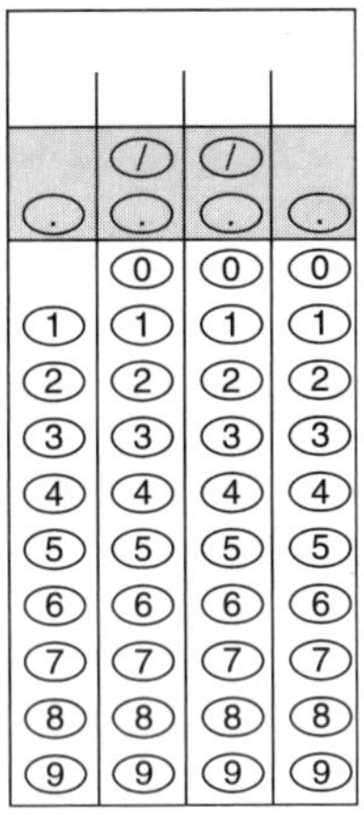

13. A video store sells a certain video for $32, which is 60 percent more than it costs the store to purchase this video. During an inventory sale, employees are invited to purchase remaining videos at 25 percent off the store's cost. If an employee purchases this video during the sale, the employee's purchase price would be what percent of the price the store originally charged for the video? (Disregard the % sign when gridding your answer.)

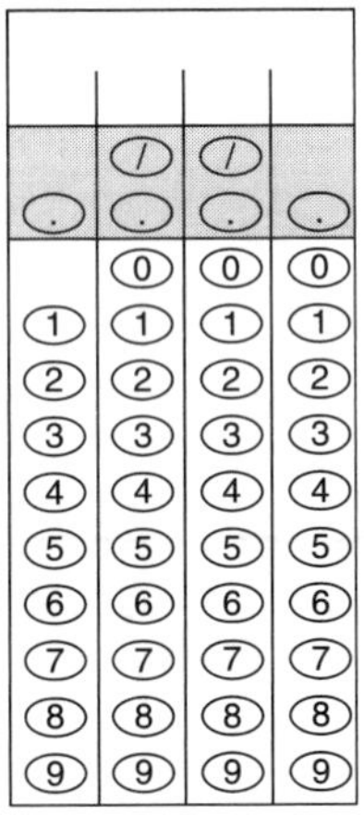

Explanations: Grid-In Practice

12. $\frac{13}{5}$ or 2.6

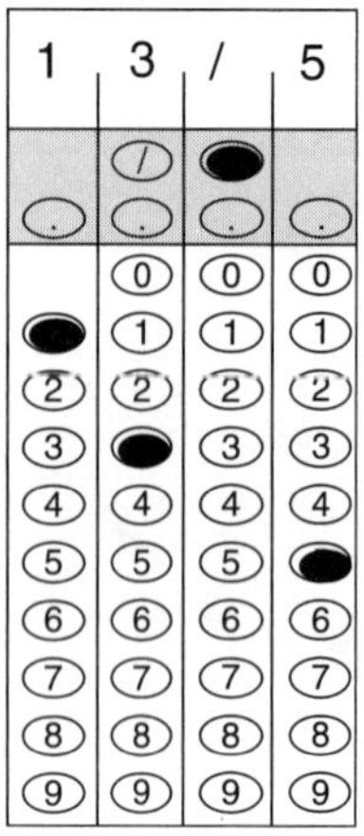

or

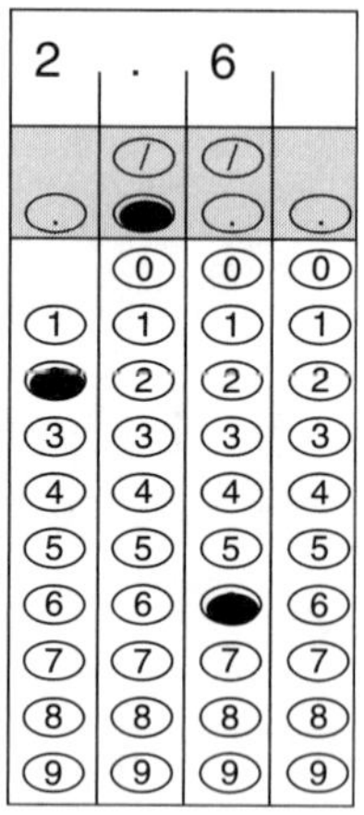

This problem may look funny at first because it's an algebra problem and yet Grid-In answers can't have variables. Just have faith. There are two ways to answer this question, depending on how much you enjoy doing algebra.

Let's say that algebra is not your first love. In that case you can pick a number for x to get rid of the algebra. Just make it a nice and easy number. For instance, you could pick $x = 1$. In that case:

$\frac{7x + 11}{5} - \frac{2x - 2}{5} = \frac{7 + 11}{5} - \frac{2 - 2}{5} = \frac{18}{5}$. Since $\frac{18}{5}$ is $\frac{13}{5}$ more than 1, the answer is $\frac{13}{5}$ or 2.6.

Alternatively, you could just do the algebra:

$\frac{7x + 11}{5} - \frac{2x - 2}{5} = \frac{7x + 11 - (2x - 2)}{5} = \frac{5x + 13}{5} = \frac{5x}{5} + \frac{13}{5} = x + \frac{13}{5}$, which is $\frac{13}{5}$ more than x.

A 1600 test taker knows that there's usually more than one way to the correct answer, and chooses the approach that she finds safest and quickest.

13. 46.8 or 46.9

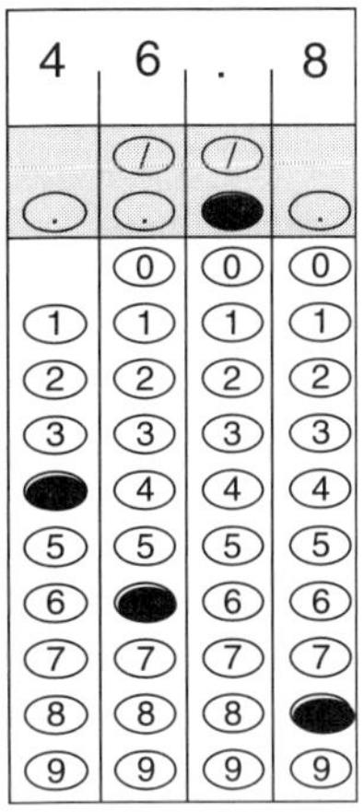

or

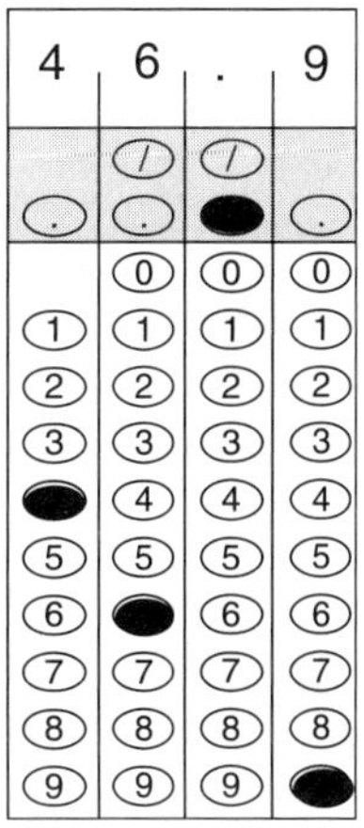

Okay, so this problem is as tough as it gets on the SAT, maybe even a bit tougher. That's all right, you're tough too. On long, multiple-step word problems such as this one, just take it one step at a time.

First you're told that a store sells a certain video for $32, which is 60 percent more than it costs the store. So to figure out the store's cost, translate the English into math: $32 = 1.6x$, where x is the cost to the store. $x = \frac{32}{1.6} = 20$, so the store's cost is $20. During a sale it's offered to employees at 25 percent off the store's cost, or $.75 \times \$20 = \$15$, so $15 is the final price to the employee.

But wait! The question asks what percent of the original price the employee pays, so pull out your calculator and divide 15 by 32. You should get .46875, or 46.875 percent, which you can grid as either 46.8 or 46.9.

> A 1600 test taker handles lengthy word problems by taking it one sentence at a time.

Now that you've had a chance to see what the SAT math challenge is all about, our next chapter will show our favorite strategies for taking on the challenge.

CHAPTER ELEVEN

Essential SAT Math Strategies

- Picking Numbers
- Backsolving
- QC Strategies

In the last chapter we looked at what the SAT 1600 math challenge is all about, and we introduced you to some of our favorite strategies for meeting the challenge. In this chapter we'll explore our favorite strategies in more detail. Many of these strategies will avail themselves over and over again as you work your way through the remaining math chapters. Even more important, they should prove extremely useful when you take an actual SAT.

We'll begin by taking a closer look at our old friend, picking numbers.

PICKING NUMBERS

As we saw in the last chapter, picking numbers is an extremely handy strategy for handling "abstract" problems—you know, the ones that insist on dealing with variables rather than good old numbers. Picking numbers makes abstract problems concrete. We've already seen that picking numbers can be an effective strategy for dealing with certain Regular Math problems, as well as QCs with variables, and even the occasional Grid-In.

But let's take a minute to break down the process as it relates to our most common case, the Regular Math problem with variables in the question and in the answer choices. Without any further ado, here's the method:

Step 1: Pick simple numbers to stand in for the variables.

Step 2: Answer the question using the numbers you picked.

Step 3: Try out all the answer choices using the numbers you picked, eliminating those that give you a different result.

Step 4: Try out different values if more than one answer choice works.

Don't worry. Step 4 is rarely necessary.

And since you're an aspiring 1600 hotshot and have already seen this strategy in action, we'll give you a few problems, and let you try out this strategy for yourself. You can then compare your technique with ours in the explanations that follow.

STRATEGY TIP

When a problem involves a unit conversion—for instance, from minutes to hours or cents to dollars—you can pick numbers that do the converting for you, such as 60 for the number of minutes, or 100 for the number of cents.

Questions 1–3

1. If a sausage-making machine produces 3,000 sausages in h hours, how many sausages can it produce in m minutes?

   (A) $\frac{m}{50h}$

   (B) $\frac{50h}{m}$

   (C) $\frac{mh}{50}$

   (D) $\frac{50m}{h}$

   (E) $50mh$

2. If $a > 1$, what is the value of $\frac{2a + 6}{a^2 + 2a - 3}$?

   (A) a

   (B) $a + 3$

   (C) $\frac{2}{a - 1}$

   (D) $\frac{2a}{a - 3}$

   (E) $\frac{a - 1}{2}$

STRATEGY TIP

When picking numbers for several related variables, start with the smallest variable—i.e., the one all the other ones build upon.

3. If $r = 3s$, $s = 5t$, $t = 2u$, and $u \neq 0$, what is the value of $\frac{rst}{u^3}$?

   (A) 30

   (B) 60

   (C) 150

   (D) 300

   (E) 600

Explanations: Questions 1–3

1. D

You may feel like solving this problem algebraically, but picking numbers here is just as quick, and a whole lot safer. The key is to pick numbers that do the unit converting for you. For instance, here the rate is given as 3,000 sausages in h hours, but the question asks you how many sausages can be made in m minutes. So let's begin by picking 60 for m, thus converting our minutes into an hour. And now make h an easy number, such as $h = 2$. Now the question asks: If 3,000 sausages can be made in 2 hours, how many sausages can be made in 60 minutes? The answer is quite obviously 1,500. Now go to the answer choices to find 1,500.

(A) $\frac{m}{50h} = \frac{60}{50 \times 2}$, which is way too small.

(B) $\frac{50h}{m} = \frac{50 \times 2}{60}$, which is still too small.

(C) $\frac{mh}{50} = \frac{60 \times 2}{50}$, which is also too small.

(D) $\frac{50m}{h} = \frac{50 \times 60}{2} = 1{,}500$. That's the ticket!

(E) $50mh = 50 \times 60 \times 2$. Too big.

So **(D)** is the answer.

2. C

Again, you may be itching to do this one using algebra, but let's try our approach. The question tells you that $a > 1$, so you could begin by picking 2 for a here.

Thus, $\frac{2a + 6}{a^2 + 2a - 3} - \frac{2(2) + 6}{2^2 + 2(2) - 3} = \frac{10}{5} = 2.$

So you are looking for an answer choice that equals 2 when $a = 2$.

(A) $a = 2$, so keep it.

(B) $a + 3 = 2 + 3 = 5$. Eliminate.

(C) $\frac{2}{a - 1} = \frac{2}{2 - 1} = 2$, so keep it.

(D) $\frac{2a}{a - 3} = \frac{2 \times 2}{2 - 3} = -4$. Eliminate.

(E) $\frac{a - 1}{2} = \frac{2 - 1}{2} = \frac{1}{2}$. Eliminate.

All right, we confess. We did this deliberately, just to make you go through step 4. Now pick a different number for a, say $a = 3$. If we run that through the expression in the question stem we get:

$$\frac{2a + 6}{a^2 + 2a - 3} - \frac{2(3) + 6}{3^2 + 2(3) - 3} = \frac{12}{12} = 1$$

So 1 is our new target number. Now if we put $a = 3$ into the remaining answer choices, there's only one choice that works:

(A) $a = 3$. No good.

(C) $\frac{2}{a - 1} = \frac{2}{3 - 1} = 1$, so **(C)** is the answer. Okay, it took some effort, but it wasn't so bad.

A 1600 test taker tries out all the answer choices when picking numbers, and picks a second time if necessary.

---

3. E

The other variables all build upon u, so pick a small number for u and figure out values for r, s and t.

For instance, if $u = 1$, then $t = 2u$, so $t = 2$; $s = 5t$, so $s = 10$; and $r = 3s$, so $r = 30$.

So $\frac{rst}{u^3} = \frac{30 \times 10 \times 2}{1 \times 1 \times 1} = 600$, and **(E)** is the answer.

You'll notice that picking numbers worked in question 3, even though there were numbers, rather than variables, in the answer choices. We often employ a different strategy when there are numbers in the answer choices, which we will look at soon. But there are two other times when there won't be variables in the answer choices, or even explicitly in the questions, but the questions will be perfect candidates for picking numbers.

We refer to those funky word problems that contain percents or fractions in the answer choices, and unknown values in the questions. By picking numbers for the unknown values in these questions, they become much easier to answer. The key is to know what numbers to pick.

Here, take a look. Try answering the following questions on your own by picking numbers, and then we'll see how your method squares with ours.

Questions 4–5

4. An antique dealer usually charges 20 percent more than his purchase price for any vase sold in his store. During a clearance sale, all items are marked 10 percent off. If the dealer sells a vase during the clearance sale, his profit on the vase (sale price minus purchase price) is what percent of the purchase price of the vase?

   (A) 8%
   (B) 9%
   (C) 10%
   (D) 11%
   (E) 12%

STRATEGY TIP

On percent questions that contain unknown values, such as the price of the vase in question 4, try picking 100 for the value.

5. In a certain orchestra, each musician plays exactly one instrument. If $\frac{1}{5}$ of the musicians play brass instruments, and the number of musicians playing wind instruments is $\frac{2}{3}$ greater than the number of musicians playing brass instruments, what fraction of the musicians in the orchestra play neither brass nor wind instruments?

   (A) $\frac{1}{5}$
   (B) $\frac{2}{5}$
   (C) $\frac{7}{15}$
   (D) $\frac{8}{15}$
   (E) $\frac{2}{3}$

STRATEGY TIP

On fraction problems that contain unknown values, such as the number of musicians in the orchestra in question 5, try picking the largest denominator in the answer choices for the value.

Explanations: Questions 4–5

4. A

Let's begin by picking $100 for the original cost of the vase. So the dealer pays $100 for the vase, but he usually charges 20 percent more, or $120 for it. During the sale the vase's price is reduced 10 percent. Ten percent of $120 is $12, so the final sale price of the vase is $108, meaning the dealer made a profit of $\frac{8}{100}$ or 8 percent of his original purchase price. So the correct answer is **(A)**.

5. C

Since 15 is the largest denominator in the answer choices, let's assume there are 15 musicians in the orchestra. Since $\frac{1}{5}$ of these were brass musicians, that means there are 3 brass musicians in the orchestra. The number of wind musicians is $\frac{2}{3}$ greater than this, that is $\frac{2}{3}$ greater than 3, so there are 2 more wind musicians than brass musicians, or 5 wind musicians altogether. So, of the 15 musicians, $3 + 5 = 8$ play either wind or brass instruments. That leaves 7 people who play neither instrument. So the fraction of musicians who play neither instrument is $\frac{7}{15}$. **(C)** is the correct answer.

Now let's look at our next strategy for dealing with ugly math questions.

BACKSOLVING

Some of the nastiest SAT math problems have numbers in the answer choices, and the picking numbers technique just won't cut it. On these questions, you can try backsolving instead. When you backsolve, you simply plug the answer choices back into the question until you find one that works. If you do it systematically, it shouldn't take you too much time. Here's the system.

Step 1: Start with **(C)**.
Step 2: Eliminate choices you know are too big or too small.
Step 3: Keep going until you find the choice that works.

Let's take a look.

6. Employee *X* is paid $12.50 an hour for the first 36 hours he works in a week, and is paid double that rate for every hour over that. Employee *Y* is paid $15.00 an hour for the first 40 hours she works in a week, and is paid 1.5 times that rate for every hour over that. On a certain week, both employees worked the same number of hours and were paid the same amount. How many hours did each employee work that week?

   (A) 48
   (B) 50
   (C) 54
   (D) 60
   (E) 64

Notice that the problem itself is long and nasty. The pay scales don't match, and overtime kicks in at different points and at different rates. But the question itself is clear enough. "How many hours did each employee work that week?" Since there are numbers in the answer choices, let's go ahead and backsolve.

By the way, here's a good occasion to pull out your calculator. Let's begin with choice **(C)** and assume that each employee worked 54 hours. That means that Employee X earned $(36 \times 12.50) + (18 \times 25.00) = \$900$, and Employee Y earned $(40 \times 15.00) + (14 \times 22.50) = \$915$. So **(C)** is out. But can we eliminate anything else? Employee Y here earned more than Employee X, but the more hours each employee works, the more Employee X's earnings close in on Employee Y's, since Employee X earns a higher overtime wage. So we want a larger number, meaning **(A)** and **(B)** are out.

Now let's try **(D)**, and assume that they each worked 60 hours. Now Employee X earns $(36 \times 12.50) + (14 \times 25.00) = \$1{,}050$, and Employee Y earns $(40 \times 15.00) + (20 \times 22.50) = \$1{,}050$.

The wages match! We found the answer, and it's **(D)**.

Now try some backsolving problems on your own.

Questions 7–8

7. At Central Park Zoo, the ratio of sea lions to penguins is 4 to 11. If there are 84 more penguins than sea lions, how many sea lions are there?

    (A) 24
    (B) 36
    (C) 48
    (D) 72
    (E) 121

8. What is the value of x if $\frac{x+1}{x-3} - \frac{x+2}{x-4} = 0$?

    (A) −2
    (B) −1
    (C) 0
    (D) 1
    (E) 2

STRATEGY TIP

If you don't know which direction to go after you've tried and eliminated **(C)**, pick the next easiest number to work with.

Explanations: Questions 7–8

7. C

The correct answer should yield a ratio of sea lions to penguins of 4 to 11, so try out choice **(C)**. If there are 48 sea lions, there are 48 + 84 = 132 penguins, so the ratio of sea lions to penguins is $\frac{48}{132} = \frac{4}{11}$, which is just what we want. That means we're done.

8. D

As always, we'll start with **(C)**. We're looking for an answer choice that gives us zero on the right side of the equation:

(C) $\frac{x+1}{x-3} - \frac{x+2}{x-4} = \frac{0+1}{0-3} - \frac{0+2}{0-4} = -\frac{1}{3} + \frac{1}{2} \neq 0$, so we have to keep fishing.

But in this case it may not be easy to know which number to pick next, so pick one of the remaining numbers that's easy to work with:

(D) $\frac{x+1}{x-3} - \frac{x+2}{x-4} = \frac{1+1}{1-3} - \frac{1+2}{1-4} = -1 + 1 = 0$

Since the equation is true for **(D)**, it must be the answer.

Now it's time to look at some strategies for dealing with QCs.

QC STRATEGIES

We've already seen how picking numbers can be a useful strategy on QCs. But there are several other strategies that will help you to breeze through this question type. Never forget that on this question type you're just looking for the relative size of the two quantities. So look for ways to compare rather than calculate. Here are a couple of ways to do that.

Make One Column Look Like the Other

Let's take a look at what we mean.

9.

Column A	Column B
Joe has 2 nickels and 3 dimes in his pocket.	
The ratio of nickels to dimes in Joe's pocket	.6

You should know that a ratio can always be expressed in fractional form, and that a fraction can always be expressed as a decimal, so let's express Column A as a decimal.

The ratio of nickels to dimes expressed as a decimal is $2 : 3 = \frac{2}{3} \approx 0.67$, so **(A)** is the answer.

That was pretty obvious, so let's take a look at a tougher example.

10. Column A | Column B

$x > 0 > y$

Column A	Column B
$(2x + 2y)^2$	$4x^2 + 4y^2$

Let's begin by making Column A look more like Column B by using FOIL:

$(2x + 2y)^2 = (2x + 2y)(2x + 2y) = 4x^2 + 8xy + 4y^2$.

So we have $4x^2 + 8xy + 4y^2$ in Column A, and $4x^2 + 4y^2$ in Column B. If we disregard the terms in common we have $8xy$ in Column A, and zero in Column B. So is $8xy$ greater than or less than zero? Well, according to the centered information, $x > 0 > y$, so x is positive and y is negative, which means that $8xy$ must be negative. The correct answer is **(B)**.

This business about disregarding the terms in common gets us to our next QC strategy.

Do the Same Thing to Both Columns

Some QC questions become a lot clearer when you change the appearance of the values in both columns. Treat the two columns like two sides of an inequality, with the sign temporarily hidden. There are several things that you can do that do not change the relationship between the columns:

- You can always safely add or subtract the same value from both columns.
- You can also multiply or divide both columns by the same *positive* value without altering the relationship. Be careful though. Multiplying or dividing by a quantity that is (or could be) *negative* does not work!
- You can square both columns. (Just make sure that neither side is negative before you do so.)

Try out this strategy in the following problem.

11. Column A | Column B

$x > 2$

Column A	Column B
$x^3 - 1$	$\frac{7x^2 - 3}{3}$

For starters, you can add 1 to both columns once you realize that $\frac{7x^2 - 3}{3} = \frac{7x^2}{3} - \frac{3}{3} = \frac{7x^2}{3} - 1$.

So now you have:

x^3	$\frac{7x^2}{3}$

Now you can divide both sides by x^2:

x	$\frac{7}{3}$

So that means that if x is greater than $\frac{7}{3}$, Column A will be greater. But if $x = \frac{7}{3}$, the columns will be equal, and if x is between 2 and $\frac{7}{3}$, say $\frac{13}{6}$, Column B will be greater. Clearly **(D)** is the answer.

In the next QC problem, you don't have to bother to pull out your calculator. It's much easier (we think) to just do the same thing to both columns.

12.

Column A	Column B
$\frac{7^8}{5^2}$	$\frac{7^7}{5}$

Here's what you could do to both columns:

Multiply both columns by 5^2, to get rid of the fractions:

$\frac{7^8}{5^2} \times 5^2 = 7^8$ $\qquad$ $\frac{7^7}{5} \times 5^2 = 7^7 \times 5$

Divide both columns by 7^7 to get:

$\frac{7^8}{7^7} = 7$ $\qquad$ $\frac{7^7 \times 5}{7^7} = 5$

$7 > 5$, so Column A is greater than Column B. **(A)** is correct.

A 1600 test taker knows what she can and cannot do to both columns in order to get a better fix on the relationship.

Let's look at one more example.

13.

Column A	Column B
$\frac{\sqrt{2}}{2\sqrt{6}}$	$\frac{\sqrt{3}}{3\sqrt{8}}$

Even with a calculator, square roots are annoying to have to deal with. So why bother? Since we know both of the quantities are positive, we can square them without affecting the relationship between the columns.

Column A: $\left(\frac{\sqrt{2}}{2\sqrt{6}}\right)^2 = \frac{\sqrt{2}}{2\sqrt{6}} \times \frac{\sqrt{2}}{2\sqrt{6}} = \frac{2}{4 \times 6} = \frac{1}{12}$

Column B: $\left(\frac{\sqrt{3}}{3\sqrt{8}}\right)^2 = \frac{\sqrt{3}}{3\sqrt{8}} \times \frac{\sqrt{3}}{3\sqrt{8}} = \frac{3}{9 \times 8} = \frac{1}{24}$

So **(A)** is the correct answer. Now let's review our next QC strategy.

Compare Piece by Piece

One helpful rule for dealing with QCs, and SAT math in general, is that whenever it seems that you have a lot of tedious calculations to make, there's got to be an easier approach. Often that easier approach is to compare piece by piece. Take a look.

14. <u>Column A</u> <u>Column B</u>

Column A	Column B
$\frac{1}{2} + \frac{4}{5} + \frac{7}{10} + \frac{9}{7}$	$\frac{1}{3} + \frac{4}{7} + \frac{8}{9} + \frac{6}{11}$

Column A: $\frac{1}{2} + \frac{4}{5} + \frac{7}{10} + \frac{9}{7}$ = A tedious calculation.

Column B: $\frac{1}{3} + \frac{4}{7} + \frac{8}{9} + \frac{6}{11}$ = A tedious calculation.

Try to compare the fractions one at a time. You don't have to compare the items in a series in order. What you are trying to determine is whether every fraction in one column is larger than (or at least equal to) a corresponding fraction in the other, like so:

$\frac{1}{2} > \frac{1}{3}$ $\quad \frac{4}{5} > \frac{4}{7}$ $\quad \frac{7}{10} > \frac{6}{11}$ $\quad \frac{9}{7} > \frac{8}{9}$

So for every piece of column B, there is a corresponding larger piece of column A. Without adding things up, column A must be the larger. **(A)** is correct.

A 1600 test taker rarely uses a calculator when solving QCs.

Sometimes you may have to apply a bit of reasoning in order to compare piece by piece, but it's almost always the quickest way to go. Let's try another.

15. <u>Column A</u> <u>Column B</u>

$w > x > y > z > 0$

Column A	Column B
$w - z$	$x - y$

When comparing piece by piece, the term you're adding should be greater than its corresponding piece, and the term you're subtracting should be less than its corresponding piece. Here: $w > x$ and $z < y$. So $w - z$ is greater than $x - y$. Although these are variables, we don't have to pick numbers, because we can see by comparing piece by piece that Column A is bigger.

"Backsolve" with the Centered Information

We've seen that picking numbers can be a worthwhile strategy on QCs. The same is true of backsolving, but once again you have to be careful. When you have centered information, a number in one column, and a variable in the other column, sometimes you can plug in the number for the variable in the centered information and see whether the number is too large, too small, or just right. You can think of this as the "Goldilocks" approach. But watch out! The Goldilocks approach has a bear trap. If the number appears just right, you *must* double-check to see whether another number could work too, making **(D)** the correct answer.

16.

Column A	Column B
y	6

y is a positive integer

$$1.15 < \frac{y+1}{y} < 1.2$$

Let's see if y could equal 6:

$$\frac{y+1}{y} = \frac{6+1}{6} = \frac{7}{6} = 1.1\overline{66}$$

$$1.15 < 1.1\overline{66} < 1.2$$

So 6 feels just right. But could y be anything else? Let's see if y could equal 5:

$$\frac{y+1}{y} = \frac{5+1}{5} = \frac{6}{5} = 1.2$$

But y is less than 1.2, so 5 is too small. Let's see if y could equal 7:

$$\frac{y+1}{y} = \frac{7+1}{7} = \frac{8}{7} \cong 1.142$$

But y is greater than 1.15, so 7 is too big. The only integer y could be is 6, so the answer is **(C)**.

A 1600 test taker always makes sure that the relationship cannot change when the QC contains a variable.

ESSENTIAL MATH STRATEGIES RECAP

How to Attack SAT Math Sections Strategically

- Do all the questions you can handle easily first. Do the tough stuff after you've answered all of the other questions in a set.
- Look for shortcuts and backdoor approaches to the answer. Choose the approach that works best for you.
- Make sure, especially towards the end of a question set, that you have read the question carefully and are answering the question that's been asked of you.

Grid-In Strategies

- Sometimes Grid-Ins have more than one possible answer. Just pick a safe answer, and fill in the grid carefully.
- Start with the left-most column when filling in the grid.
- Don't bother to round up on decimal answer choices.

QC Strategies

- Pick numbers, making sure to pick twice and to pick different kinds of numbers the second time.
- Make one column look like the other.
- Do the same thing to both columns.
- Compare piece by piece.
- "Backsolve" with the centered information.

Regular Math Strategies

- Pick numbers.
- Backsolve.

How to pick numbers on regular math questions

Step 1: Pick simple numbers to stand in for the variables.
Step 2: Answer the question using the number(s) you picked.
Step 3: Try out all the answer choices, eliminating those that give you a different result.
Step 4: Try out different values if more than one answer choice works.

How to backsolve on regular math questions

Step 1: Start with (C).
Step 2: Eliminate choices you know are too big or too small.
Step 3: Keep going until you find the choice that works.

We know that you're just dying to test out all of these strategies. That's what the next chapter is all about.

CHAPTER TWELVE

SAT Math Strategies Practice Set and Explanations

Notes:

(1) Calculator use is permitted.

(2) All numbers used are real numbers.

(3) Figures are provided for some problems. All figures are drawn to scale and lie in a plane UNLESS otherwise indicated.

Reference Information

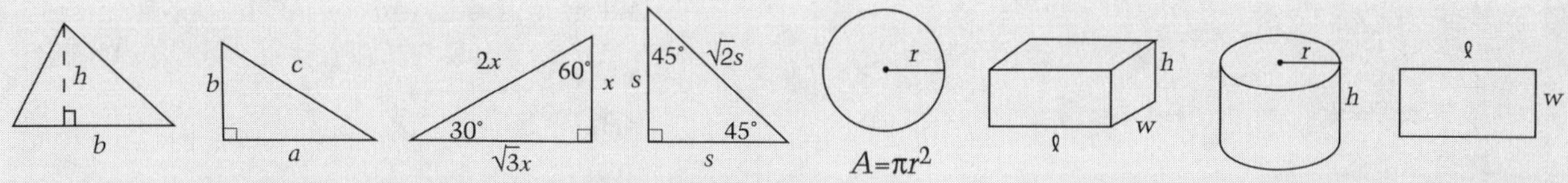

$A=\frac{1}{2}bh$ $c^2 = a^2 + b^2$ Special Right Triangles $A=\pi r^2$ $C=2\pi r$ $V=\ell wh$ $V=\pi r^2 h$ $A=\ell w$

The sum of the degree measures of the angles of a triangle is 180.
The number of degrees of arc in a circle is 360.
A straight angle has a degree measure of 180.

1. If n is an even number, which of the following must be odd?

   (A) $\frac{3n}{2}$

   (B) $2(n - 1)$

   (C) $n(n + 1)$

   (D) $\frac{n}{2} + 1$

   (E) $2n + 1$

2. If $\frac{3x}{4} + 10 = \frac{x}{8} + 15$, then $x =$

   (A) 4

   (B) 8

   (C) 10

   (D) 12

   (E) 16

3. A water tower is filled to $\frac{3}{4}$ of its capacity. If $\frac{3}{5}$ of the water it is currently holding were to be released, what fraction of its capacity would it hold?

   (A) $\frac{3}{20}$

   (B) $\frac{1}{4}$

   (C) $\frac{3}{10}$

   (D) $\frac{1}{5}$

   (E) $\frac{1}{20}$

4. Louis is three times as old as his sister Denise, who is five years older than their cousin Celeste. If in 18 years Louis will be twice as old as Celeste will be then, how old is Denise?

(A) 7
(B) 8
(C) 9
(D) 10
(E) 12

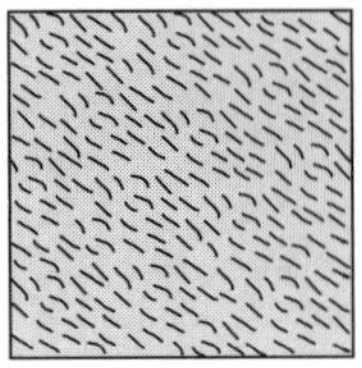

5. The diagram above represents a square garden. If each side of the garden is increased in length by 50 percent, by what percent is the area of the garden increased?

(A) 50%
(B) 100%
(C) 125%
(D) 150%
(E) 225%

6. The cost to rent a boat for a fishing trip is x dollars, which is to be shared equally among the people taking the trip. If 12 people go on the trip rather than 20, how many more dollars, in terms of x, will it cost per person?

(A) $\frac{x}{8}$
(B) $\frac{x}{12}$
(C) $\frac{x}{16}$
(D) $\frac{x}{20}$
(E) $\frac{x}{30}$

7. A car rental company charges for mileage as follows: x dollars per mile for the first n miles and $x + 1$ dollars per mile for each mile over n miles. How much will the mileage charge be in dollars for a journey of d miles where $d > n$?

(A) $d(x + 1) - n$
(B) $xn + d$
(C) $xn + d(x + 1)$
(D) $x(n + d) + d$
(E) $(x + 1)(d - n)$

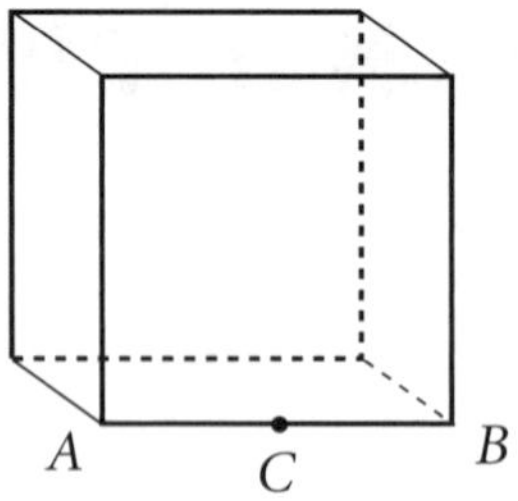

8. The surface area of the cube above is 294 square centimeters. If C is the midpoint of AB, what is the length of AC in centimeters?

(A) 3
(B) 3.5
(C) 4
(D) 4.5
(E) 6

9. Twenty percent of the trees in an orchard are apple trees, and $\frac{1}{3}$ of the trees that are not apple trees are cherry trees. If $\frac{3}{4}$ of the trees in the orchard are fruit trees, and the only types of fruit trees in the orchard are apple trees, cherry trees, and plum trees, what fraction of the trees in the orchard are plum trees?

(A) $\frac{1}{30}$
(B) $\frac{3}{40}$
(C) $\frac{1}{12}$
(D) $\frac{17}{60}$
(E) $\frac{13}{45}$

10. At a light bulb factory, one out of every 30 light bulbs produced is defective. Ninety-two percent of the defective light bulbs are discarded at the factory, and the remaining defective light bulbs are shipped to customers. If 1,200 defective light bulbs were shipped to customers over the course of one year, how many light bulbs were produced by the factory during that year?

(A) 300,000
(B) 450,000
(C) 500,000
(D) 540,000
(E) 600,000

11. If y is a positive number, which of the following is equivalent to increasing y by 40 percent and then decreasing the result by 50 percent?

(A) Decreasing y by 30%
(B) Decreasing y by 25%
(C) Decreasing y by 10%
(D) Increasing y by 10%
(E) Increasing y by 20%

12. If a speedboat travels at a rate of $\frac{x}{10}$ miles every y seconds, how many miles will the speedboat travel in z minutes?

(A) $\frac{xy}{10z}$
(B) $\frac{xz}{10y}$
(C) $\frac{xyz}{10}$
(D) $\frac{6xy}{z}$
(E) $\frac{6xz}{y}$

13.

Column A	Column B
$7^5 + 7^6$	8×7^5

14.

Column A	Column B

The remainder when n is divided by 5 is 3. The remainder when m is divided by 5 is 4.

Column A	Column B
The remainder when $n + m$ is divided by 5	The remainder when $n \times m$ is divided by 5

15.

Column A	Column B
$\sqrt{15} + \sqrt{7}$	$\sqrt{8} + 4$

16.

Column A	Column B

$y > 0$

Column A	Column B
$\frac{y^2 - 1}{y + 1}$	$y - 1$

17. Column A | Column B

Lisa's weekly income is 68 percent of Bart's weekly income. Lisa's weekly income is \$476.

Column A	Column B
Bart's weekly income	\$700

18. Column A | Column B

$ab = 25$
$a^3 < 0$

Column A	Column B
$a - b$	$a + b$

19. Column A | Column B

N is the set of all fractions respresented in the form $\frac{s-1}{s}$, where s is an integer such that $1 < s < 30$.

Column A	Column B
The product of all the fractions that are in N.	$\frac{1}{30}$

20. A candy jar contains only grape, cherry, orange, and lemon candies. In the jar there are twice as many grape candies as cherry candies, and twice as many cherry candies as orange and lemon candies combined. If there are three times as many orange candies as lemon candies, what's the probability that a candy drawn at random from the jar will be an orange candy?

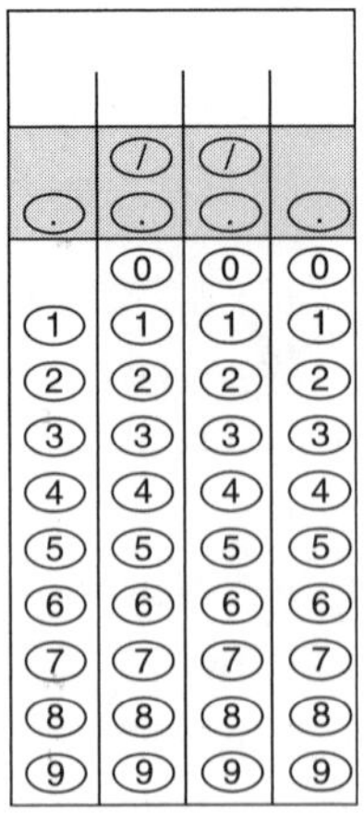

Explanations

1. E

Try picking an even number for n to plug into the answer choices, such as 2.

(A): $\frac{3n}{2} = \frac{3 \times 2}{2} = \frac{6}{2} = 3$. Keep it for now.

(B): $2(n - 1) = 2(2 - 1) = 2$. This is not odd. Discard.

(C): $n(n + 1) = 2(2 + 1) = 6$. This is not odd. Discard.

(D): $\frac{n}{2} + 1 = \frac{2}{2} + 1 = 2$. This is not odd. Discard.

(E): $2n + 1 = 2 \times 2 + 1 = 5$. Keep it for now.

Now try picking a different even number for n, such as 4:

(A): $\frac{3n}{2} = \frac{3 \times 4}{2} = \frac{12}{2} = 6$. This is not odd. Discard.

(E): $2n + 1 = 2 \times 4 + 1 = 9$. This is odd. Bingo!

2. B

Let's backsolve to answer this. Normally we would begin with **(C)**, but since it's clear that 10 does not yield nice round numbers when plugged into $\frac{3x}{4}$ or $\frac{x}{8}$, we'll start with an easier number, such as **(B)**, $x = 8$:

$$\frac{3 \times 8}{4} + 10 = \frac{8}{8} + 15 \ ?$$

$$\frac{24}{4} + 10 = 1 + 15$$

$$6 + 10 = 16 \qquad \text{Bingo!}$$

3. C

Here we want to pick a number for the capacity of the water tower, making sure the number works well with the fractions in the problem. Let's use the largest denominator in the answer choices and say that the water tower holds 20 gallons.

Thus, if the tower is filled to $\frac{3}{4}$ of its capacity, it contains 15 gallons. And if $\frac{3}{5}$ of that were to be released, 9 gallons would be released, leaving 6 gallons. Thus the tower would be left holding $\frac{6}{20} = \frac{3}{10} =$ of its capacity.

4. B

Here's another opportunity to backsolve, so let's start with **(C)**:

If Denise is 9, then Louis is 27 and Celeste is 4. In 18 years Louis will be 45 and Celeste will be 22, so Louis will be *slightly more than* twice as old as Celeste.

That didn't work, so let's try **(B)**:

If Denise is 8, then Louis is 24 and Celeste is 3. In 18 years Louis will be 42 and Celeste will be 21, so Louis will be twice as old as Celeste will be then. That works, so **(B)** is the answer.

5. C

Since we are dealing with a square garden, both sides are the same, and the area = $(\text{side})^2$. And because this is also a percent problem, we can make the original dimensions 10 ft. by 10 ft., so that the original area would be 100 sq. ft. Thus if we increase each side length by 50%, the new dimensions would be 15 ft. by 15 ft., for a new area of $15 \times 15 = 225$ sq. ft.

If you figured this much out and then picked **(E)**, you didn't read the question carefully enough. The question asks by what percent the area of the garden is *increased*. The amount of increase is $(225 - 100) =$ 125 sq. ft., which is 125% of 100 sq. ft., making **(C)** the correct answer.

6. E

Pick a number for x, making sure that the number you pick works well with the numbers in the problem. You want a number that both 12 and 20 divide into evenly, so let's try $x = 60$:

If 12 people go on the trip, the cost will be $\frac{60}{12} = 5$ dollars per person.

If 20 people go on the trip, the cost will be $\frac{60}{20} = 3$ dollars per person.

Consequently, the additional cost per person will be $5 - 3 = 2$ dollars, and 2 is the target number:

(A) $\frac{x}{8} = \frac{60}{8}$, which is not 2. Discard.

(B) $\frac{x}{12} = \frac{60}{12} = 5$. Discard.

(C) $\frac{x}{16} = \frac{60}{16}$, which is not 2. Discard.

(D) $\frac{x}{20} = \frac{60}{20} = 3$. Discard.

(E) $\frac{x}{30} = \frac{60}{30} = 2$. This is it!

7. A

Say you picked $x = 2$ and $n = 3$, and $d = 4$. Use these numbers to work out how much a journey of 4 miles costs.

The first 3 miles costs 2 dollar per mile, so the charge for the first 3 miles is 6 dollars.

The final mile costs $2 + 1 = 3$ dollars per mile, so the charge here is 3 dollars.

The total charge is $6 + 3 = 9$ dollars. This is your target number. Look for it when you substitute $x = 2$ and $n = 3$, and $d = 4$ into the answer choices.

(A) $d(x + 1) - n = 4(2 + 1) - 3 = 9$. Keep this.

(B) $xn + d = 2(3) + 4 = 10$. Eliminate.

(C) $xn + d(x + 1) = 2(3) + 4(2 + 1) = 18$. Eliminate.

(D) $x(n + d) + d = 2(3 + 4) + 4 = 18$. Eliminate.

(E) $(x + 1)(d - n) = (2 + 1)(4 - 3) = 3$. Eliminate.

Only choice **(A)** gives you your target number, so that's the answer.

8. B

Let's backsolve this confusing geometry problem. Let's assume $AC = 4$: If $AC = 4$, the edge length of the cube is 8, so each face of the cube is $8^2 = 64$ square centimeters. There are 6 faces to a cube, so the entire surface area would be $64 \times 6 = 384$ square centimeters. This is too large so **(C)**, **(D)**, and **(E)** are all out.

Try $AC = 3.5$: If $AC = 3.5$, the edge length of the cube is 7, so each face of the cube is $7^2 = 49$ square centimeters. There are 6 faces to a cube, so the entire surface area would be $49 \times 6 = 294$ square inches, which is what we want, so the answer is **(B)**.

9. D

We'll treat this as we would any fraction problem with an unknown value, and plug in the largest denominator in the answer choices for the number of trees in the orchard. So we'll assume there are 60 trees. Twenty percent, i.e., $\frac{1}{5}$ of these, or 12 of the trees, are apple trees, leaving 48 trees, of which $\frac{1}{3}$, or 16 trees, are cherry trees. $\frac{3}{4}$ of all the trees, or 45 trees, are fruit trees, and since all the fruit trees are either apple, cherry or plum, that leaves $45 - (12 + 16) = 17$ plum trees. Thus, the fraction of all the trees in the orchard that are plum trees is $\frac{17}{60}$.

10. B

Let's backsolve this one. If you start with **(C)**, you quickly see that 500,000 cannot be the answer because 1 in 30 light bulbs are defective, and 500,000 is not divisible by 30. Eliminate.

Let's try **(B)**: Out of 450,000 light bulbs, 1 in 30, or $450{,}000 \div 30 = 15{,}000$ light bulbs are defective. If 92 percent of these are discarded, 8 percent are shipped out: $15{,}000 \times 0.08 = 1{,}200$. So **(B)** is the answer.

11. A

This question begs to be solved by picking numbers. Let $y = 100$. Increasing 100 by 40 percent gives you 140. Decreasing that by 50 percent leaves you with 70. Going from 100 to 70 is the same as decreasing by 30 percent. That was too easy.

12. E

Here's another opportunity to pick numbers, and since the problem involves a unit conversion from seconds to minutes, we want to pick numbers that do the converting for us. For instance, we could make $x = 20$ and $y = 60$, so that the speedboat travels $\frac{20}{10}$, or 2 miles every 60 seconds, or one minute. So if we make $z = 2$ the number of minutes, then the boat travels 2 miles a minute, so it must travel 4 miles in 2 minutes. So 4 is your target number when $x = 20$, $y = 60$, and $z = 2$. Now try out the answer choices.

(A) $\frac{xy}{10z} = \frac{20 \times 60}{10 \times 2}$, which is too large.

(B) $\frac{xz}{10y} = \frac{20 \times 2}{10 \times 60}$, which is too small.

(C) $\frac{xyz}{10} = \frac{20 \times 60 \times 2}{10}$, which is way too large.

(D) $\frac{6xy}{z} = \frac{6 \times 20 \times 60}{2}$, which is even larger.

(E) $\frac{6xz}{y} = \frac{6 \times 20 \times 2}{60} = 4$. We finally found it!

13. C

You could pull out a calculator, but there's a quicker approach. Remember: Compare, don't calculate. But in order to compare, you need to put both columns into a similar form. Factoring 7^5 out of both terms in Column A will help you to do just that:

Column A: $7^5 + 7^6 = 7^5(1 + 7) = 7^5 \times 8 = 8 \times 7^5$

So the two quantities are equal.

14. C

Pick numbers on QC remainder problems: Since n leaves a remainder of 3 when divided by 5, let's pick $n = 8$. And since m leaves a remainder of 4 when divided by 5, let's pick $m = 9$. Now let's plug these numbers into the columns.

In Column A: The remainder when $8 + 9 = 17$ is divided by 5 is 2.

In Column B: The remainder when $8 \times 9 = 72$ is divided by 5 is also 2.

So the columns appear equal, but because this is a hard QC you should pick numbers again, such as $n = 13$ and $m = 14$. When you do, you still get remainders of 2 in both columns, so the answer is in fact **(C)**.

15. B

Compare piece by piece: $\sqrt{8}$ is greater than $\sqrt{7}$, and 4 is greater than $\sqrt{15}$. (If this is not intuitive, remember that $\sqrt{16} = 4$.) Column B is greater than Column A. You might have been tempted to square both sides to remove the radical signs, but that would have involved unnecessary work.

16. C

You could pick numbers, but it's probably easier here to make Column A look more like Column B by factoring the numerator.

Column A: $\frac{y^2 - 1}{y + 1} = \frac{(y + 1)(y - 1)}{y + 1} = y - 1$

17. C

Here, the easiest approach is the Goldilocks approach. In other words, take 68 percent of \$700 and see whether the result you get for Lisa's income is too big, too small, or just right. Pulling out a calculator, $.68 \times 700 = 476$, so the two quantities are equal, **(C)**.

18. A

This seems tricky, because it's hard to get a fix on the values for a or b, but our job is to compare, not calculate. You're told that $ab = 25$, so a and b must have the same sign since they have a positive product. Since $a^3 < 0$, a must be negative. So both a and b are negative. Comparing the columns piece by piece, $-b$ is greater than $+b$, so Column A is greater.

19. A

This problem is confusing, and it would seem to involve a painful amount of calculating. But as we know, there must be a simpler way. The smallest value for s is 2. If s is 2, the fraction $\frac{s-1}{s}$ is $\frac{1}{2}$. If s is 3, the fraction is $\frac{2}{3}$. If s is 4, the fraction is $\frac{3}{4}$, and so on until if s is 29, the fraction is $\frac{28}{29}$. So that means that in Column A, after some canceling, we get:

$$\frac{1}{\cancel{2}} \times \frac{\cancel{2}}{\cancel{3}} \times \frac{\cancel{3}}{\cancel{4}} \cdots \frac{\cancel{28}}{29} = \frac{1}{29}$$

$\frac{1}{29} > \frac{1}{30}$, so Column A is greater than Column B.

20. 3/28, 6/56, 9/84 or .107

As you should know, every now and then you can pick numbers even on a Grid-In. Here's a perfect example. Let's assume there's 1 lemon candy (since all the other numbers seem to build on this one). Read carefully through the question, and you'll see that that means there are 3 orange candies, 8 cherry candies, and 16 grape candies.

So the probability of picking an orange candy is:

$$\frac{\text{Number of orange candies}}{\text{Total number of candies}} = \frac{3}{1+3+8+16} = \frac{3}{28}$$

or .107.

section five

STRAIGHT MATH ON THE SAT

CHAPTER THIRTEEN

SAT Arithmetic

- Number properties
- Roots and exponents

Okay, now that you've seen the basic math strategies Kaplan has to offer a top-notch test taker, it's time to see how they come into play on straight-ahead math questions. More often than not, the math tested on the SAT doesn't get too fancy. But what can get tricky at times is how the questions are put together.

But don't worry. A systematic approach to these questions is all it takes for a 1600 test taker to demonstrate the straight-ahead math knowledge they've already mastered in junior high and high school math class.

NUMBER PROPERTIES

Questions concerning number properties are some of the toughest non–word problem questions on the SAT.

But what do we mean by number properties?

"Number properties" refer to ideas such as: Is a number odd or even? Positive or negative? Greater or smaller than another number? It sounds simple enough, but these kinds of questions can get tough since we tend not to think in these terms when we do everyday math.

On number properties questions, you need to think about how numbers behave and how certain numbers behave differently than others. For instance, if a question asks about even numbers, remember that 0 is even. If a question asks about prime numbers, think about 2, since it's the smallest prime number, and the only even prime number. Understanding how numbers "behave" is what number properties questions are all about.

Let's look at some tough number properties questions.

Questions 1–2

1. If j and k are integers, and $2j + k = 15$, which of the following must be true?

   I. j is odd.

   II. k is odd.

   III. $j + k$ is even.

   (A) None
   (B) I only
   (C) II only
   (D) III only
   (E) I, II, and III

2. Column A | Column B

   a is a positive integer

Column A	Column B
remainder when a is divided by 5	remainder when a^2 is divided by 5

   (A) the quantity in Column A is greater
   (B) the quantity in Column B is greater
   (C) the quantities in both columns are equal
   (D) the relationship cannot be determined

Explanations: Questions 1–2

1. C

Roman numeral questions can be tricky since you need to work through the statements first, and then see how they affect the answer choices. A quick scan of the statements tells you that you're dealing with properties of odd and even numbers. If you remember the properties (such as ODD + EVEN = ODD and ODD × EVEN = EVEN) you could try to reason the problem out, but in our humble opinion there's an easier approach.

You may have guessed it. It's time to pick numbers. The question asks which of the following MUST be true, and statement I says j is odd, so let's see if we can make j even by picking 2 for j. $2(2) + 11 = 15$. Since 2 works, statement I doesn't have to be true, and **(B)** and **(E)** are out. Now look at statement II, which says k is odd. When we picked 2, an even number, for j we got 11, an odd number, for k. So let's try an odd number for j, say 3. $2(3) + 9 = 15$. Since we tried both even and odd numbers for j and both times k came out odd, we know now that statement II must be true. Now look at the answer choices and see what you can eliminate. **(A)** and **(D)** are both out, so the answer has to be **(C)**, without even looking at statement III.

> A 1600 test taker handles Roman numeral questions one statement at a time, eliminating answer choices as she goes along. That way, she sometimes doesn't have to evaluate all three statements.

But what the heck, we'll check out statement III anyway. It says $j + k$ is even. Let's look at the numbers we've already picked. We first picked $j = 2$ and $k = 11$; $2 + 11 = 13$, which is odd, so statement III is out, just as we suspected.

2. D

Both remainder questions and QCs with variables are highly amenable to picking numbers. Let's start with the simple case where $a = 5$. If $a = 5$, Column A is the remainder when 5 is divided by 5, or 0, and Column B is the remainder when 5^2, or 25, is divided by 5, which is also 0. Both columns equal 0, so either **(C)** or **(D)** is correct. Remember, once you establish a relationship by picking numbers on QCs with variables, the correct answer will either be that relationship or **(D)**.

Now that we've established that the columns can be equal, we need to see if the relationship can change. Let's try $a = 7$. If $a = 7$, then Column A is the remainder when 7 is divided by 5, or 2, and Column B is the remainder when 7^2, or 49, is divided by 5, or 4. In this case, Column B is greater. Since the relationship changes, we know that we do not need to pick any more numbers, and **(D)** is correct.

Questions 3–4

3. If the sum of five consecutive integers is a, then the sum of the next five consecutive integers is

   (A) $a + 1$
   (B) $a + 5$
   (C) $a + 25$
   (D) $2a$
   (E) $5a$

4. If P is the product of the first seven positive integers, then P is NOT a multiple of

   (A) 27
   (B) 35
   (C) 42
   (D) 63
   (E) 72

Explanations: Questions 3–4

3. C

If the sum of five consecutive integers in a set is a, then each of the next five consecutive integers will be five greater than the corresponding integer in the original set. Since there are five integers in the new set, the sum of the five integers in the new set must be $a + 5(5) = a + 25$. **(C)** is correct. You can easily prove this to yourself by picking numbers, if you have the time.

A 1600 SAT test taker relies on logic and reasoning to handle questions like this one, and then confirms his work by picking numbers if time permits.

4. A

If P is the product of the first seven positive integers, then all of its factors will be combinations of these integers, or at least their prime factors. Break down the first seven positive integers into their prime factors, and see which answer choice cannot be the product of some combination of these prime factors. 2, 3, 5, and 7 are prime. $4 = 2 \times 2$ and $6 = 2 \times 3$. So the prime factorization of P is $1 \times 2 \times 3 \times (2 \times 2) \times 5 \times (2 \times 3) \times 7 = 2 \times 2 \times 2 \times 2 \times 3 \times 3 \times 5 \times 7$. Only **(A)**, $27 = 3 \times 3 \times 3$, cannot be produced from these prime factors since 3 only appears twice in the prime factorization of P.

A 1600 test taker knows how to work with prime factors in order to get a better handle on questions involving multiples.

Questions 5–6

5. If $-1 < b < 0$, which must be true?

   (A) $b^2 < b < 0$
   (B) $0 < b < b^2$
   (C) $b < b^3 < b^5$
   (D) $b < b^2 < b^3$
   (E) $b < b^2 < b^4$

6. Column A | Column B

$P = \{-2, -1, 1, 2\}$
The members of set Q are squares of the numbers in set P

Column A	Column B
The number of members in set P	The number of members in set Q

   (A) the quantity in Column A is greater
   (B) the quantity in Column B is greater
   (C) the quantities in both columns are equal
   (D) the relationship cannot be determined

Explanations: Questions 5–6

5. C

Once again this question tests your ability to understand how a number behaves. In this case, b is a negative fraction. Since b is negative, b will be positive when raised to an even exponent, and negative when raised to an odd exponent. This allows you to quickly eliminate **(A)**, **(B)**, and **(D)**.

You're left with **(C)** and **(E)**. Now it may be time to pick an easy negative fraction, say $-\frac{1}{2}$.

$\left(-\frac{1}{2}\right)^2 = \frac{1}{4}, \left(-\frac{1}{2}\right)^3 = -\frac{1}{8}, \left(-\frac{1}{2}\right)^4 = \frac{1}{16}$, and $\left(-\frac{1}{2}\right)^5 = -\frac{1}{32}$. Now $-\frac{1}{2} < -\frac{1}{8} < -\frac{1}{32}$, so choice **(C)** is correct.

A 1600 test taker uses logic and insight whenever possible, but is never afraid to confirm her results using concrete numbers.

6. A

Your first instinct on a question like this one might be to choose **(C)** since you are simply squaring the members of set P to determine the members of set Q. But be careful. Tricky QCs, most often those towards the end of a question set, contain traps.

In this case, there are few enough elements in the set to allow you to square each value and see what you come up with. Remember that negative values when squared become positive. So the squares of the set containing $\{-2, -1, 1, 2\}$ would be $\{4, 1, 1, 4\}$ respectively. Since two terms appear twice in this set, set Q is really $\{1, 4\}$. So set P contains four elements, and set Q contains two elements. Column A is greater, **(A)** is correct.

The previous two questions covered number properties with a few exponents mixed in. In the next section, you'll see some roots and exponents questions with a touch of number properties.

ROOTS AND EXPONENTS

Along with questions about number properties, those testing roots and exponents are among the toughest straightforward arithmetic questions on the SAT. To get a top-notch score on the SAT, you'll need to get comfortable with square roots and with all rules concerning adding and multiplying exponents.

The following questions should give you a pretty good (or gruesome) idea of your current skill level.

Questions 7–8

7. $3^5 + \frac{1}{3^5} =$

   (A) 1

   (B) 3

   (C) $\frac{3^6 - 1}{3}$

   (D) $\frac{3^{10} + 1}{3^5}$

   (E) $\frac{3^{25}}{3^5 + 1}$

8. $\frac{3\sqrt{3}}{\sqrt{2}} \times \frac{4\sqrt{3}}{3} =$

   (A) 3
   (B) $6\sqrt{2}$
   (C) 12
   (D) $12\sqrt{2}$
   (E) 36

Explanations: Questions 7–8

7. D

Remember that you can add only fractions with the same denominator.

Convert 3^5 to a fraction with a denominator of 3^5. Then the numbers can be added.

$$3^5 + \frac{1}{3^5} = \frac{3^5}{1} \times \left(\frac{3^5}{3^5}\right) + \frac{1}{3^5}$$

$$= \frac{3^{10}}{3^5} + \frac{1}{3^5} = \frac{3^{10} + 1}{3^5}$$

Answer **(D)** it is.

A 1600 test taker knows that when you multiply exponential expressions with the same base, you add the exponents, and when you divide exponential expressions with the same base, you subtract the exponents.

8. B

Get comfortable plowing through calculations like those you see below:

$$\frac{3\sqrt{3}}{\sqrt{2}} \times \frac{4\sqrt{3}}{3} = \frac{3\sqrt{3} \times 4\sqrt{3}}{\sqrt{2} \times 3}$$

$$= \frac{4 \times \sqrt{3} \times \sqrt{3}}{\sqrt{2}}$$

$$= \frac{4 \times 3}{\sqrt{2}}$$

$$= \frac{12}{\sqrt{2}}$$

This isn't one of the answer choices because having a radical alone in the denominator is not considered "proper format." Rewrite the expression by multiplying both the numerator and denominator by $\sqrt{2}$ to get rid of the radical in the denominator: $\frac{12}{\sqrt{2}} \times \frac{\sqrt{2}}{\sqrt{2}} = \frac{12\sqrt{2}}{2} = 6\sqrt{2}$, or **(B)**.

A 1600 test taker "rewrites" her answer to match the form used in the answer choices.

Questions 9–10

9. If $2^x = y$, which of the following equals $8y$ in terms of x?

(A) 2^{2+x}
(B) 2^{2x}
(C) 2^{3+x}
(D) 2^{3x}
(E) 2^{8x}

10.

Column A	Column B
$(x-2)^2 = 16$	
$y^2 = 25$	
x	y

(A) the quantity in Column A is greater
(B) the quantity in Column B is greater
(C) the quantities in both columns are equal
(D) the relationship cannot be determined

Explanations: Questions 9–10

9. C

Questions like this one are susceptible to one of two approaches, and it's important that you understand yourself as a test taker, and use the approach you are most comfortable with. Let's begin with the arithmetic approach.

We are told that $2^x = y$ and asked to express $8y$ in terms of x. If $2^x = y$, then $8(2^x) = 8y$. In order to multiply 8 and 2^x together, we need to rewrite 8 so that it has the same base of 2. Since $8 = 2^3$, we can rewrite the expression as:

$8(2^x) = 2^3 \times 2^x = 2^{3+x}$. **(C)** is correct.

The alternative approach is to pick numbers. When picking numbers, choose numbers that are easy to work with. In this case, let's say $x = 2$. If x is 2, then $y = 2^x = 2^2 = 4$. If $y = 4$, then $8y = 32$. Now we can plug in 2 for x for each answer choice looking for the choice that gives us 32 as its outcome. Quickly work through the calculations:

(A) $2^{2+x} = 2^{2+2} = 2^4 = 16$

(B) $2^{2x} = 2^{2\times 2} = 2^4 = 16$

(C) $2^{3+x} = 2^{3+2} = 2^5 = 32$. Bingo!

(D) $2^{3x} = 2^{3\times 2} = 2^6 = 64$

(E) $2^{8x} = 2^{8\times 2} = 2^{16}$ = Way too big.

Once again, **(C)** is correct.

A 1600 test taker understands the methods that work best for her, chooses an approach quickly, and follows through to the correct answer. Indecision kills.

---

10. D

QCs can get tricky when they have squared values in the centered information. Always remember to consider negative values on questions like this one. Both equations will most likely yield two solutions, and your instincts should nudge you towards **(D)** as an answer.

Let's solve for x and y:

$(x - 2)^2 = 16$, so $x - 2 = 4$ or -4, and x could equal 6 or -2.

$y^2 = 25$, so y could equal 5 or -5.

We'll review how to solve these sorts of equations algebraically in the next section. What's important now is to see how to compare the columns. If $x = 6$, and $y = 5$, Column A is greater. If $x = -2$ and $y = 5$, Column B is greater. The relationship can change, and **(D)** is correct.

A 1600 test taker knows that there will almost always be two solutions to an equation involving a squared variable. For instance, if $x^2 = 16$, then x can equal 4 or –4. He also knows that this is one of the test makers' favorite traps, especially on QCs.

This concludes our treatment of straightforward arithmetic questions. In the next chapter we'll discuss how a 1600 test taker handles SAT algebra.

CHAPTER FOURTEEN

SAT Algebra

- Algebraic manipulation
- Inequalities
- Simultaneous equations
- Quadratics
- Symbol questions

The algebra tested on the SAT is of the straightforward junior high or high school variety: evaluate an expression, solve an equation or inequality, you know the drill. But that doesn't mean you have to solve these questions the way your high school algebra teacher has taught you. You never have to show your work—all that counts is bubbling in the correct answer.

> A 1600 test taker is all about results. He doesn't care how she gets to the correct answer, as long as she gets there and gets there quick.

STRAIGHTFORWARD ALGEBRA

Most often, algebra questions test your ability to translate English into math, perform basic algebraic manipulations, and solve for a single variable.

The first question in the following practice set is a good example of a straightforward algebra problem.

Questions 1–2

1. If $x = \frac{x + y}{z,}$ which of the following must be equal to z?

   (A) $\frac{x}{y} + x$

   (B) $\frac{x}{y} + 1$

   (C) $\frac{y}{x} + y$

   (D) $\frac{y}{x} + x$

   (E) $\frac{y}{x} + 1$

2. $(R^c)(R^d)(R^e) = R^{-12}$. If $R > 0$, and c, d, and e are each different negative integers, what is the smallest number that c could be?

   (A) –1
   (B) –6
   (C) –9
   (D) –10
   (E) –12

Explanations: Questions 1–2

1. E

Now you could always go ahead and pick numbers on a question like this one, but let's just see if your algebra is up to the challenge. We want to solve for z here, so let's begin by taking z out of the denominator by multiplying both sides by z:

$x = \frac{x + y}{z}$, so $zx = x + y$. Now you can divide both sides by x:

$z = \frac{x + y}{x}$. And now you can distribute out the denominator on the right side of the equation:

$z = \frac{x}{x} + \frac{y}{x} = 1 + \frac{y}{x} = \frac{y}{x} + 1$. So **(E)** is the correct answer here. By the way, did we mention that you can pick numbers here?

2. C

This question tests your basic understanding of exponents and algebra. When numbers with the same base are multiplied together, you add the exponents. So $(R^c)(R^d)(R^e) = R^{c+d+e} = R^{-12}$. We know now that $c + d + e = -12$. In order for c to be as small as possible, d and e must be as large as possible. The question states that c, d, and e are each *different negative* integers. Remember that negatives get larger as they approach zero, so the greatest values we can choose for d and e are -1 and -2. Plug in these numbers to determine the value of c if $d = -1$ and $e = -2$.

$$
\begin{aligned}
c + d + e &= -12 \\
c + (-1) + (-2) &= -12 \\
c - 3 &= -12 \\
c &= -9
\end{aligned}
$$

(C) is correct.

A 1600 test taker never forgets that a negative number becomes greater as its absolute value becomes smaller.

INEQUALITIES

Inequalities appear quite often on the SAT. Treat them as you would regular equations, but remember to flip the sign when you multiply or divide both sides by a negative value. Also note that an inequality represents a range of values as opposed to an equation, which represents a single value.

Questions 3–4

3. If $-2 < x < 2$ and $3 < y < 8$, which of the following represents the range of all possible values of $y - x$?

   (A) $5 < y - x < 6$
   (B) $1 < y - x < 5$
   (C) $1 < y - x < 6$
   (D) $5 < y - x < 10$
   (E) $1 < y - x < 10$

4. If $8 < \sqrt{(n + 6)(n + 1)} < 9$, then n could equal

   (A) 5
   (B) 6
   (C) 7
   (D) 8
   (E) 9

Explanations: Questions 3–4

3. E

The range of possible values can be found by subtracting the smallest possible value from the largest possible value. The greatest value of $y - x$ will occur when y is as large as possible and x is as small as possible. That is, $y - x < 8 - (-2)$, or 10. The smallest value of $y - x$ will occur when y is as small as possible, and x is as large as possible. That is $y - x > 3 - 2$, or 1. So $1 < y - x < 10$. **(E)** is correct.

> A 1600 test taker applies reasoning to determine what the least or greatest possible value of something could be.

4. A

When solving an inequality like this one, treat it like an equation, that is, by doing the same thing to all its parts. There are two important things to remember when dealing with inequalities: (1) multiplying or dividing an inequality by a negative number reverses the sign, and (2) you are solving for a range of values rather than a single value.

For starters, you can get rid of that nasty radical sign by squaring all the elements in the inequality $8 < \sqrt{(n + 6)(n + 1)} < 9$. The direction of the signs won't change since all the elements are greater than 0.

So $64 < (n + 6)(n + 1) < 81$. Now you could try backsolving; the answer choice for which this relationship is true will be correct.

As always, start with choice **(C)**: $(n + 6)(n + 1) = (7 + 6)(7 + 1) = 104$. This is greater than 81, so discard and move onto a smaller answer choice.

(B) $(n + 6)(n + 1) = (6 + 6)(6 + 1) = 84$. This is still greater than 81, so the correct answer choice must be smaller still, which only leaves **(A)**.

> A 1600 test taker isn't afraid to combine a backdoor approach like backsolving with a front-door approach like algebraic manipulation.

SIMULTANEOUS EQUATIONS

Sometimes the SAT requires you to deal with more than one equation in a single question. We refer to these kinds of questions as simultaneous equations. The two ways to handle simultaneous equations are *substitution* and *combination.*

See which technique works best in each of the next two questions.

Questions 5–6

5. For the positive values a, b, c, and d, $a = 2b$, $\frac{1}{2}b = c$, and $4c = 3d$. What is the value of $\frac{d}{a}$?

   (A) $\frac{1}{3}$

   (B) $\frac{3}{4}$

   (C) 1

   (D) $\frac{4}{3}$

   (E) 3

6. Column A — Column B

$$p + q - r = 15$$
$$2p + 2q + r = 45$$

Column A	Column B
r	5

(A) the quantity in Column A is greater
(B) the quantity in Column B is greater
(C) the quantities in both columns are equal
(D) the relationship cannot be determined

Explanations: Questions 5–6

5. A

To find the ratio of d to a, you need to get a and d together in a single equation. You can do this by substituting for the variables b and c in order to eliminate them. Working from the information that $a = 2b$, we get $\frac{a}{2} = b$. We can substitute this into the equation, $\frac{1}{2}b = c$ to get $\frac{1}{2}\left(\frac{a}{2}\right) = c$ or $\frac{a}{4} = c$. Since $4c = 3d$, we can substitute for c to get $4\left(\frac{a}{4}\right) = 3d$, or $a = 3d$. So $\frac{d}{a} = \frac{d}{3d} = \frac{1}{3}$, **(A)** is correct.

Of course you could also solve this problem by picking numbers, but you'd have to be a bit thoughtful. You're told that for the positive values a, b, c, and d, $a = 2b$, $\frac{1}{2}b = c$, and $4c = 3d$. You could try to pick a value for a, but you're better off starting on the other end. If $4c = 3d$, then you could pick $c = 3$ and $d = 4$. Thus $\frac{1}{2}b = 3$, so $b = 6$, and $a = 2b$, so $a = 12$. So $\frac{d}{a} = \frac{4}{12} = \frac{1}{3}$.

A 1600 test taker knows whether he's better off trusting his algebra skills or picking numbers, and proceeds accordingly.

6. C

At first glance, this looks like a prime candidate for choice **(D)** since you're looking at three variables and two equations. But if you add the centered equations together, things begin to fall into place:

$$\begin{array}{r} p + q - r = 15 \\ +2p + 2q + r = 45 \\ \hline 3p + 3q = 45 \end{array}$$

If you now divide both sides by 3, you'll find that $p + q = 20$. Now you can solve for r by plugging 20 in for $p + q$ in the first equation:

$$\begin{aligned} (p + q) - r &= 15 \\ 20 - r &= 15 \\ -r &= -5 \\ r &= 5 \end{aligned}$$

The columns are equal, and **(C)** is correct.

QUADRATICS

Quadratic equations appear quite often on the SAT. Quadratic expressions are what you get when you multiply two binomials, for instance, $x + 2$ and $x - 3$, to get $(x + 2)(x - 3) = x^2 - x - 6$.

Fortunately, these questions tend not to test more than your ability to FOIL and reverse FOIL an expression. Take a crack at the following examples of tricky quadratic questions.

Questions 7–8

7. If $s \neq -2$, then $\frac{2s^2 - 8}{s + 2}$
   (A) $s - 4$
   (B) $s + 4$
   (C) $s^2 + 4$
   (D) $s^2 - 4$
   (E) $2s - 4$

8. If $n > 0$ and $4x^2 + kx + 25 = (2x + n)^2$ for all x, what is the value of $k + n$?
   (A) 5
   (B) 15
   (C) 20
   (D) 25
   (E) 30

Explanations: Questions 7–8

7. E

When asked to simplify an expression like this one, use the clues the test maker gives you. If you see $s + 2$ in the denominator, there's a strong chance that you will be able to factor out the numerator so that an $(s + 2)$ appears there as well. Here's how to work through this one:

$\frac{2s^2 - 8}{s + 2} = \frac{2(s^2 - 4)}{s + 2} = \frac{2\cancel{(s + 2)}(s - 2)}{\cancel{s + 2}} = 2(s - 2)$. Distribute the 2 into the parentheses to get $2s - 4$, **(E)**.

> A 1600 test taker knows the common quadratics and knows automatically that when an expression is in the form $a^2 - b^2$, she should rewrite it as $(a + b)(a - b)$, and vice versa.

Did we mention, by the way, that you could pick numbers here? Try picking $s = 3$ and see what happens.

8. D

The question tells us we are dealing with the square of a binomial of the form $(2x + n)^2$, and we know that n is positive and equals 25 when squared (remember FOIL). So n must equal 5 (it could have also been −5, but you're told here that $n > 0$). Thus, $(2x + n)^2 = (2x + 5)^2$. FOIL that expression to find k. $(2x + 5)(2x + 5) = 4x^2 + 20x + 25$. $4x^2 + kx + 25 = 4x^2 + 20x + 25$, so $k = 20$. Once again, it would be very tempting to choose **(C)** at this point, but the question is asking for $k + n$, not k. $k + n = 20 + 5 = 25$, **(D)**.

> A 1600 test taker always double-checks on tough questions to make sure he's answering the question that's being asked.

SYMBOL QUESTIONS

Some difficult SAT math questions require you to deal with weird symbols and functions. Don't panic when you see something you haven't seen before. Any weird symbols that are introduced will be defined for you, and you just need to work with those definitions.

In the end, symbol questions wind up testing your ability to do some straightforward algebra.

Questions 9–10

The following two questions refer to the following definitions for integers *c* greater than 1.

$\text{\textcircled{c}} = c^2 - 2c$

$\boxed{c} = c^2 + 2c$

9. $\boxed{3} + \text{\textcircled{2}} =$
   (A) 3
   (B) 7
   (C) 11
   (D) 15
   (E) 19

10. If c is an integer greater than 1, then $\text{\textcircled{(c + 2)}} =$
   (A) c^2
   (B) $c^2 + 2$
   (C) $\text{\textcircled{c}}$
   (D) $\text{\textcircled{c}} + 2$
   (E) $\boxed{c}$

Explanations: Questions 9–10

9. D

Don't be intimidated by the unfamiliar symbols here. This question is really a simple algebraic computation question in disguise. Just refer to the right-hand sides of the symbolism equations. All you need to do is plug 3 in for c in $\boxed{c} = c^2 + 2c$, and 2 in for c in $\enclose{circle}{c} = c^2 - 2c$.

$\boxed{3} + \enclose{circle}{2} = 3^2 + 2(3) + 2^2 - 2(2) = 9 + 6 + 4 - 4 = 15$. **(D)** is correct.

A 1600 test taker is never intimidated by weird-looking symbols.

10. E

This question can be handled algebraically or by picking numbers. Since our focus in this chapter is on algebra, we'll lead with the algebraic solution, then quickly run through how to handle this question by picking numbers.

Each technique is effective. The key, as always, is to quickly decide on the approach that works best for you.

We're asked to find $\enclose{circle}{(c + 2)}$. Just as we plugged in numbers for c on the previous question, here we will plug in the expression $(c + 2)$ for c.

$\enclose{circle}{c} = c^2 - 2c$, so $\enclose{circle}{(c + 2)} = (c + 2)^2 - 2(c + 2)$.

This expression can be simplified as follows:

$$\begin{aligned}(c + 2)^2 - 2(c + 2) &= (c^2 + 4c + 4) - (2c + 4)\\ &= c^2 + 4c + 4 - 2c - 4\\ &= c^2 + 2c\end{aligned}$$

$\boxed{c} = c^2 + 2c$ and **(E)** is correct.

If you prefer to pick numbers here, see what happens when $c = 2$. $\enclose{circle}{(c + 2)} = \enclose{circle}{4} = 4^2 - 2(4) = 16 - 8 = 8$. Now plug 2 in for c for each answer choice, and select the choice which gives you an outcome of 8:

(A) $c^2 = 2^2 = 4$

(B) $c^2 + 2 = 2^2 + 2 = 4 + 2 = 6$

(C) $\enclose{circle}{c} = c^2 - 2c = 2^2 - 2(2) = 4 - 4 = 0$

(D) $\enclose{circle}{c} + 2 = (c^2 - 2c) + 2 = 2^2 - 2(2) + 2 = 4 - 4 + 2 = 2$

(E) $\boxed{c} = c^2 + 2c = 2^2 + 2(2) = 4 + 4 = 8$

Only **(E)** produces the desired outcome, so **(E)** is correct.

Of course, you always have to try all the answer choices any time you pick numbers. Sometimes two or more answer choices will work for the particular value that you chose. When this happens, you must go back and pick another value to eliminate the remaining incorrect answer choices.

This concludes the algebra chapter. Next we'll cover the last piece of straight-ahead math, geometry.

CHAPTER FIFTEEN

SAT Geometry

- Triangles, rectangles, and circles
- Mixed figures
- Coordinate geometry
- Solid geometry

As with the other math topics, SAT geometry draws from topics covered in junior high and high school math. It's a sampling of angles, triangles, rectangles, circles, and the (x, y) coordinate plane. This is true for both the straight math problems and—as you'll soon see—the word problems.

The defining feature of SAT geometry problems, to the extent they can be said to have one, is that they tend to combine different topics in the same question. That is, you will rarely get a question testing only a triangle or only a rectangle. More common is a question that tests your ability with both.

TRIANGLES, RECTANGLES, and CIRCLES

Triangles, rectangles, and circles are the SAT "Gang of Three" when it comes to geometry. These figures are by far the most commonly tested. And as you will soon see, they are most commonly tested together.

Geometry Practice Set 1

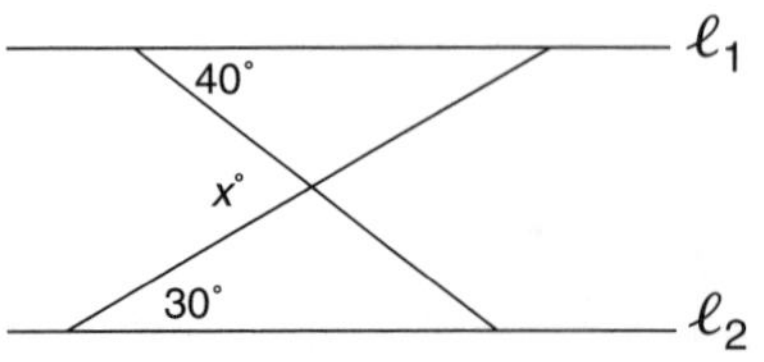

1. In the figure above, if $\ell_1 \parallel \ell_2$, what is the value of x ?
   (A) 70
   (B) 100
   (C) 110
   (D) 140
   (E) 150

2. Column A — Column B

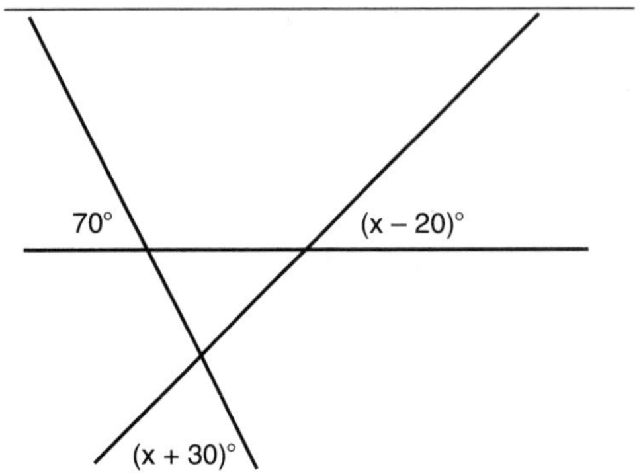

Note: Figure not drawn to scale.

Column A	Column B
x	60

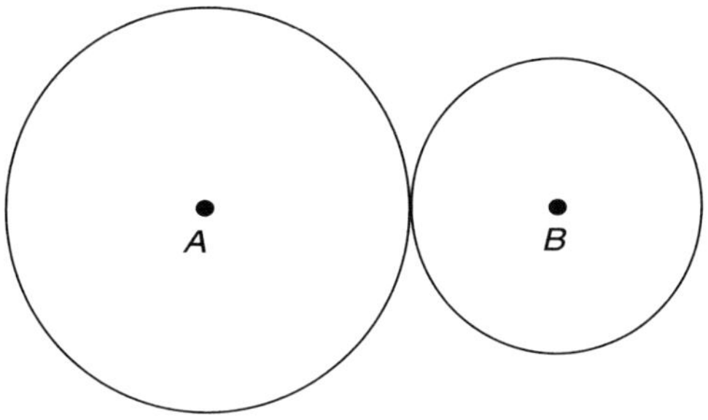

3. In the figure above, circles *A* and *B* are tangent. The circumference of circle *A* is 6π and the circumference of circle *B* is 4π. If point *P* lies on circle *A* and point *Q* lies on circle *B*, what is the greatest possible distance between points *P* and *Q*?

   (A) 5
   (B) $5\sqrt{2}$
   (C) 10
   (D) 5π
   (E) 10π

Explanations: Geometry Practice Set 1

1. A

Fill information into the diagram as you go along. The transversals form two pairs of alternate interior angles, as below.

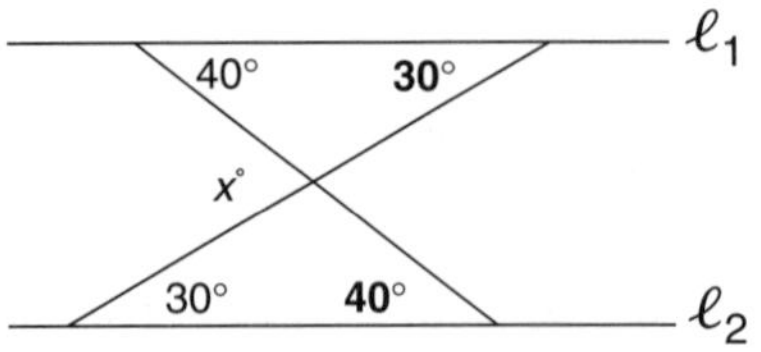

The interior angles of a triangle sum to 180°, so the angle supplementary to x is 180° – 30° – 40° = 110°.

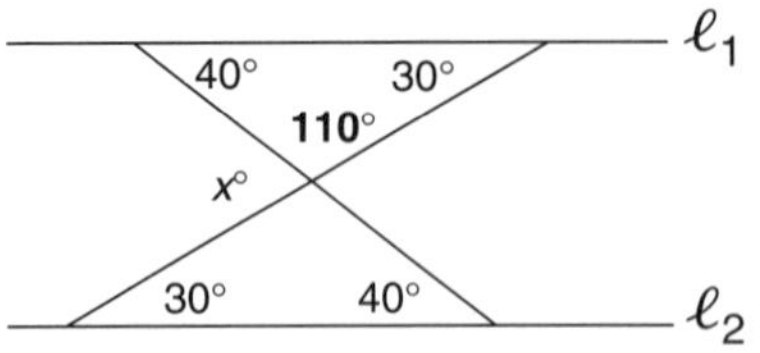

If the angle marked x is supplementary to an angle of 110°, then $x = 180 - 110 = 70$.
(A) is correct.

2. B

Vertical angles are equal. Therefore, each of the angle measures given is also the measure of its vertical angle, and each vertical angle happens to be an interior angle of the triangle. The sum of the interior angles of a triangle is 180°. So the three angles together measure 180°, and $70 + (x - 20) + (x + 30) = 180$. So $70 + 2x + 10 = 180$, $2x + 80 = 180$; $2x = 100$, $x = 50$. So Column A has a value of 50, Column B has a value of 60. Column B is greater so **(B)** is correct.

3. C

The diagram below shows that P and Q are as far apart as possible when separated by a diameter of both circles.

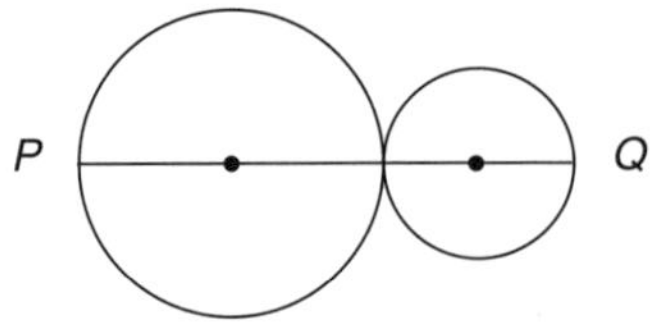

The circumference of circle A is 6π, so the diameter of A is 6 ($2\pi \times$ radius = $\pi \times$ diameter = circumference). Circle B's circumference is 4π, so its diameter is 4. Therefore, the greatest possible distance between point P and point Q is 6 + 4, or 10. **(C)** it is.

Geometry Practice Set 2

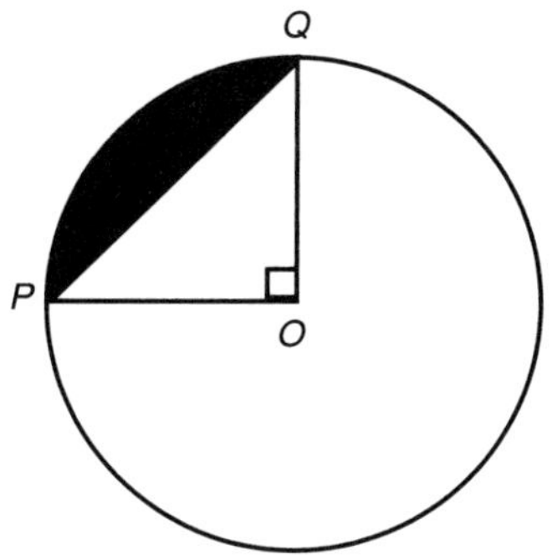

4. In circle O above, if ΔPOQ is a right triangle and radius $OP = 2$, what is the area of the shaded region?

   (A) $4\pi - 2$
   (B) $4\pi - 4$
   (C) $2\pi - 2$
   (D) $2\pi - 4$
   (E) $\pi - 2$

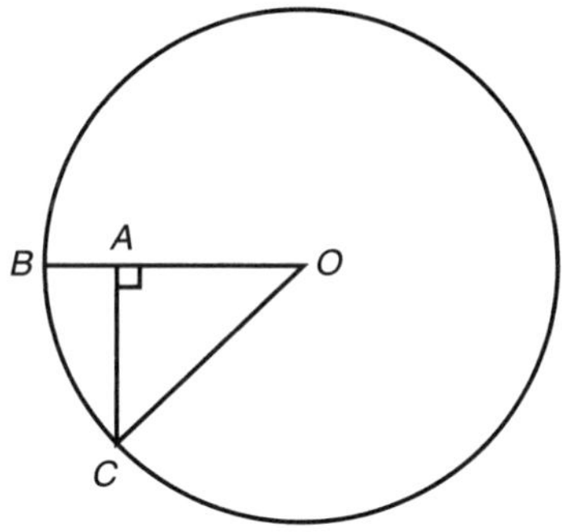

Note: Figure not drawn to scale.

5. If the area of the circle with center O above is 100π and AC has a length of 6, what is the length of AB ?

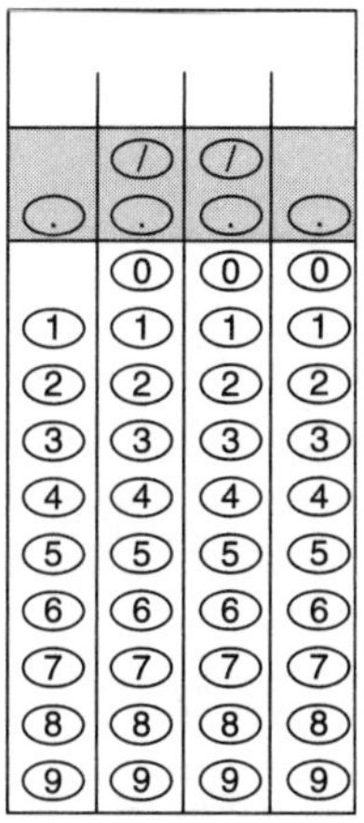

Explanations: Geometry Practice Set 2

4. E

The area of the shaded region is the area of sector *OPQ* minus the area of ΔPOQ. Since $\angle POQ$ is 90°, sector *OPQ* is a quarter-circle. The circle's radius, *OP*, is 2, so its area is $\pi(2^2) = 4\pi$. Therefore, the quarter-circle's area is π.

ΔPOQ's area is $\frac{1}{2}(b \times h) = \frac{1}{2}(2 \times 2) = 2$. So the area of the shaded region is $\pi - 2$. **(E)** is correct.

5. 2

Since we know the area of the circle, we can find the length of radii *OB* and *OC*. We can't find *AB* directly, but if we can find the length of *OA*, then *AB* is just the difference between *OB* and *OA*.

The circle's area, πr^2, is 100π, so its radius is $\sqrt{100}$ or 10. So *OC* is 10 and, as we've been told, *AC* is 6. ΔAOC is a right triangle so we can use the Pythagorean theorem to find *OA*. Ideally, you should recognize that ΔAOC is a 3-4-5 right triangle; *OC* is twice 5, *AC* is twice 3, so *OA* must be twice 4, or 8. (If you didn't see this: $(OA)^2 + 6^2 = 10^2$, $(OA)^2 + 36 = 100$, $(OA)^2 = 64$, $OA = 8$.) *AB* is the difference between the radius *OB* and segment *OA*, so its length is $10 - 8$, or 2.

A 1600 test taker "sees" lengths and regions that need to be measured as parts of larger lengths and areas with already known measurements.

Geometry Practice Set 3

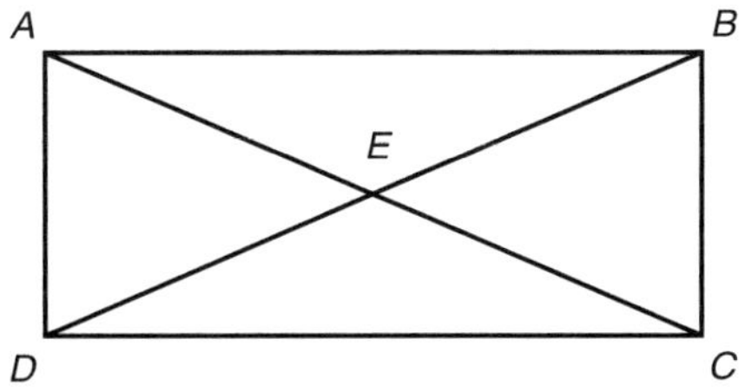

6. In the figure above, *ABCD* is a rectangle. If the area of ΔAEB is 8, what is the area of ΔACD ?

   (A) 8
   (B) 12
   (C) 16
   (D) 24
   (E) 32

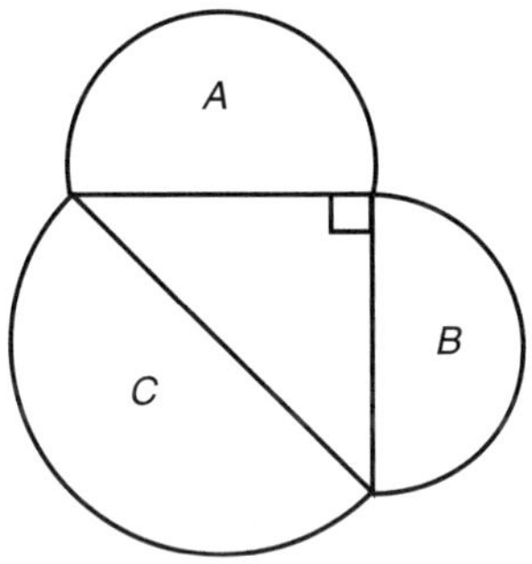

7. In the figure above, if semicircles *A* and *B* each have area 4π, what is the area of semicircle *C* ?

   (A) 4π
   (B) $4\pi\sqrt{2}$
   (C) 6π
   (D) 8π
   (E) 16

Explanations: Geometry Practice Set 3

6. C

ΔCDE has the same area as ΔAEB; they're congruent triangles. But we want the area of ΔACD, which means that we need to know ΔADE's area as well. So we want to find a relationship between ΔADE's area and ΔCDE's area.

Let's make AD the base of ΔADE. Its height, a line drawn perpendicularly from E (the rectangle's midpoint, where its diagonals meet) to AD is just one-half the length of side DC. So the area of ΔADE is $\frac{1}{2} \times AD \times \frac{DC}{2} = \frac{1}{4} \times AD \times DC$.

Applying similar reasoning, let DC be the base of ΔCDE. Its height is then a line drawn perpendicularly from E to DC, which is one-half the length of side AD. So ΔCDE's area is: $\frac{1}{2} \times DC \times \frac{AD}{2} = \frac{1}{4} \times DC \times AD$.

The two triangles are equal in area; each has an area of 8. Therefore, the area of ΔACD is $8 + 8 = 16$. **(C)** is correct.

7. D

The areas of semicircles A and B are equal, so their diameters are equal. Therefore, ΔABC is an isosceles right triangle, and the ratio of each leg to the hypotenuse (the diameter of semicircle C) is $1:1:\sqrt{2}$.

Method I: Move step-by-step from the area given for semicircles A and B to the radius of semicircle C, and find its area with that. The area of a small semicircle is $\frac{1}{2} \times \pi r^2 = 4\pi$; $\pi r^2 = 8\pi$; $r^2 = 8$; $r = \sqrt{8}$. Each leg of the triangle is a diameter, so its length is twice the radius or $2\sqrt{8}$. Therefore, the hypoenuse of the triangle, h, is found with the Pythagorean theorem:

$$(2\sqrt{8})^2 + (2\sqrt{8})^2 = h^2$$
$$32 + 32 = h^2$$
$$64 = h^2$$
$$8 = h$$

. . . which is also the diameter of semicircle C. The radius is half of 8, or 4. The area of semicircle C is $\frac{1}{2} \times \pi 4^2 = 8\pi$.

Method II: Use the ratios more directly. Since the diameters of circles A, B, and C are in the ratio $1:1:\sqrt{2}$, the ratio of their areas will be $1^2:1^2:(\sqrt{2})^2$ or $1:1:2$. C must have twice the area of A, or 8π. **(D)** is correct.

A 1600 test taker uses the diagrams to record, and then derive, important information.

Geometry Practice Set 4

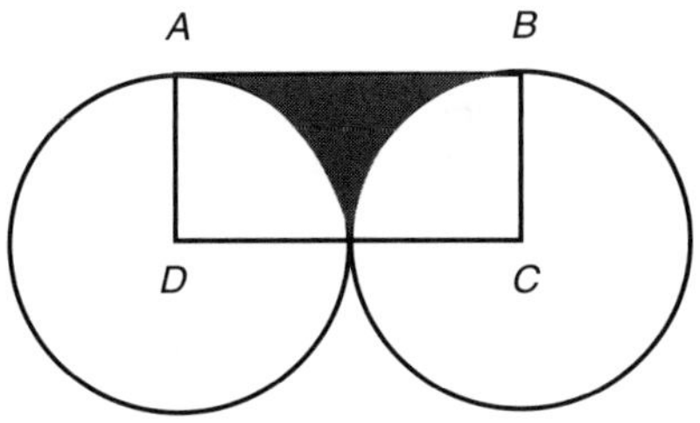

8. In the figure above, *ABCD* is a rectangle and *DA* and *CB* are radii of the circles shown. If $AB = 4$, what is the perimeter of the shaded region?

   (A) $2\pi + 4$
   (B) $4\pi + 4$
   (C) $4\pi + 8$
   (D) $8\pi + 8$
   (E) $8\pi + 16$

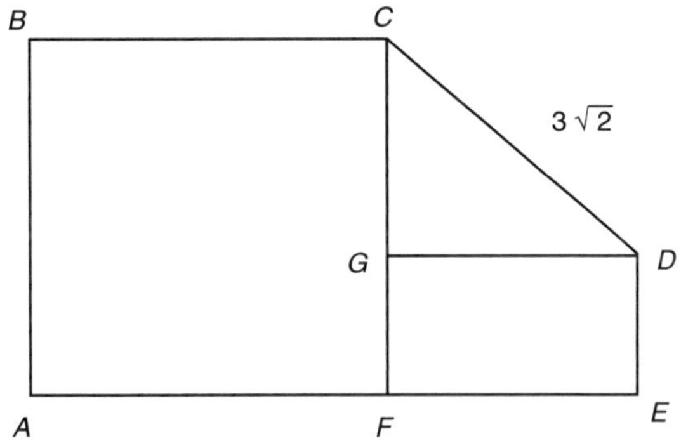

9. In the figure above, the area of square *ABCF* is 25 and $\triangle CDG$ is an isosceles right triangle. What is the area of rectangle *DEFG*?

   (A) 15
   (B) 12
   (C) 9
   (D) $6\sqrt{2}$
   (E) 6

Explanations: Geometry Practice Set 4

8. A

The perimeter of the shaded region is the length of *AB*, plus the length of the two arcs which are part of the perimeter of the shaded region. We already know $AB = 4$, so we have only to find the length of the two arcs.

Since *ABCD* is a rectangle, $DA = CB$ and the two circles have equal radii. *DC* consists of a radius of the circle on the left and a radius of the circle on the right, so $DC = 2r$. But $DC = AB = 4$. Therefore, $2r = 4$, $r = 2$. The sectors are both quarter-circles (the central angle is a right angle). The arc length of a quarter-circle is $\frac{1}{4}$ of the circumference of the whole circle, or $\frac{1}{4} \times 2\pi r$. So, the perimeter of each quarter-circle is $\frac{1}{4} \times 2 \times \pi \times 2 = \pi$. The perimeter of the shaded region is $4 + 2 \times \pi$, or $4 + 2\pi$. That makes **(A)** the winner.

9. E

You have to find the area of rectangle *DEFG* which is embedded in a diagram with two other shapes. The area of rectangle $DEFG$ = length $\times$ width = $GD \times GF$.

Remember in multiple figure problems that the solution usually lies in the features that the shapes share.

The length of *GF* is equal to $CF - CG$, so we need to find *CF* and *CG* in order to find *GF*.

We're also told that triangle *CDG* is an isosceles right triangle. You can use the Pythagorean theorem or the known ratios of the sides of a right isosceles triangle to find the length of leg *GD*, which is what we'll call the length of the rectangle. Also, $GD = CG$, and *CG* is one of the two lengths you need to find in order to find the width, *GF*.

We're told that the area of the square *ABCF* is 25. The area of a square is the length of one side squared. So each side is equal to $\sqrt{25} = 5$. *CF*, then, equals 5.

The leg length to leg length to hypotenuse length ratio of an isosceles right triangle is $1:1:\sqrt{2}$. We know that here the hypotenuse is $3\sqrt{2}$. So the legs *CG* and *GD* each have a length of 3. Now let's go back and try to figure out what *GF* equals. $GF = CF - CG$. So $GF = 5 - 3$ or 2.

Now we know that the width *GF* of rectangle *DEFG* is 2. The length, *GD*, is 3. So the area is 3×2 or 6, **(E)**.

COORDINATE GEOMETRY

Coordinate geometry deals with two-dimensional planes. The planes are defined by an x-axis (which runs horizontally) and a y-axis (which runs vertically).

A location on the plane is expressed in (x, y) coordinates.

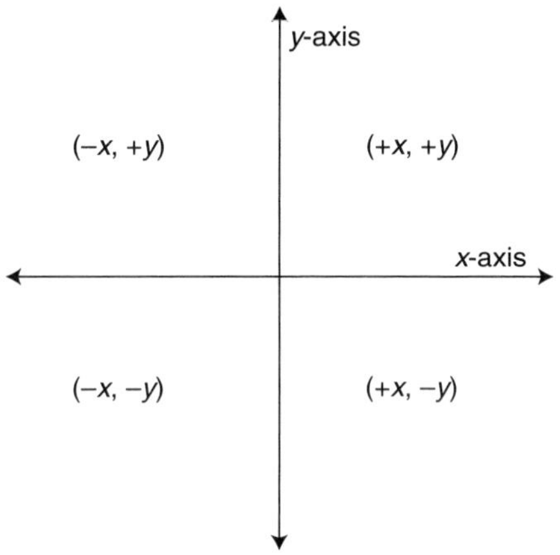

Now try a few questions. Bear in mind that you can always draw a quick coordinate plane if it helps you (and the question doesn't provide one).

Geometry Practice Set 5

10. In the xy-plane, at what point does the graph of the equation $x + 3y = 9$ cross the y-axis?

    (A) (–3, 0)
    (B) (0, –3)
    (C) (0, 3)
    (D) (0, 9)
    (E) (9, 0)

11. Point Q is on the same line as (0, 0) and (3, 9). Which of the following could be point Q?

    (A) (0, 1)
    (B) (1, 3)
    (C) (2, 4)
    (D) (–3, 9)
    (E) (–6, –2)

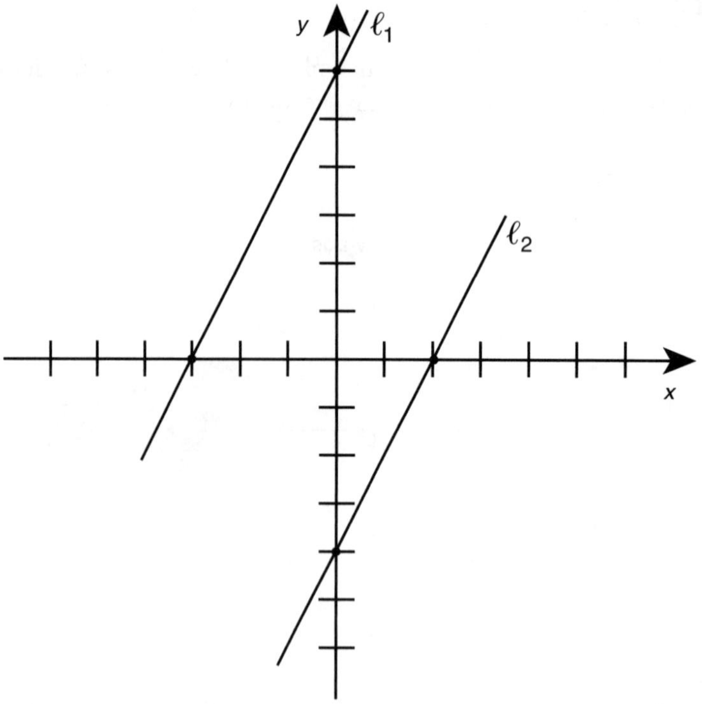

12. The equation of line ℓ_1 is $y = 2x + 6$. Line ℓ_2 is parallel to line ℓ_1. Which of the following is the equation of line ℓ_2?

(A) $y = -4x + 2$
(B) $y = -2x + 4$
(C) $y = 2x - 4$
(D) $y = 2x + 4$
(E) $y = 4x + 2$

Explanations: Geometry Practice Set 5

10. C

Since every point on the y-axis has an x-coordinate of 0, when a line crosses the y-axis, its x-coordinate is 0 (that already eliminates (**A**) and (**E**)). We can substitute $x = 0$ into the equation to find the y-coordinate of the line when it crosses the y-axis. $x + 3y = 9$, $0 + 3y = 9$; $3y = 9$, $y = 3$. So the line crosses the y-axis at (0, 3), making **(C)** correct.

11. B

You can directly figure out the equation for the line through (0, 0) and (3, 9). The slope of a line is $\frac{y_2 - y_1}{x_2 - x_1}$, so the slope of this line is $\frac{9-0}{3-0} = \frac{9}{3} = 3$. The equation for a line is $y = mx + b$ where m is the slope and b is the y-coordinate at which the line crosses the y-axis. This line crosses the y-axis at (0,0), so $b = 0$. Therefore, the equation for the line is $y = 3x$. Among the points given, only (1, 3) fits that equation, making **(B)** the right answer.

If you forgot the formula for a line, you could have done the same thing informally by noticing that, starting from the origin, the y-coordinate increases by 3 for every 1 the x-coordinate increases (and conversely, the y-coordinate must decrease by 3 for every 1 the x-coordinate decreases). Only one of the points can be reached from the origin (0, 0) this way.

> A 1600 test taker sometimes uses scratch paper to sketch the coordinate plane when it isn't provided, in order to visualize what's going on.

12. C

Since parallel lines on the coordinate plane have the same slope, the correct answer must have the same slope as $y = 2x + 6$.

The answer choices are in $y = mx + b$ form, where m is the slope and b is the y-intercept. Find the slope and the y-intercept of ℓ_2.

$y = 2x + 6$ is in the $y = mx + b$ form, so the slope is the coefficient of the x term, or 2. This means we can eliminate (**A**), (**B**), and (**E**)—none of them has slope +2. Since line ℓ_2 crosses the y-axis at the point (0, –4), the y-intercept is –4, and the equation of the line must be $y = 2x - 4$. **(C)** is correct.

Finally, a little taste of the geometry of solids.

Geometry Practice Set 6

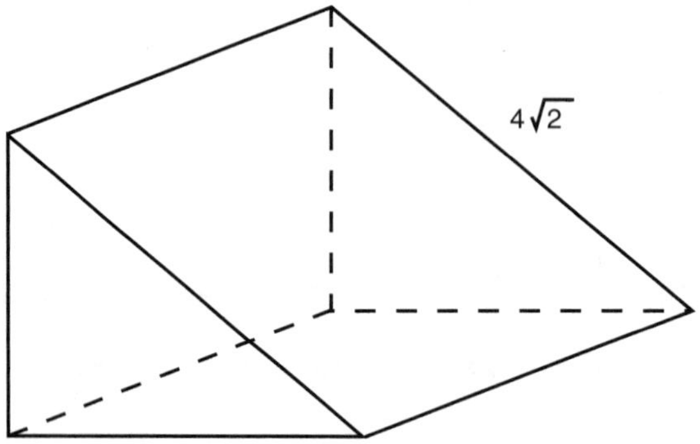

13. If the solid above is half of a cube, then the volume of the solid is

 (A) 16
 (B) 32
 (C) 42
 (D) 64
 (E) $64\sqrt{2}$

Explanations: Geometry Practice Set 6

13. B

This requires some intuition. The solid is half of a cube; you can imagine an identical solid lying on the top of this one to form the complete cube. Then it becomes clear that the line segment with length $4\sqrt{2}$ is the diagonal of a square face. The diagonal is the hypotenuse of a right isosceles triangle with the two edges of the cube as legs; you can find the length of an edge by using the sides ratio for such triangles. In right isosceles triangles, the hypotenuse is $\sqrt{2}$ times either of the legs. Since the hypotenuse has length $4\sqrt{2}$, the legs (which are also the edges of the cube) have length 4. So the cube's volume is $4^3 = 64$. *But be careful, that's not the answer to the question!* The volume of the solid in the diagram is half the cube's volume, or 32. (**B**) it is.

That wraps up our tour of the difficult "straight math" SAT questions. Try your hand at the Straight Math practice set that follows.

CHAPTER SIXTEEN

Straight Math Practice Set and Explanations

Notes:

(1) Calculator use is permitted.

(2) All numbers used are real numbers.

(3) Figures are provided for some problems. All figures are drawn to scale and lie in a plane UNLESS otherwise indicated.

Reference Information

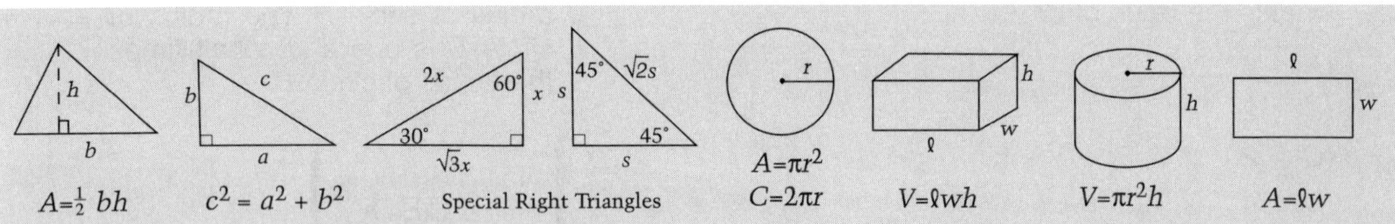

The sum of the degree measures of the angles of a triangle is 180.
The number of degrees of arc in a circle is 360.
A straight angle has a degree measure of 180.

1. If x is the sum of n odd integers, which of the following must be true?

   (A) x is odd.

   (B) x is even.

   (C) $x \neq 0$

   (D) If x is even, n is even.

   (E) If n is odd, x is even.

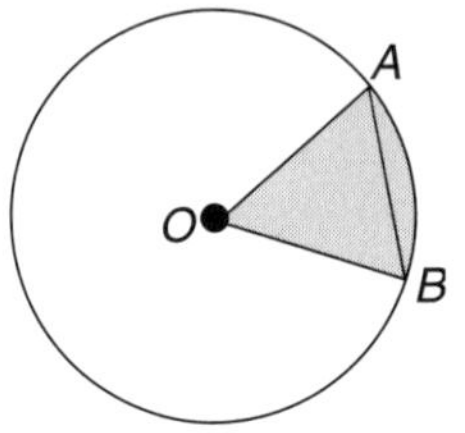

2. If $OA = AB = 6$ in the figure above, what is the area of the shaded region?

   (A) 36π

   (B) 12π

   (C) 6π

   (D) $9\sqrt{3}$

   (E) 18

3. For all $x > 0$ and all $y > 0$ such that $x \neq y$,

$$\frac{\frac{x}{y} - \frac{y}{x}}{\frac{1}{x} - \frac{1}{y}} =$$

(A) $y(x + y)$
(B) $y(-x - y)$
(C) $-x + y$
(D) $x + y$
(E) $-x - y$

4. If $x^2 - 9 < 0$, which of the following is true?

(A) $x < -3$
(B) $x > 3$
(C) $x > 9$
(D) $x < -3$ or $x > 3$
(E) $-3 < x < 3$

5. If 4 is one of the solutions of $x^2 + cx - 24 = 0$, what is the value of c?

(A) -6
(B) -2
(C) 2
(D) 4
(E) 6

6. If the lengths of all three sides of a triangle are integers, and the length of one side is 7, what is the least possible perimeter of the triangle?

(A) 9
(B) 10
(C) 15
(D) 21
(E) 24

7. If $9^{2x - 1} = 3^{3x + 3}$, then $x = $?

(A) -4
(B) $-\frac{7}{4}$
(C) $-\frac{10}{7}$
(D) 2
(E) 5

8. If $f(x) = x^3 - x^2 - x$, what is the value of $f(-3)$?

(A) -39
(B) -33
(C) -21
(D) -15
(E) 0

9. If a certain line in the coordinate plane contains points (3, 8) and (5, 2), which of the following represents the equation for that line?

(A) $y = -\frac{1}{3}x + 9$
(B) $y = 3x - 1$
(C) $y = 3x - 13$
(D) $y = -3x + 17$
(E) $y = -3x + 2$

10. Column A / Column B

The radius of circle A is half the radius of circle B. The radius of circle C is one and a half times the radius of circle B.

Column A	Column B
$\frac{\text{Area of circle C}}{\text{Area of circle A}}$	9

11. Column A / Column B

$x > 0$

Column A	Column B
$4\sqrt{x} + 4\sqrt{x}$	$\sqrt{8x}$

12. Column A — Column B

Column A	Column B
The number of distinct prime factors of 84	The number of distinct prime factors of 96

13. Column A — Column B

$\frac{n}{x} = 8$ and $\frac{n}{y} = 2$

Column A	Column B
x	y

14. Column A — Column B

m is a positive integer.

Column A	Column B
$(-3)^{2m}$	$(-3)^{2m+3}$

15. Column A — Column B

$xy \neq 0$

$\frac{x}{y} = \frac{y}{x}$

Column A	Column B
x	y

16. Column A — Column B

$y > 0$

Column A	Column B
$\frac{(y-1)(y+1)}{y^2}$	$\frac{(y-2)(y+2)}{y^2}$

17. Column A — Column B

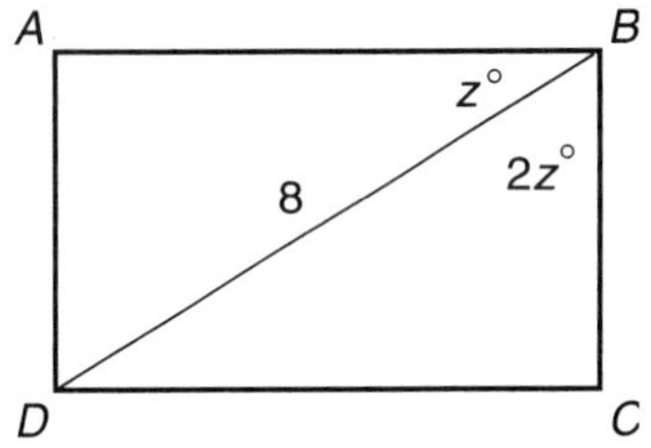

Column A	Column B
The area of rectangle *ABCD*	30

18. How many positive integers less than 50 are multiples of 4 but <u>not</u> multiples of 6?

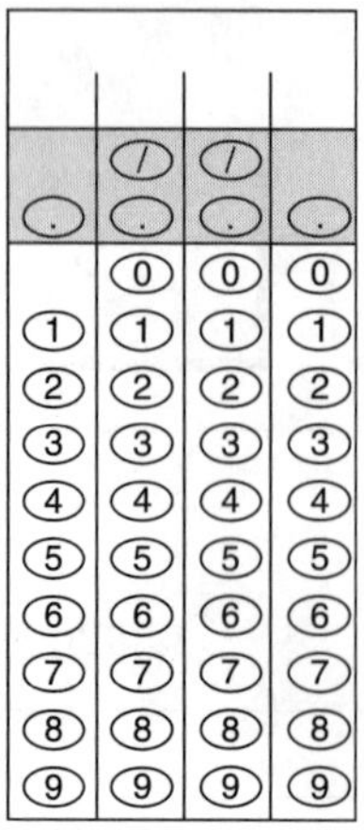

19. If $x^2 + 2xy + y^2 = 1{,}296$ and $x + y > 0$, then $\sqrt{x + y} =$

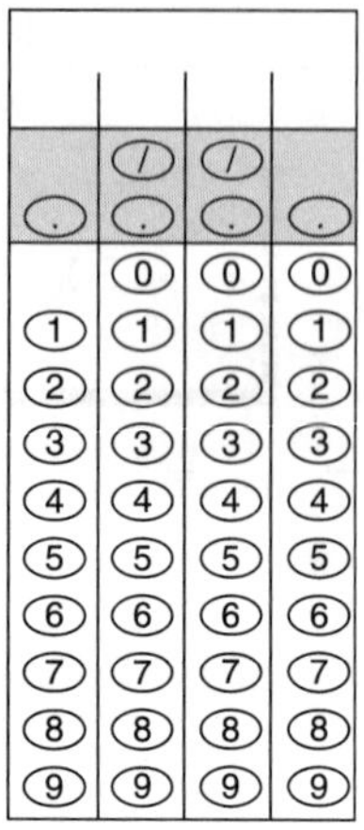

20. If 5,544n is the square of an integer, what is the least possible value of n ?

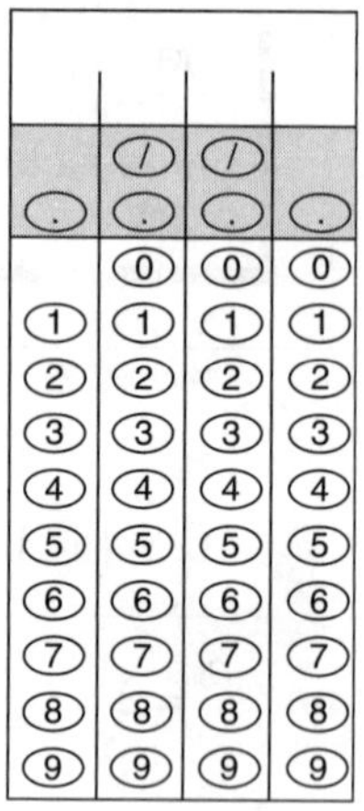

Explanations

1. D

You want to try out a few possibilities since n could be even or odd.

For instance, n could be 3 and all the odd integers could equal 1 for a sum of $x = 3$. Eliminate **(B)** and **(E)**.

Or n could be 2 and all the odd integers could equal 1 for a sum of $x = 2$. Eliminate **(A)**.

Or x could be the sum of –1 and 1; thus $x = 0$ and choice **(C)** is out as well.

2. C

Notice two sides of the triangle are radii. This means they must be the same length, so $OB = OA = AB = 6$, which means the triangle is equilateral. Since all three angles of an equilateral triangle are 60 degrees, the shaded region must take up 60 degrees of the 360 degrees in the circle; in other words, $\frac{1}{6}$ of the circle $\left(\frac{60}{360} = \frac{1}{6}\right)$.

We know that the area of the entire circle is πr^2 or 36π. We want only $\frac{1}{6}$ of that though, which is 6π. So the area of the shaded region is 6π.

3. E

Now here's an ugly problem. Both the numerator and the denominator involve the subtraction of fractions. In both cases you can use xy as a common denominator:

$$\frac{\frac{x}{y} - \frac{y}{x}}{\frac{1}{x} - \frac{1}{y}} = \frac{\frac{x^2}{xy} - \frac{y^2}{xy}}{\frac{y}{xy} - \frac{x}{xy}}$$

$$= \frac{\frac{x^2 - y^2}{xy}}{\frac{y - x}{xy}}$$

$$= \frac{x^2 - y^2}{y - x}$$

The numerator is in the factorable "difference-of-squares" form:

$$\frac{x^2 - y^2}{y - x} = \frac{(x - y)(x + y)}{y - x}$$

Because $x - y = -1(y - x)$, you can cancel them out, leaving a factor of –1:

$$\frac{(x - y)(x + y)}{y - x} = -1(x + y) = -x - y$$

4. E

Rearrange $x^2 - 9 < 0$ to get $x^2 < 9$. We're looking for all the values of x that would fit this inequality. We need to consider both *positive* and *negative* values of x. Remember that $3^2 = 9$ and also that $(-3)^2 = 9$. If x is positive, and $x^2 < 9$, we can simply say that $x < 3$. But what if x is negative? x can take on only values whose square is less than 9. In other words, x cannot be less than or equal to –3. (Think of smaller numbers like –4 or –5; their squares are greater than 9.) So if x is negative, $x > -3$. x can also be 0. Therefore, $-3 < x < 3$. If you had trouble solving algebraically, you could have tried each answer choice:

(A) Say $x = -4$. $(-4)^2 - 9 = 16 - 9 = 7$. No good.

(B) Say $x = 4$. $4^2 - 9 = 16 - 9 = 7$. No good.

(C) Since 4 was too big, anything greater than 9 is too big. No good.

(D) Combination of **(A)** and **(B)**, which were both wrong. No good.

Clearly, **(E)** must be correct.

5. C

Because 4 is one of the solutions of the equation $x^2 + cx - 24 = 0$, we know that one of the factors of $x^2 + cx - 24$ is $(x - 4)$. In order to get the last term of -24, $(x - 4)$ would have to be multiplied by $(x + 6)$. FOIL out $(x - 4)(x + 6)$ to get $x^2 + 2x - 24 = 0$. So $c = 2$, **(C).**

Alternately, you could substitute 4 for x into the equation $x^2 + cx - 24 = 0$ and then solve the resulting equation for c:

$$4x^2 + c(4) - 24 = 0$$

$$16 + 4c - 24 = 0$$

$$4c - 8 = 0$$

$$c = 2$$

6. C

You are told that the 2 unknown side lengths are integers, and if the length of the known side is 7, you should know the sum of the 2 unknown lengths has to be greater than 7, because the Triangle Inequality Theorem states that the length of any side of a triangle must be less than the sum of the other two sides. So the least amount the 2 unknown sides could add up to is 8, which would make the perimeter $7 + 8 = 15$.

7. E

Rewrite the left side of the equation so that both sides have the same base:

$$9^{2x - 1} = 3^{3x + 3}$$

$$(3^2)^{2x - 1} = 3^{3x + 3}$$

When you raise a power to another power, you multiply the exponents, so you now have:

$$3^{4x - 2} = 3^{3x + 3}$$

Now that the bases are the same, just set the exponents to be equal:

$$4x - 2 = 3x + 3$$

$$4x - 3x = 3 + 2$$

$$x = 5$$

8. B

This looks like a question in which you have to understand how functions work, but in fact it's just a "plug in the number and see what you get" question.

$$f(x) = x^3 - x^2 - x$$

$$f(-3) = (-3)^3 - (-3)^2 - (-3)$$

$$= -27 - 9 + 3$$

$$= -33$$

9. D

There are, as usual, a couple of ways you could approach this question. If you wanted to try a backdoor approach, you could plug in the values for the two points you're given into answer choices until you find an equation that works for both points. If you tried this approach, we would recommend that you start with **(E)** and work your way up, because of the SAT's tendency for **(D)** and **(E)** to be the more likely answer choices on "which of the following" questions.

But let's try answering this the old fashioned way. The first thing you want to do is figure out the slope of the line, which is equal to $\frac{y_2 - y_1}{x_2 - x_1}$, so here, that equals $\frac{8 - 2}{3 - 5} = \frac{6}{-2} = -3$. Since the slope equals m when the linear equation is in the form $y = mx + b$, you know that this equation will be written $y = -3x + b$, so **(A)**, **(B)**, and **(C)** are all out. Now just plug in the values for one of the points in order to solve for b. If you plug in (3, 8), you get $8 = -3(3) + 17$, so the answer is **(D)**.

10. C

Here it might help to pick numbers for the radii of the circles, starting with circle A. Let's say the radius of circle A is 1; thus the radius of circle B would be 2, and the radius of circle C would be one and a half times 2, or 3. Since the area of a circle equals πr^2, the area of circle A equals π, and the area of circle C equals 9π, so in Column A you have $\frac{9\pi}{\pi}$, or 9. So the two columns are equal, and the answer is **(C)**.

11. A

Make the columns look more alike. First, add the terms in Column A, giving you $8\sqrt{x}$. Then break Column B into parts. $\sqrt{8x}$ is the same as $\sqrt{8} \times \sqrt{x}$. Now, both columns have $\sqrt{x}$, so it's the coefficients that make the difference. Since 8 is greater than $\sqrt{8}$, Column A is greater than Column B.

12. A

Here we have to figure out the prime factors for the numbers in the columns. In Column A, $84 = 4 \times 21 = 2 \times 2 \times 3 \times 7$, so 2, 3, and 7 are its distinct factors, for a total of 3.

In Column B, $96 = 8 \times 12 = 2 \times 2 \times 2 \times 2 \times 2 \times 3$, so 2 and 3 are its distinct factors, for a total of 2. Thus Column A is greater, and **(A)** is correct.

13. D

The value for n could be anything, so pick simple numbers for n to come up with possible values for x and y, making sure to try out both positive and negative values. For starters, you could pick $n = 8$.

$\frac{8}{x} = 8$ and $\frac{8}{y} = 2$, so $x = 1$ and $y = 4$, making Column B greater. Eliminate **(A)** and **(C)**. Now try a negative value for n, such as $n = -8$:

$\frac{-8}{x} = 8$ and $\frac{-8}{y} = 2$, so $x = -1$ and $y = -4$, making Column A greater.

So **(B)** is out, and the relationship between the columns cannot be determined.

14. A

Remember that a negative number raised to an even exponent is positive, while a negative number raised to an odd exponent is negative. $2m$ will always be even, so Column A will produce a positive number since -3 is being raised to an even exponent. Conversely, $(-3)^{2m+3}$ will always be odd since an even number plus an odd number is always odd. Column B is negative, so **(A)** is the correct answer.

15. D

Like many QCs that consist entirely of variables, the trick here is to avoid making assumptions and looking only at obvious possibilities. One of these is that x and y must be equal. To show that that's not the only possibility, you could pick numbers, making sure to pick twice. The first time you might pick $x = 2$ and $y = 2$. $\frac{x}{y} = \frac{y}{x}$, and in this case Column A = Column B. But how about $x = 2$ and $y = -2$? Now $\frac{x}{y} = \frac{y}{x}$ but Column A is greater than Column B. Without more information, it's impossible to find a consistent relationship between x and y, so the answer is **(D)**.

16. A

Because the square of any nonzero number is positive, y^2 must be positive, so multiply both columns by y^2. You're left with $(y - 1)(y + 1)$ in Column A and $(y - 2)(y + 2)$ in Column B. You should recognize these as differences of squares. You could also multiply out the columns using FOIL.

Column A: $(y - 1)(y + 1) = y^2 - 1$.

Column B: $(y - 2)(y + 2) = y^2 - 4$.

Now you can subtract y^2 from both columns, leaving -1 in Column A and -4 in Column B. **(A)** wins.

17. B

You are dealing with a favorite SAT triangle here. One of the 90° corner angles of the rectangle is made up of the angles z and $2z$. So, $z + 2z = 90$, or $z = 30$ and $2z = 60$.

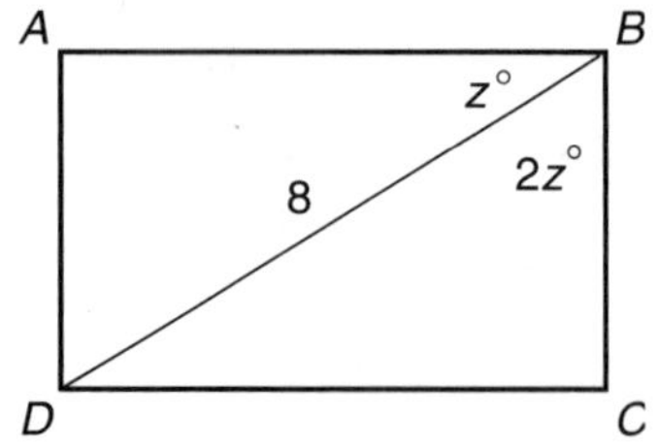

If $z = 30$, then ΔBCD has interior angles of 30°, 60° and 90°. Since ΔADC is a 30-60-90 triangle, it has sides in the ratio of $1 : \sqrt{3} : 2$. So if the hypotenuse is 8, the legs of ΔBCD are 4 and $4\sqrt{3}$: Now BC and DC are the length and width of the rectangle, so the area of rectangle $ABCD$ = length × width = $4 \times 4\sqrt{3} = 16\sqrt{3}$, which is less than 30 (You don't need a calculator for this if you know that $\sqrt{3} \approx 1.7$).

18. 8

On questions such as this, the safest strategy is to list all the possibilities. Also, realize that multiples of both 4 and 6 are multiples of 12 (the least common multiple of the two), so skip over all multiples of 12:

4
8
~~12~~
16
20
~~24~~
28
32
~~36~~
40
44
~~48~~

for a total of 8.

19. 6

Notice that $x^2 + 2xy + y^2$ factors to $(x + y)^2$. So $(x + y)^2 = 1{,}296$.

You are looking for $\sqrt{x + y}$, so break it down as follows:

$$\sqrt{(x + y)^2} = \sqrt{1{,}296}$$
$$x + y = 36$$

So:

$$\sqrt{x + y} = \sqrt{36} = 6$$

20. 154

Here's a very tricky problem that is best solved by prime factorization. For a number to be a square of an integer, all of its prime factors have to pair up. For instance, $36 = 6 \times 6 = 3 \times 2 \times 3 \times 2 = (3 \times 3) \times (2 \times 2)$. So to figure out the smallest number that you would have to multiply 5,544 by to get a square of an integer, figure out the prime factors of 5,544. $5{,}544 = 11 \times 504 = 11 \times 4 \times 126 = 11 \times 2 \times 2 \times 2 \times 63 = 11 \times 2 \times 2 \times 2 \times 21 \times 3 = 11 \times 2 \times 2 \times 2 \times 7 \times 3 \times 3$. We already have two 2s and two 3s that pair up, but we still need to pair up 11, 7, and one more 2. So the smallest number we would need to multiply 5,544 by to get a square of an integer would be $11 \times 7 \times 2 = 154$.

section six

SAT MATH WORD PROBLEMS

CHAPTER SEVENTEEN

Arithmetic and Algebra Word Problems

- Fractions, ratios, and proportions
- Percent problems
- Rate problems
- Average problems
- Algebra word problems

The majority of word problems you'll encounter on the SAT will test either arithmetic or algebra, and very often both. Since you will frequently be solving for an unknown, you'll often have to use some algebra even on arithmetic questions. To muddy the waters even more, word problems will often concern two or more math topics or techniques.

The trick, of course, is to unpack the English to get at the specific math being tested, and then to answer the *question being asked*. Since many word problems contain more than one step, you may have to solve for more than one value. Picking the answer choice with the value that is asked for, rather than another value, is a crucial but often messed up last step.

Before we examine some of the most common arithmetic and algebra word problem questions, what follows are some overarching strategies for handling any type of word problem you might encounter on the SAT.

WORD PROBLEM STRATEGIES

Here's the general approach to any word problem:

1. Read through the whole question. Do this to get a sense of what's going on. You want to know the basic situation described, the type of information you've been given, and—most important of all—what exactly you are being asked.

2. Identify the different variables or unknowns and label them. For example, if the problem discusses Charlie's and Veronica's warts, you may wish to use "c" to represent Charlie's warts and "v" to represent Veronica's warts. Notice that we didn't use "x" and "y." If we had, we might later forget whether x represented Charlie's warts or Veronica's.

3. Translate the problem into math. This usually entails rewriting the English sentences into equations or statements. The sentence "Veronica has four fewer warts than Charlie has" would become: $v = c - 4$. Notice that the math terms are not in the same order as the English terms in the sentence. When you translate, you are translating the ideas. The idea here is "four fewer warts than Charlie." That means $c - 4$, not $4 - c$!

4. Tackle the math. Solve the equations. Use a calculator, where needed, to help crunch the numbers. Make sure you've determined the value that the question is asking you for.

5. Check your work, if you have time.

The Translation Table

It's a good idea to familiarize yourself with the mathematical meanings of some of the most common words used in word problems. Knowing these equivalencies can provide you with a specific, concrete starting point, especially when a word problem seems incomprehensible.

The table below can be a lifesaver—the sort of thing you might want to tattoo on your inside forearm. But that would be wrong.

English	"Mathish"
equals is, was, will be has costs adds up to is the same as	$=$
times of multiplied by product of twice, double, triple, half	$\times$
per out of divided by each ratio of __ to __	$\div$
and plus added to sum combined total	$+$
minus subtracted from less than decreased by difference between	$-$
what how much how many a number	x, n (variable)

Remember: If you are completely baffled by a word problem, look for some of the words in the left-hand column. Then work from their math equivalent and try to construct an equation.

FRACTIONS, RATIOS, AND PROPORTIONS

The most straightforward word problems test the related concepts of fractions, ratios, and proportions. Look at these two:

Questions 1–2

1. At College X, the faculty-to-student ratio is 1:9. If two-thirds of the students are female and one-quarter of the faculty is female, what fraction of the combined students and faculty are female?

   (A) $\frac{11}{24}$

   (B) $\frac{5}{8}$

   (C) $\frac{25}{56}$

   (D) $\frac{11}{12}$

   (E) It cannot be determined from the information given.

2. An empty metal box weighs 10 percent of its total weight when filled with varnish. If the weight of a partly filled box is one-half that of a completely filled box, what fraction of the box is filled?

   (A) $\frac{3}{5}$

   (B) $\frac{5}{9}$

   (C) $\frac{1}{2}$

   (D) $\frac{4}{9}$

   (E) $\frac{2}{5}$

Don't worry about the fact that the second question includes percents and fractions. That is common; a percent is a fraction with 100 as the denominator. As previously mentioned, the boundaries between types of questions—especially in word problems—aren't very clear-cut. Because they are so common, percent questions will be covered separately in this chapter.

Both of the previous examples are susceptible to picking numbers. For example, in the second question, assume a full box of varnish weighs a nice, round 100 lbs. Then attack the problem. While this sort of shortcut may be frowned on by math purists, the SAT couldn't care less how you get to the answer. Do it the way that is fastest for you.

A final reminder: Pick *useful* numbers. *Intelligent* numbers. You don't get extra credit for making the job tougher. When you're working with percents, use 100. For other questions, pick the numbers that are easiest to work with.

Explanations: Questions 1–2

1. B

Pick a number for the smallest given quantity described in the question—the number of female faculty: if there's 1 female member of the faculty, then the total number of faculty is 4 times 1, or 4. There are 9 times as many students, or 36 students. $\frac{2}{3}$ of 36 students are female, so there are 24 female students. Therefore, the total number of females is 1 + 24, or 25, and the total number of students and faculty is 36 + 4, or 40. That makes the fraction $\frac{25}{40}$, or $\frac{5}{8}$. **(B)** is correct.

2. D

Pick numbers. Since you are dealing with percents, pick 100, so say the box weighs 100 pounds when full. In this case, the weight of the metal box is 10 percent, or $\frac{1}{10}$, of 100 pounds, which is 10 pounds. That leaves 90 pounds of varnish to fill the box. The weight of the partly filled box is half of 100 pounds, or 50 pounds. Since the box itself weighs 10 pounds, 40 pounds of varnish are in the partly filled box. Since the box has the capacity to hold 90 pounds of varnish, the box is $\frac{4}{9}$ full. **(D)** is correct.

Now, how much fun would it have been to work with 47 female faculty members? Or a full box of varnish that weighs 217.18 kg? Not very . . . . Of course, you could solve the problems using these bizarre numbers, but that's a strategy for the Funky Number Admissions Test, not the SAT.

A 1600 test taker often decides to pick numbers when working with word problems. This works best when the numbers picked are smart numbers.

Now let's tackle a few more fraction and ratio questions.

Questions 3–5

3. Column A | Column B

A piece of string is marked in segments of $\frac{1}{4}$ the length of the string and also in segments of $\frac{1}{3}$ the length of the string. The string is then cut at each mark.

Column A	Column B
Number of different lengths of the bits of string	3

4. An assortment of candies consists of x chocolates and y buttercreams. If 2 chocolates are added and 3 buttercreams are removed, what fraction of the remaining candies, in terms of x and y, are chocolates?

(A) $\frac{x+2}{y}$

(B) $\frac{x}{y-1+2}$

(C) $\frac{x-1}{x+y+2}$

(D) $\frac{x+2}{x+y-1}$

(E) $\frac{x+3}{x+y}$

5. A batch of cookies was divided among three tins: $\frac{2}{3}$ of all the cookies were placed in either the blue tin or the green tin, and the rest were placed in the red tin. If $\frac{1}{4}$ of all the cookies were placed in the blue tin, what fraction of the cookies that were placed in the other tins were placed in the green tin?

(A) $\frac{15}{2}$

(B) $\frac{9}{4}$

(C) $\frac{5}{9}$

(D) $\frac{7}{5}$

(E) $\frac{9}{7}$

Explanations: Questions 3–5

3. C

When working with a word problem, it is often helpful to make a diagram. This is especially true with geometry word problems that don't come with one (we'll tackle geometry problems a little later). But it can also be useful when dealing with nongeometry word problems, such as the present example. Here you have a piece of string marked into fourths and thirds. To make things easy, assume that the string is 1 foot long. Whatever the actual length, the relative lengths of the pieces will be the same. 1 foot is also convenient, as it equals 12 inches, and 12 is the least common denominator of the fractions in the problem. Making cuts every one-fourth the length of the string means making cuts every 3 inches. A cut every third the length of the string means a cut every 4 inches.

Draw the diagram:

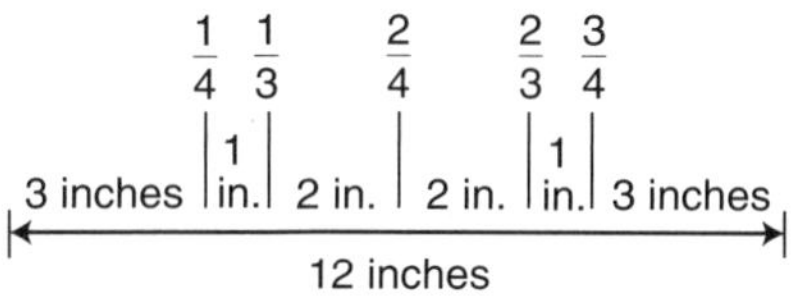

So there are 3 different possible lengths of string, and the columns are equal. **(C)** is correct.

> A 1600 test taker doesn't hesitate to make a diagram whenever it is helpful for conceptualizing the problem.

4. D

You are asked to find what fraction of all the candies will be chocolates after the total has been adjusted. This fraction is simply the number of chocolates over the total number of candies after the change has been made.

Find the number of chocolates and buttercreams by translating the stem. Then divide the number of chocolates by the total number of chocolates and buttercreams. Alternatively, since all the answer choices contain variables, you could try picking numbers.

You initially had x chocolates, but now have two more, or $x + 2$. The original number of buttercreams was y, and 3 were removed, so the number of buttercreams is $y - 3$.

So the fraction of candies which are chocolates =

$$\frac{\text{Number of chocolates}}{\text{Number of candies}} = \frac{x+2}{x+2+y-3} = \frac{x+2}{x+y-1}$$

Once again, if translating this problem was difficult—many people have trouble sorting out parts and totals—you should have tried plugging in numbers. For instance, say there are initially 5 chocolates and 5 buttercreams—10 candies total. After the 2 chocolates are added and the 3 buttercreams are removed, there are 7 chocolates and 9 candies total. Plugging in 5 and 5 for x and y in the answer choices, only choice **(D)** works out to $\frac{7}{9}$.

5. C

Pay attention to what you're asked for—it can be written as follows:

$$\frac{\text{Number of cookies in green tin}}{\text{Number of cookies in green tin} + \text{Number of cookies in red tin}}$$

You are told that $\frac{1}{4}$ of the cookies are in the blue tin and, since $\frac{2}{3}$ of the cookies were placed in either the blue or the green tin, $\frac{1}{3}$ must go in the red tin. Also notice that actual numbers for the cookies are not given; you have only fractions to work with.

You already know the fraction of the cookies that go in the red tin and blue tin, so work out the fraction of cookies that go in the green tin.

The fractions of the total cookies in each tin must add up to 1, so the fraction of all the cookies in the green tin is given by the equation $\frac{1}{3} + \frac{1}{4}$ + (fraction in green tin) = 1. That is, fraction in green tin =

$$1 - \frac{1}{3} - \frac{1}{4} = \frac{12}{12} - \frac{4}{12} - \frac{3}{12} = \frac{5}{12}$$

So:

$$\frac{\text{Number of cookies in green tin}}{\text{Number of cookies in green tin} + \text{Number of cookies in red tin}} =$$

$$\frac{\frac{5}{12}}{\frac{5}{12} + \frac{1}{3}} = \frac{\frac{5}{12}}{\frac{5}{12} + \frac{4}{12}} = \frac{\frac{5}{12}}{\frac{9}{12}} = \frac{5}{9}.$$

PERCENTS

Percents show up frequently in SAT word problems. And that just makes sense, really. Word problems rely on "real life" scenarios (well, *somebody's* real life, if not yours). Percents are common in everyday life—money, taxes, etc. Thus, they make excellent material for the bitter gnomes that devise word problems.

Let's look at a representative pair.

Questions 6–8

6. In 1966, the operative mortality rate in open heart surgery at a certain hospital was 8.1 per 100 cases. By 1974, the operative mortality rate had declined to 4.8 per 100 cases. If the rate declined by 20 percent from 1973 to 1974, by approximately what percent did it decline from 1966 to 1973?

   (A) 6%
   (B) 21%
   (C) 26%
   (D) 41%
   (E) 49%

7. If Ms. DeLong travels to state A to purchase camping equipment, she must pay the prevailing sales tax of 8 percent on what she buys. The store will ship her purchase to her home in state B without charging tax, but with a fixed shipping fee of $3.20. What is the least amount of money she can spend, so that having the purchase shipped will not be more expensive than paying the sales tax? (Disregard the $ sign when gridding in your answer.)

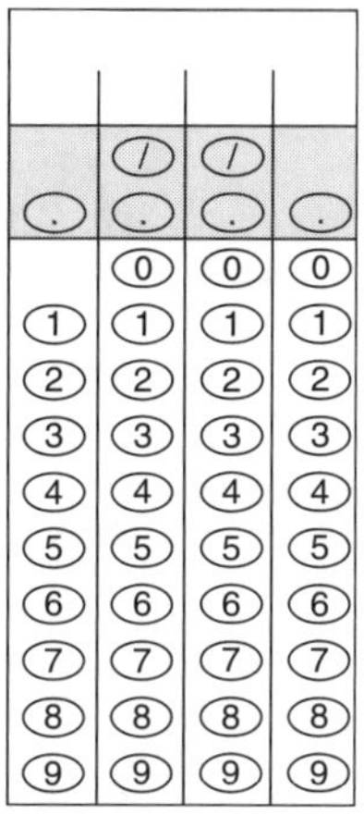

8. At a certain store, each item that normally costs \$20.00 or less is on sale for 80 percent of its normal price, and each item that normally costs more than \$20.00 is on sale for 75 percent of its normal price. If a customer purchases c items, each of which normally costs \$15.00, and d items, each of which normally costs \$24.00, what is the average (arithmetic mean) amount, in dollars, that she pays for each item?

   (A) $\frac{c+d}{30}$

   (B) $\frac{12}{c}+\frac{18}{d}$

   (C) $\frac{12c+18d}{2}$

   (D) $\frac{12c+18d}{c+d}$

   (E) $\frac{30}{c+d}$

Explanations: Questions 6–8

6. C

To determine the percent decrease in the rate from 1966 to 1973 you need to find the rate for 1973. You know the actual rate for 1974, and since you also know the percent decrease from 1973 to 1974, you can find the 1973 rate. The rate dropped 20% from 1973 to 1974, so the 1974 rate represents 100% – 20% = 80% of the 1973 rate. Let the 1973 rate be represented by x, and plug into the percent formula: Percent × Whole = Part, so $8x = 4.8$, $x = \frac{48}{8} = 6$. So the rate decreased by $8.1 - 6 = 2.1$ from 1966 to 1973.

Percent decrease $= \frac{\text{Part decrease}}{\text{Whole}} \times 100\%$, or in this case, $\frac{2.1}{8.1} \times 100\%$. It's time to pull out your calculator. $2.1 \div 8.1 = .\overline{259}$. Convert this decimal into a percent by multiplying by 100% and you get $25.\overline{925}\%$. **(C)** comes closest, and it's the correct answer.

7. 40

The sales tax on her purchase must equal the fixed shipping fee of \$3.20. So you must find the purchase amount at which the sales tax equals the shipping fee of \$3.20. Let x = the purchase amount. 8% of x = \$3.20, so $.08x = \$3.20$, and $x = \frac{3.20}{.08}$. Pull out your caculator and divide; $3.20 \div .08 = 40$. $x = \$40.00$. So when x is \$40.00, the tax will equal the shipping fee. Grid in 40 as the correct answer.

As you can see, the tendency of word problems to involve more than one technique or type of math is borne out again. Here using a little algebra made finding the solutions easier and quicker.

Let's look at some other, difficult percent word problems.

8. D

This is a complicated word problem; translate it one step at a time. Items that are less than or equal to \$20.00 are discounted by 80%, items that are over \$20.00 are discounted by 75%. The customer purchases c items costing \$15.00 and d items costing \$24.00, that is, c items discounted by 80% and d items discounted by 75%. The average price then is

$$\frac{\text{Total discounted cost of articles purchased}}{\text{Number of articles purchased}}$$

Find the average of the discounted prices of all the articles.

80% of \$15.00 = \$12.00; total amount spent on these c items: \$12c

75% of \$24.00 = \$18.00; the total amount spent on these d items: \$18d

$$\text{Average} = \frac{\text{Total discounted cost of articles purchased}}{\text{Number of articles purchased}}$$

$$= \frac{12c + 18d}{c + d}\text{, or } \textbf{(D)}.$$

As you are probably starting to realize, one of the keys to not fouling up a word problem is to read carefully. Often, similar terms will be employed and you must keep them straight.

If these next questions spin your head around like a gyroscope, consider employing a strategy like backsolving or picking numbers.

Questions 9–10

9. At car dealership X, the total profit from sales increased by 10 percent over the previous year, while the number of cars sold decreased by 10 percent over the previous year. Approximately what was the average percent increase in profit per car over the previous year?

   (A) 18%
   (B) 20%
   (C) 22%
   (D) 23%
   (E) 25%

10. A magazine's survey of its subscribers finds that 20 percent are male. If 70 percent of the subscribers are married, and 10 percent of these are male, what percent of the male subscribers are not married? (Disregard % sign when gridding your answer.)

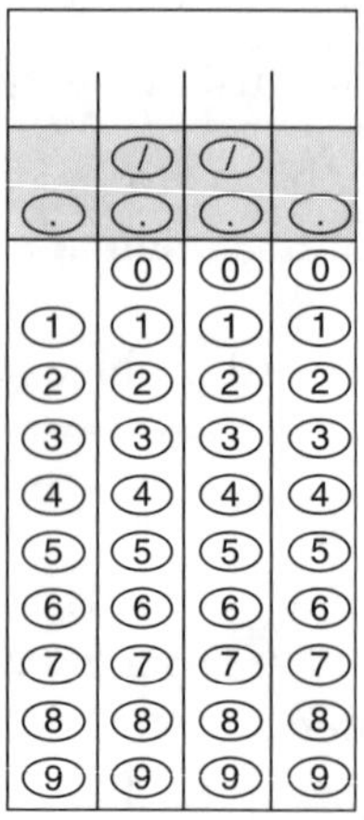

Explanations: Questions 9–10

9. C

Pick numbers for the original number of cars sold and the original profit per car. If the car dealership sold 10 cars at a \$10 profit per car it originally made \$100 profit total. The next year it sold 10% fewer cars, or 9 cars. The profit, however, increased by 10%, or equaled \$100 + (10% of \$100) = \$110. The profit per car increased from \$10 to $\frac{\$110}{9}$. If you pull out your calculator, you'll see that $\frac{\$110}{9} \approx \$12.22$, so the amount of increase is \$12.22 − \$10.00 = \$2.22. The percent increase in profit per car is the amount of increase divided by the original profit per car: $\frac{\$2.22}{\$10.00}$, or approximately 22%. **(C)** is correct.

> A 1600 test taker is able to quickly choose an alternative strategy when the situation demands it.

10. 65

Pick a number to represent magazine subscribers. Pick 100 because it's easy to find percents of 100. 70% of the magazine subscribers are married, so there are 70 married subscribers. 10% of the married subscribers are male, so there are 10% × 70 = 7 married male subscribers. 20% of all the subscribers are male, so 20 of them are males. If 7 of the 20 males are married, 20 – 7 = 13 of them are not married. So the percent of male subscribers who are not married is given by $\frac{\text{Part}}{\text{Whole}} \times 100\%$, which is $\frac{13}{20} \times 100\% = 65\%$. Fill in the grid with **65**.

RATES

The paradigmatic SAT word problem is probably the "rates" word problem. A rate is just a ratio involving units. It expresses the units of one item per units of another. So we can solve for a rate like so:

$$\text{Rate} = \frac{\text{Units of } A}{\text{Unit of } B}$$

The rate that you'll most often encounter on the SAT is speed. Speed is specifically the ratio of distance to time. Here's the formula:

$$\text{Rate} = \frac{\text{Distance}}{\text{Time}}$$

This can also be written as either of the following:

$$\text{Time} = \frac{\text{Distance}}{\text{Rate}}$$

$$\text{Distance} = \text{Rate} \times \text{Time}$$

All three equations say the same thing. And if we have any two of the three components (Rate, Time, and Distance), we can solve for the third.

Let's take a look at some of the tougher rate problems the SAT may throw at you. Here are two problems with the characteristic SAT twist: You have to work with more than just one speed. Give them a try.

Questions 11–12

11.

Column A	Column B
A motorist travels 90 miles at a rate of 20 miles per hour. He returns the same distance at a rate of 40 miles per hour.	
30 miles per hour	Average speed for entire trip

12. A riverboat leaves Mildura and travels upstream to Renmark at an average speed of 6 miles per hour. It returns by the same route at an average speed of 9 miles per hour. What is its average speed for the round trip, in miles per hour?

(A) 7.0
(B) 7.2
(C) 7.5
(D) 7.8
(E) 8.2

Explanations: Questions 11–12

11. A

To find the average speed for the entire trip you need to plug into the formula for average speed: Average speed $= \dfrac{\text{Total distance}}{\text{Total time}}$. The total distance is easy to find: He travels 90 miles there and 90 miles back for a total of 180 miles. Use a version of the distance formula, Time $= \dfrac{\text{Distance}}{\text{Rate}}$, to figure the time spent on each half of the trip, then add these for the total time. Leaving, he travels 90 miles at 20 miles per hour, so it takes $\dfrac{90 \text{ miles}}{20 \text{ miles per hour}} = \dfrac{9}{2}$ hours. Returning, he travels 90 miles at 40 miles per hour, so it takes $\dfrac{90 \text{ miles}}{40 \text{ miles per hour}} = \dfrac{9}{4}$ hours. So the total time $= \dfrac{9}{2} + \dfrac{9}{4} = \dfrac{18}{4} + \dfrac{9}{4} = \dfrac{27}{4}$, or 6.75 hours. So the average speed for the full trip $= \dfrac{180}{6.75} = 26.\overline{6}$, which is less than 30, so Column A is greater, and **(A)** is correct.

12. B

Once again, you cannot simply average the two speeds; each leg of the trip will take a different amount of time and you must weight the average to account for this. The average speed for the entire trip equals the total distance traveled divided by the total amount of time it took. Pick a number for the distance from Mildura to Renmark; try 18 since it is evenly divisible by both speeds. On the first leg of the trip, traveling 18 miles at 6 miles per hour will take 3 hours. On the return trip, traveling 18 miles at 9 miles per hour will take 2 hours. So the average speed for the entire trip is $\dfrac{18 + 18}{3 + 2} = \dfrac{36}{5} = 7\dfrac{1}{5}$ or 7.2 miles per hour. **(B)** wins.

> A 1600 test taker knows the formulas cold for determining Time, Rate, and Distance.

AVERAGES

A couple of word problems on the SAT will invariably deal with averages, and they may also include the related concepts of median and mode. Mostly, these questions simply test your ability to use the average formula and/or understand the difference between mean, median, and mode.

Let's take a look and see if you're sufficiently above average when it comes to handling average problems.

Questions 13–14

13. The average age of the members of a five-man rock group is 42. After the original drummer quits and is replaced by a 27-year-old, the average age of the rock group is now 38. What was the age of the original drummer?

    (A) 44
    (B) 45
    (C) 46
    (D) 47
    (E) 48

14. If Tim's test scores in math class were 92, 78, 92, 77, and 86, which of the following is greater than 85?

    I. The mode of the test scores
    II. The median of the test scores
    III. The average (arithmetic mean) of the test scores

    (A) I only
    (B) II only
    (C) I and II only
    (D) I and III only
    (E) I, II, and III

Explanations: Questions 13–14

13. D

The average formula states that Average = $\frac{\text{Sum of the terms}}{\text{Number of terms}}$. So there are three components to the formula, and just as with a rate question, whenever you have two out of three of the components, you should automatically calculate the third component. Let's apply that strategy here.

You are first told that the average age of the members of the five-man group is 42, so the sum of their ages is $42 \times 5 = 210$. After the original drummer is replaced with a 27-year-old, the new average age of the group is 38, so the sum of the ages of the new group is $38 \times 5 = 190$. After you subtract out the age of the new drummer, or 27, you have the age of the original members minus the drummer: $190 - 27 = 163$. So the age of the original drummer must be the sum of the ages of the original five members minus the sum of the ages of the other four members: $210 - 163 = 47$. Thus, the answer is **(D)**.

14. C

This question isn't that hard, but you need to know the definitions of median and mode. You are asked to determine which of the three values is greater than 85, so start with option I, the mode of the test scores. "Mode" simply means the most frequently appearing number in a set, and in this case there's only one number that appears more than once—92—so 92 is the mode. Since 92 is greater than 85, you can eliminate any answer choice that does not contain option I, in this case **(B)**.

Now check option II, the median of the test scores. "Median" means the number that falls in the middle after the numbers have been arranged in ascending order, so let's rearrange the test scores: 77, 78, 86, 92, 92. The number in the middle is 86, so that's the median, and $86 > 85$, so option II is good as well. You can eliminate **(A)** and **(D)**, but it looks like we'll also have to check out option III in this case.

The average (arithmetic mean) of the test scores is the sum of the scores divided by the number of scores, or $\frac{92 + 78 + 92 + 77 + 86}{5} = \frac{425}{5} = 85$, which is equal to, but not greater than 85, so option III is out, making **(C)** the answer.

A 1600 test taker knows the definitions for all the math terms that could appear on the SAT.

ALGEBRA

You may be surprised to learn that straightforward algebra accounts for relatively few SAT Word Problems. But algebra will nonetheless rear its ugly head from time to time. The good news is that when these problems do appear, they can almost always be solved by picking numbers or backsolving.

If you are rusty with equations, variables, and all that good stuff, you may want to brush up a bit. Use the next four algebra word problems to measure yourself.

Questions 15–16

15. On four successive days, a farmer picks exactly twice as many apples each day as on the previous day. If in the course of the four days he picks a total of 12,000 apples, how many apples does he pick on the second of the four days?

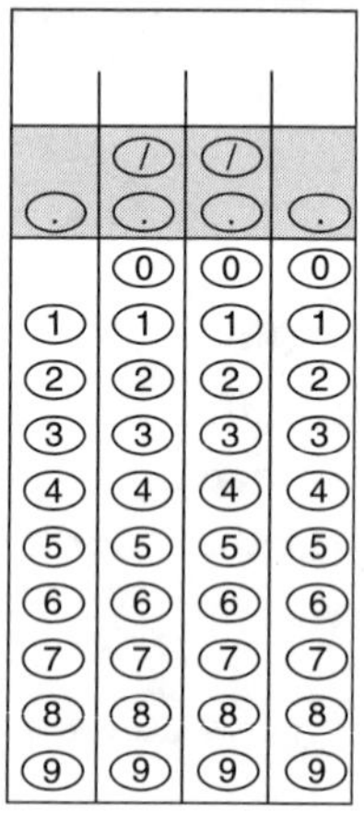

16. If $8 < x < 9$, and $x^2 = (10 - y)(10 + y)$, which of the following is a possible value for y?

    (A) –7
    (B) –6
    (C) 3
    (D) 4
    (E) 5

Explanations: Questions 15–16

15. 1600

Solve for the number of apples picked on the first day, then double that amount to get the number picked on the second day. Let x represent the number of apples that the farmer picks on the first day. Then on the second, third, and fourth days, the farmer picks $2x$, $4x$, and $8x$ apples, respectively. Since he picks a total of 12,000 apples, $12{,}000 = x + 2x + 4x + 8x$, and $12{,}000 = 15x$. Therefore, $x = \frac{12{,}000}{15}$, or 800 apples. But that's for the first day. On the second day, he picks twice as many: $800 \times 2 = 1{,}600$.

16. E

This problem is best solved by working backwards from the answer choices. If $8 < x < 9$, then $64 < x^2 < 81$. Multiplying through the expression given for x^2, you get $x^2 = 10^2 - y^2$ or $x^2 = 100 - y^2$. Each answer choice gives a possible value for y, so try plugging each of these values into the equation, starting with **(E)**, until you get a value for x^2 such that $64 < x^2 < 81$. (You should know why you're starting with **(E)** for this problem by now. But if not, read below.)

(E) $x^2 = 100 - 5^2 = 100 - 25 = 75$; $64 < 75 < 81$, so this choice is correct. Let's check the other answer choices just for the sake of the discussion.

(D) $x^2 = 100 - 4^2 = 100 - 16 = 84$—eliminate.

(C) $x^2 = 100 - 3^2 = 100 - 9 = 91$—eliminate.

(B) $x^2 = 100 - (-6)^2 = 100 - 36 = 64$—eliminate.

(A) $x^2 = 100 - (-7)^2 = 100 - 49 = 51$—eliminate.

A 1600 test taker starts with **(E)** and works back to **(A)** whenever the question asks: *Which of the following . . . ?*

Questions 17–18

17. A travel agent offers a vacation plan which costs z dollars for the first day, and $\frac{z}{6}$ dollars for each additional day. How much does a vacation of y days cost, in dollars, where $y > 1$?

(A) $\frac{yz}{6}$

(B) $\frac{yz}{3}$

(C) $\frac{yz + 6z}{6}$

(D) $\frac{yz + 5z}{6}$

(E) $\frac{y^2z + 5yz + z^2}{3}$

18. Last year, the P members of a partnership divided D dollars profit evenly among themselves. If N people join the partnership during the year, how much more profit in the course of the year must the partnership make for the amount of profit per partner to remain the same?

(A) $\frac{NP}{D}$

(B) $\frac{ND}{P}$

(C) $\frac{N + P}{D}$

(D) $\frac{N}{PD}$

(E) $\frac{P}{ND}$

Explanations: Questions 17–18

17. D

Pick numbers for y and z that are easy to work with: Since $y > 1$, try $y = 2$; to make $\frac{z}{6}$ an integer, try $z = 6$. In that case, the first day costs 6 dollars and the second day costs $\frac{6}{6}$, or 1 dollar. So the total cost for the 2 days is 7 dollars. Now see which answer choices yield 7 when $y = 2$ and $z = 6$. Remember to try all the answer choices, just in case more than one answer choice works for the numbers you picked.

(A) $\frac{2 \times 6}{6} = 2$, eliminate.

(B) $\frac{2 \times 6}{3} = 4$, eliminate.

(C) $\frac{2 \times 6 + 6 \times 6}{6} = 8$, eliminate.

(D) $\frac{2 \times 6 + 5 \times 6}{6} = 7$, possibly correct.

(E) $\frac{2^2 + 5 \times 2 \times 6 + 6^2}{3} = \frac{100}{3}$, eliminate.

Since only **(D)** works, it is the correct answer.

18. B

Start by finding the amount per partner when there are only P members. There are D dollars divided equally among P members. So each got $\frac{D}{P}$ dollars profit. When N more people join, if each of these also receive $\frac{D}{P}$ dollars, then the company must earn $N \times \frac{D}{P}$, or $\frac{ND}{P}$ more dollars for everyone to make the same profit. **(B)** is correct. Of course, you could also have attacked this problem by picking numbers.

CHAPTER EIGHTEEN

Geometry Word Problems

- Garden variety geometry word problems
- 3-D geometry word problems
- The tricky stuff

The SAT test makers occasionally test geometry in the form of word problems. This gives them the opportunity to combine the different areas of geometry, assigning you, the test taker, the task of working with circles *and* triangles, or triangles *and* rectangles, etc.

Of course, as stated earlier, we can't review all of high school geometry here. This book focuses on the 1600-level questions that the SAT presents. Between the examples here and those in the geometry part of the Straight Math section, however, you'll get a very good idea of what geometry skills and information you need to have.

GEOMETRY WORD PROBLEMS PRACTICE SET 1

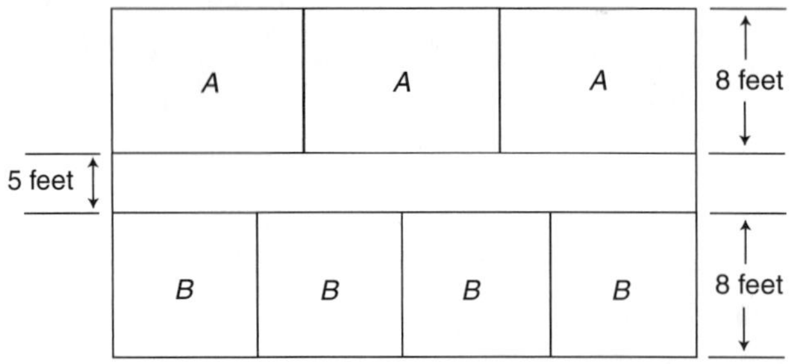

1. The figure above shows the floor plan of an office in which seven rectangular rooms are divided by a rectangular hallway. The three rooms labeled *A* have dimensions 8 feet by 12 feet, and the four rooms labeled *B* have dimensions 8 feet by 9 feet. What is the total area of the entire office in square feet (ignoring the thickness of the walls)?

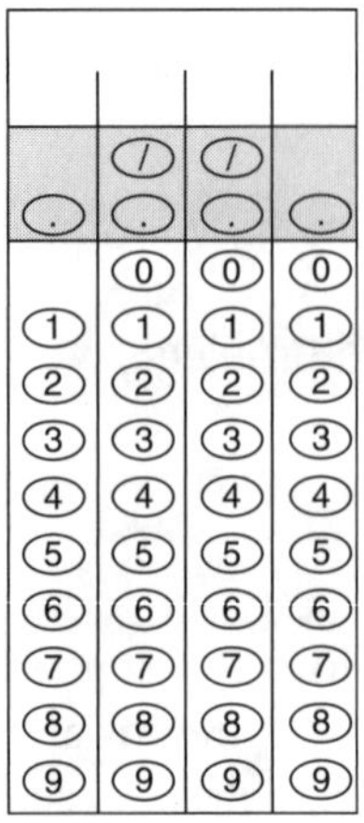

2. A garden measuring 40 meters by 50 meters is to be surrounded by a flagstone walkway 5 meters wide. If each stone is rectangular and has the dimensions 2 meters by 1 meter, how many stones will be needed to cover the walkway?

   (A) 250
   (B) 275
   (C) 425
   (D) 450
   (E) 500

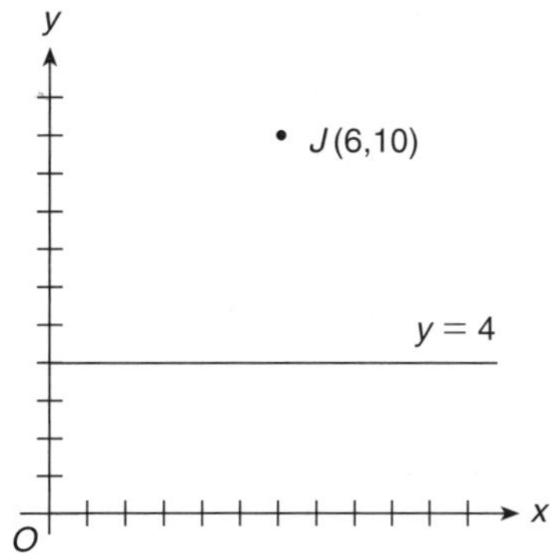

3. In the diagram above, the line $y = 4$ is the perpendicular bisector of segment JK (not shown). What is the distance from the origin to point K?

   (A) 4
   (B) $2\sqrt{10}$
   (C) 8
   (D) $6\sqrt{2}$
   (E) $4\sqrt{34}$

Explanations: Geometry Word Problems Practice Set 1

1. 756

The entire office is rectangular, so its area equals its length times its width. You can use the given information to figure out these dimensions. The vertical length is fairly easy to find: It's just the vertical length of an A-room, plus the vertical length of a B-room, plus the length of the hallway, or $8 + 8 + 5 = 21$. Now, notice that the horizontal width of the entire office is made up of three A-rooms across the top, or four B-rooms across the bottom. You're told that each A-room is 8 ft $\times$ 12 ft, and since the diagram shows the vertical length as 8 feet, the horizontal width of each A-room must be 12 feet. So the width of the entire office is equal to the sum of the widths of the 3 A-rooms, or $3 \times 12 = 36$ feet. So the area of the entire office is 21×36, or 756 square feet.

Notice that this geometry word problem included a nice, clean, helpful diagram. That will not always be the case. Very often, only part of the figure will be provided. Sometimes a figure will be described solely in words.

When you don't have all the illustration you need, it's your job to provide it. Put your pencil and scrap paper to work. Draw or redraw the diagram to fit your needs.

2. E

The easiest thing to do here is to draw a diagram:

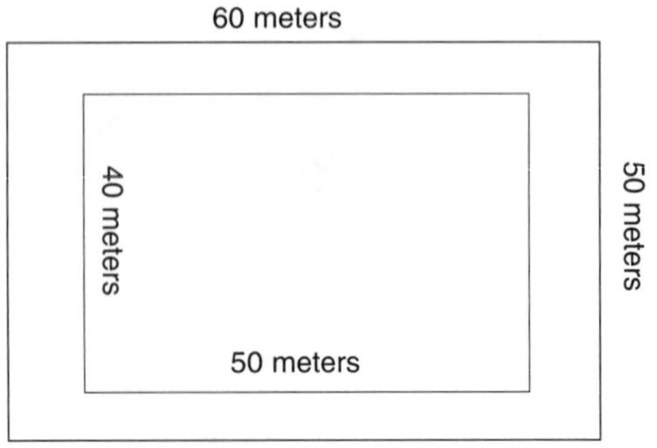

You get two rectangles: one with dimensions 40 meters by 50 meters (the lawn); one with dimensions 50 meters by 60 meters (the lawn and the walk). The area of the walk alone is the difference between the two rectangular areas, or $(50 \times 60) - (40 \times 50) = 3{,}000 - 2{,}000 = 1{,}000$ square meters. Since each stone has area $2 \times 1 = 2$ square meters, you would need 500 stones for the whole walk. **(E)** is the answer.

3. B

Don't try to keep all the information in your head—add to the diagram so you can refer to it as you solve. Horizontal line $y = 4$ is the perpendicular bisector of JK, so JK must be vertical and parallel to the y-axis. Draw in segment JK, dropping straight down from point J through the x-axis. Before you can find the distance from the origin to point K, you need to know its coordinates. K is directly below J so both points are the same distance from the y-axis and their x-coordinates must be the same. So the x-coordinate of K is 6. Since the line $y = 4$ bisects JK, the vertical distance from J to the line must be the same as the vertical distance from the line to K. Vertical distance is the positive difference between the y-coordinates, so the vertical distance from J to line $y = 4$ is $10 - 4$, or 6. Therefore the positive difference between the y-coordinates of line $y = 4$ and point K is also

6, so the y-coordinate of K is $4 - 6$, making -2 the y-coordinate of point K. So the coordinates of point K are $(6, -2)$. You will notice that K, the origin O, and the point where JK crosses the x-axis are the vertices of a right triangle, with its hypotenuse being the distance from the origin to point K. Use the Pythagorean theorem to find the length of the hypotenuse. Hypotenuse^2 = (length of the leg lying on the x-axis)^2 + (length of the leg parallel to the y-axis)^2 = $6^2 + 2^2 = 40$.

So the distance from the origin to $K = \sqrt{40} = 2\sqrt{10}$. **(B)** it is.

A 1600 test taker draws useful diagrams when the word problem doesn't provide them, and adds to diagrams information that is discovered.

Just as with straightforward geometry problems on the SAT, geometry word problems often contain circles, triangles, or a combination of the two.

GEOMETRY WORD PROBLEMS PRACTICE SET 2

4. Column A | Column B

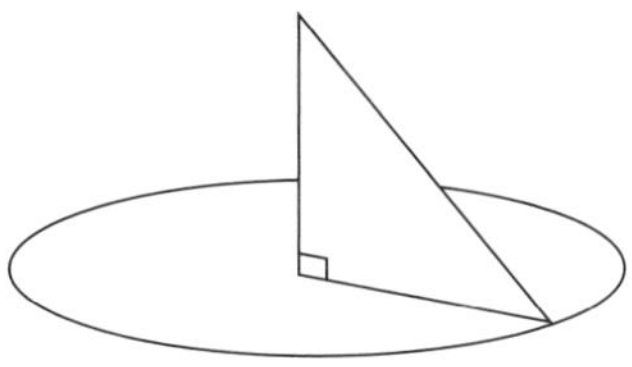

Note: Diagram not drawn to scale.

The above diagram represents a sundial, formed by attaching the shortest side of a right triangle to a radius of the circular base. The length of the two longest sides of the triangle are 13 centimeters and 12 centimeters.

Column A	Column B
25π	The area of the circular base

5. A circular manhole is covered by a circular cover which has a diameter of 32 inches. If the manhole has a diameter of 30 inches, how much greater than the area of the manhole is the area of the cover, in square inches?

(A) 2π
(B) 4π
(C) 24π
(D) 31π
(E) 124π

Explanations: Geometry Word Problems Practice Set 2

4. C

You can find the area of the circle if you can find a value for the radius. The circle's radius is equal to the length of the shorter leg of the right triangle. You might have recognized this triangle as a 5–12–13 right triangle, so the shortest side is 5. (If you didn't recognize this special right triangle, you could have used the Pythagorean theorem to find the unknown side. The longest side is the hypotenuse, so $\text{leg}_1^2 + \text{leg}_2^2 = \text{hypotenuse}^2$, that is $\text{leg}_1^2 + 12^2 = 13^2$, or $\text{leg}_1^2 = 169 - 144 = 25$, so $\text{leg}_1 = 5$.) Since this side is equal to the radius of the circle, you are now ready to plug into the area formula: area $= \pi r^2 = \pi(5)^2 = 25\pi$. Both columns are equal, and **(C)** is correct.

5. D

Knowing the diameter of a circle is enough to determine its area, since area $= \pi r^2$, and r, the radius, is half the diameter. The radius of the cover is $\frac{1}{2}(32) = 16$, so the cover has an area of $\pi(16)^2$, or 256π. The manhole has a radius of $\frac{1}{2}(30)$, or 15, so its area is $\pi(15)^2$, or 225π. So the area of the cover is $256\pi - 225\pi$ or 31π square inches greater than the area of the manhole. **(D)** it is.

The key to answering many of the most difficult SAT word problems is to see the figure differently. Often the figure presented can be broken down into smaller figures, or extended to create larger figures. By examining these "secondary" figures, you can derive the information you need to answer the question.

This is a skill best taught by example. Here are two of them.

GEOMETRY WORD PROBLEMS PRACTICE SET 3

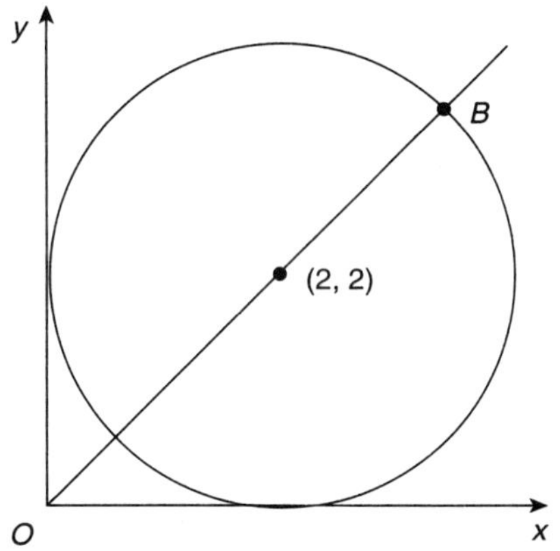

6. In the rectangular coordinate system above, the circle is tangent to the x and y axes and has center (2, 2). Line segment OB connects the origin to a point on the circle that passes through the center of the circle. What is the length of OB ?

   (A) $2\sqrt{2}$
   (B) $2 + \sqrt{2}$
   (C) 4
   (D) $2 + 2\sqrt{2}$
   (E) $4\sqrt{2}$

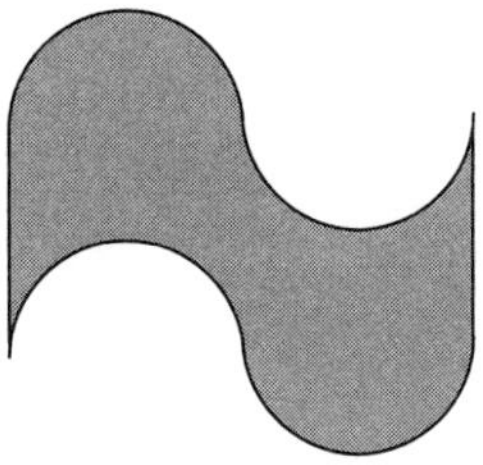

7. If each curved portion of the boundary of the figure above is formed from the circumferences of two semicircles, each with a radius of 2, and each of the parallel sides has length 4, what is the area of the shaded figure?

   (A) 16
   (B) 32
   (C) $16 - 8\pi$
   (D) $32 - 8\pi$
   (E) $32 - 4\pi$

Explanations: Geometry Word Problems Practice Set 3

6. D

Look for some way to break *OB* down into familiar segments whose lengths you are able to find. Notice that the distance from the center of the circle to *B* is a radius of the circle. The radius of the circle is the distance from point (2, 2) to the point where the circle touches the *x*-axis, or (2, 0). This distance is 2. So the radius is 2. But what about the distance from *O* to the center of the circle? Well, if you draw a perpendicular line from the center of the circle down to the *x*-axis, you form a right triangle whose hypotenuse is the distance from *O* to the center of the circle. The horizontal leg of this triangle extends from the origin to 2 on the *x*-axis, so its length is 2. The vertical leg extends from the *x*-axis to a height of 2 parallel to the *y*-axis, so its length is also 2. The triangle is an isoceles right triangle. The leg length to leg length to hypotenuse length ratio in an isosceles right triangle is $1:1:\sqrt{2}$. So the hypotenuse has a length of $2\sqrt{2}$. Therefore, the length of *OB* is $2 + 2\sqrt{2}$. **(D)** is correct.

7. B

This looks pretty tricky at first glance, but in reality is quite simple. The shaded figure looks like a rectangle which has had two semicircles removed and two added on. In other words, whatever has been cut out of the original rectangle has been added back on. In other words, what we have here is really just the area of the rectangle. What are the dimensions of this rectangle? They've told us that the width is 4 units. The area of a rectangle is length × width, so look for a way to find the length.

There are two circles along the length of the rectangle—the length is equal to four times the circle's radius.

If each radius is 2 and there are 4 of them along each horizontal side, then the length is 8 units. Since area = length × width, the area is $8 \times 4 = 32$ square units, answer **(B)**.

A 1600 test taker modifies the diagrams given to create "secondary" diagrams, which help him to discover information hidden in the original.

You will probably see one or two word problems on the SAT involving three-dimensional geometry. There's a good chance that the problem will involve cylinders, which we think you'll agree shouldn't worry you too much. But there's also a chance that the problem will involve surface area. We'll see what you think about that.

GEOMETRY WORD PROBLEMS PRACTICE SET 4

8. How many cylindrical oil drums, with a diameter of 1.5 feet and a length of 4 feet, would be needed to hold the contents of a full cylindrical fuel tank, with a diameter of 12 feet and a length of 60 feet?

   (A) 640
   (B) 720
   (C) 840
   (D) 880
   (E) 960

9. Can *A* and can *B* are both right circular cylinders. The radius of can *A* is twice the radius of can *B*, while the height of can *A* is half the height of can *B*. If it costs $4.00 to fill half of can *B* with a certain brand of gasoline, how much would it cost to completely fill can *A* with the same brand of gasoline?

   (A) $1
   (B) $2
   (C) $4
   (D) $8
   (E) $16

10. A certain box has dimensions of n, $2n$, and $3n$, where n is an integer. Which of the following could be the surface area of the box?

    (A) 48
    (B) 64
    (C) 150
    (D) 198
    (E) 220

Explanations: Geometry Word Problems Practice Set 4

8. E

To find the number of drums needed to hold the contents of the tank, set the combined volume of all the drums equal to the volume of the tank. The combined volume of the drums is the volume per drum × the total number of drums. The volume of a cylinder is the area of the circular base × the height, and the area of the circular base is equal to π × radius squared. Since the question gives the diameter of each cylinder, you'll need to halve each diameter to find the radius, and then you can find the volume. The radius of each drum is $\frac{1.5}{2} = 0.75$ or $\frac{3}{4}$. So, the volume of each drum is $\pi\left(\frac{3}{4}\right)^2(4) = \left(\frac{9}{16}\right)(4)\pi = \frac{9\pi}{4}$. The number of drums is unknown, so use a variable such as x to represent it. So the total volume of the drums is $(x)\frac{9\pi}{4}$. The volume of the tank is $\pi(6^2)(60) = (36)(60)\pi$. So $(x)\frac{9\pi}{4} = (36)(60)\pi$; $x = (36)(60)\pi\left(\frac{4}{9\pi}\right) = (4)(60)(4) = 960$. **(E)** is correct.

9. E

The volume of a cylinder is (area of the base) × (height).

Find out the volumes of the cylinders, and work out how much greater the complete volume of can A is compared to half the volume of can B.

Volume of can B: $\pi r^2 h$.

Volume of can A: $\pi(2r)^2 \times \frac{h}{2} = \pi 4r^2 \times \frac{h}{2} = 2\pi r^2 h$, which is twice the volume of can B.

Therefore, if it takes \$4 to fill half of can B, then it will take \$8 to completely fill can B, and it will take twice \$8, or \$16, to completely fill can A. **(E)** wins again.

10. D

Perhaps drawing a diagram of the box would help:

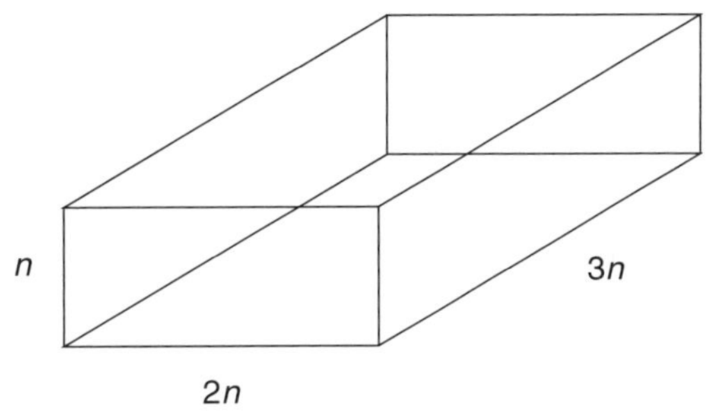

The surface area is the combined area of all the sides, or faces, of the box. There are two sides that are n by $2n$, two sides that are n by $3n$, and two sides that are $2n$ by $3n$.

Thus the surface area of the entire box is:

$2(n \times 2n) + 2(n \times 3n) + 2(2n \times 3n) = 4n^2 + 6n^2 + 12n^2 = 22n^2$

If you had trouble visualizing this, you can memorize the surface area formula:

Surface area of a box = $2lw + 2lh + 2wh$, where l = length, w = width and h = height.

So $22n^2$ must be an integer. Now you should check out the answer choices:

(A)	48	Not divisible by 22.	Eliminate.
(B)	64	Ditto.	Eliminate.
(C)	150	Ditto.	Eliminate.
(D)	$198 = 22 \times 9, 9 = 3^2$, so $n = 3$		Bingo.
(E)	$220 = 22 \times 10$, but 10 is not a perfect square.		Eliminate.

So **(D)** is correct.

A 1600 student uses visualization to help with surface area problems, or if that doesn't work, memorizes the surface area formula.

We'll finish up with two more examples of modifying a diagram. **Hint:** The first one is worth sketching so you have a diagram to modify. The second one is a suitable ending to geometry word problems.

GEOMETRY WORD PROBLEMS PRACTICE SET 5

11. If a square is formed by joining the points *A* (–2, 1), *B* (1, 5), *C* (5, 2), and *D* (2, –2), what is the area of square *ABCD* ?

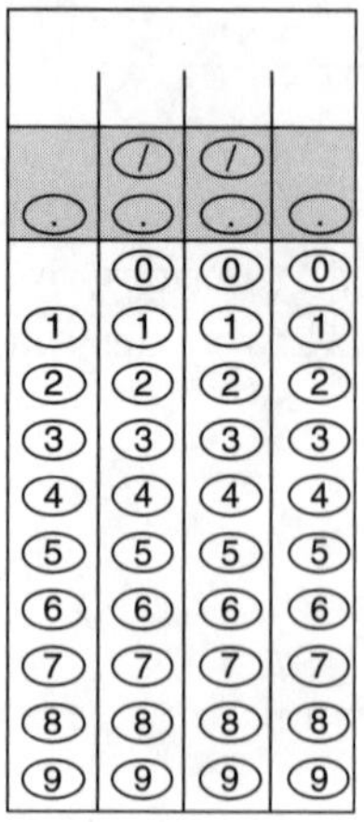

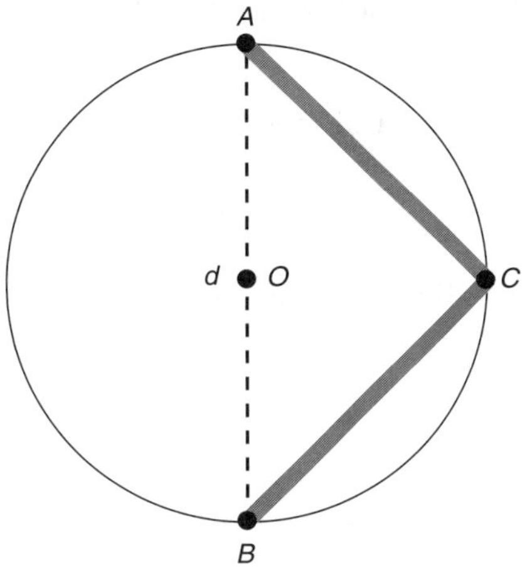

12. Points A and B are at opposite ends of a circular pond with diameter d. A bridge connects point A with point C, and another bridge connects point C with point B. The two bridges are of equal length. What is the ratio of the distance from A to B when traveling along the two bridges, to the distance when traveling along the edge of the pond?

(A) $\frac{2\sqrt{2}}{\pi}$

(B) $\frac{d\sqrt{2}}{\pi}$

(C) $\frac{2}{\pi}$

(D) $\frac{\sqrt{2}}{2\pi}$

(E) $\frac{2\sqrt{2}}{\pi d}$

Explanations: Geometry Word Problems Practice Set 5

11. 25

First sketch the square *ABCD*. The area of any square is equal to the length of one of its sides squared. So if we can find the length of any one side of square *ABCD*, we can find the area of the square.

You can find the length of side *AB*, the hypotenuse of a right triangle with legs of 4 and 3. (In fact you can construct a right triangle just like this one for all sides of the square.)

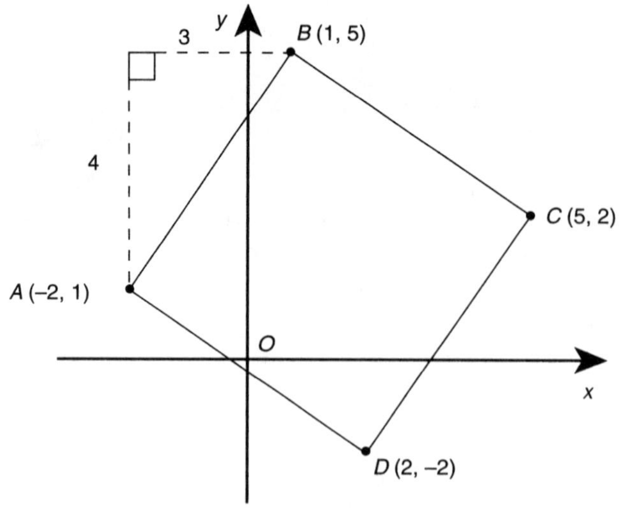

You can find the hypotenuse of this triangle using the Pythagorean theorem.

This is one of our special right triangles—it has legs in a ratio of 3:4:5, so *AB* has a length of 5. The area of the square is then $5 \times 5 = 25$.

12. A

Approach this tough geometry problem step by step, that is, unless you're running short on time and/or geometry problems aren't your strong suit to begin with, in which case you'll want to check out our alternate approach on the next page. The best place to start on this one is to first figure out the distance from A to B around the edge of the pond, which you can see is half of the circle's circumference. Circumference is π times diameter, so the circumference of the entire circle is πd, making the distance along the edge from A to B half this or $\frac{\pi d}{2}$. Finding the distance from A to B across the bridges is a bit more involved. Draw a line from point C to the center of the circle, O.

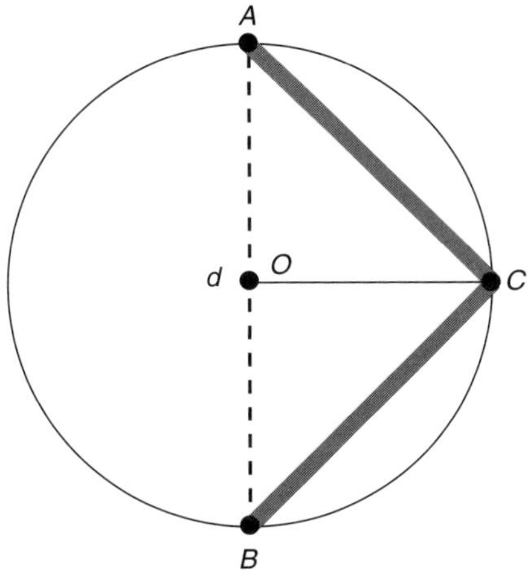

AC and BC are the same length. OA, OC, and OB are all radii of the circle so they are all the same length. So ΔAOC and ΔBOC are congruent isosceles right triangles. (That is, their interior angles and the length of their sides are the same.) The sides of an isosceles right triangle are in the ratio 1: 1:$\sqrt{2}$. Since the legs have a length of $\frac{d}{2}$, the hypotenuses, AC and BC, have a length of $\frac{d\sqrt{2}}{2}$ and $AC + BC = \frac{d\sqrt{2}}{2} + \frac{d\sqrt{2}}{2} = d\sqrt{2}$. This is the distance from A to B when traveling along the bridges. So the ratio of the route over the bridges to the route around the edge of the pond is $\frac{\sqrt{2}d}{\frac{\pi d}{2}} = \frac{\sqrt{2}d}{1} \times \frac{2}{\pi d} = \frac{2\sqrt{2}}{\pi}$, or **(A)**.

Alternate Approach: If you found the previous explanation confusing, there is another approach that works especially well on tough geometry word problems such as this one. We call this approach "eyeballing." The question asks for the ratio of the distance when traveling from point *A* to point *B* along the bridges, to the distance when traveling along the edge of the pond. Well, just take a look at the picture. Is the distance when traveling along the bridges shorter than when traveling along the edge of the pond? Yes, it is. Is it much shorter? No, it is not. So what sort of "eyeball" ratio would you come up with? Something just a little less than 1, we hope.

So now let's examine the answer choices, looking for an answer that's slightly less than 1 (and for the purposes of eyeballing, we can say $\sqrt{2} = 1.4$ and $\pi = 3.14$):

(A) $\frac{2\sqrt{2}}{\pi}, = \frac{2.8}{3.14},$ which is slightly less than 1. Looks good!

(B) $\frac{d\sqrt{2}}{\pi} = \frac{d(1.4)}{3.24}$. But since d can be any value, such as $d = 5$, that can't be right. Eliminate.

(C) $\frac{2}{\pi} = \frac{2}{3.14} < \frac{2}{3}$. That seems too small. Eliminate.

(D) $\frac{\sqrt{2}}{2\pi} = \frac{1.4}{6.28}$. That is way too small. Eliminate.

(E) $\frac{2\sqrt{2}}{\pi d} = \frac{2.8}{(3.14)d}$. There's that d again, which I know can't be right. Eliminate.

Thus, by the process of elimination the answer must be **(A)**.

A 1600 test taker is not afraid to use the strategy of "eyeballing" on tough geometry problems.

CHAPTER NINETEEN

Oddball Word Problems

- What to do when you encounter a question type you've never seen before
- How to deal with clock questions, combination questions, "weird definition" questions, pattern problems, etc., etc., etc.
- How to be ready for anything

As with other SAT question types, perhaps even more so, word problems are often oddballs. Because they deal with "real world" situations, word problems can be used to test just about every math and logic skill under the sun. You wouldn't be properly prepared for the 1600-level math questions if your practice didn't include a sampling of these.

On test day, of course, you may encounter other oddballs. That's just the nature of the game. But bear in mind that just because a question seems completely new to you, it doesn't have to be difficult.

ODDBALL WORD PROBLEMS PRACTICE SET 1

1. A computer is programmed to generate two numbers according to the following scheme: The first number is to be a randomly selected integer from 0 to 99; the second number is to be an integer which is less than the square of the units digit of the first number. Which of the following pairs of numbers could NOT have been generated by this program?

   (A) 99, 10
   (B) 60, –10
   (C) 58, 63
   (D) 13, 11
   (E) 12, 3

2. A certain clock rings two notes at quarter past the hour, four notes at half past, and six notes at three-quarters past. On the hour, it rings eight notes plus an additional number of notes equal to whatever hour it is. How many notes will the clock ring between 1:00 P.M. and 5:00 P.M., including the rings at 1:00 and 5:00?

   (A) 87
   (B) 95
   (C) 102
   (D) 103
   (E) 115

3. Each of three after-school student clubs—the chess club, the German club, and the debating society—has exactly 8 members. If exactly 4 students are members of all 3 clubs and if each pair of these 3 clubs has 5 members in common, then how many different students are members of one or more of these clubs?

   (A) 8
   (B) 13
   (C) 16
   (D) 24
   (E) 27

Explanations: Practice Set 1

1. D

Don't waste time abstractly pondering the question stem's special instructions; turn to the answer choices and start testing the given pairs of numbers. As always, start at **(D)** or **(E)** for this question, since the SAT favors these two answer choices when the question asks "which of the following."

> **(E)** The units' digit of 12 is 2 and $2^2 = 4$; $4 > 3$, so eliminate.
>
> **(D)** The units' digit of 13 is 3, and $3^2 = 9$; $9 < 11$, so this pair does not meet the conditions, making **(D)** correct.

That wasn't too bad, was it? The simple technique of backsolving allowed us to ignore all of the strangeness and focus on the task at hand.

So there are two lessons here. One, oddball word problems can be easy word problems. And two, the basic approach to oddball word problems is to focus on what is familiar—what you know—and employ the same strategies you use for common word problem types.

> A 1600 test taker doesn't panic when she encounters a strange word problem. She instead evaluates the question dispassionately, knowing that many "oddballs" are fairly easy and meant to distinguish the formulaic thinkers (who panic and screw up) from the creative thinkers (who rise to the challenge).

2. D

Even though the problem involves only simple arithmetic, don't try to do all the work in your head. Be systematic. Notice that the rings occur in an hourly pattern. The total number of rings on the hour = $(1 + 8) + (2 + 8) + (3 + 8) + (4 + 8) + (5 + 8) = 9 + 10 + 11 + 12 + 13 = 55$. The clock rings twice at a quarter past and it does this 4 times, so the total number of rings at a quarter past = $2(4) = 8$. Likewise, the total number of rings at half past = $4(4) = 16$, and the total number of rings at three-quarters past = $6(4) = 24$. Adding up, $55 + 8 + 16 + 24 = 103$.

You also could have set up a chart to organize information, like the one below. Setting up the chart will take a few extra seconds, but if arranging the information visually so you can see it all at once makes the difference between a confusing problem and an intuitively clear one, by all means, draw the chart, like this:

		:00		:15		:30		:45		
1 P.M.		9		2		4		6		
2 P.M.		10		2		4		6		
3 P.M.		11		2		4		6		
4 P.M.		12		2		4		6		
5 P.M.		13								
Total	=	55	+	8	+	16	+	24	=	103

(D) is correct.

3. B

To keep track of all the confusing information, set up a sketch like the one below and fill in the information as you go along.

Club 1: __ __ __ __ __ __ __ __
Club 2: __ __ __ __ __ __ __ __
Club 3: __ __ __ __ __ __ __ __

Since 4 students are members of all 3 clubs, fill in a letter for each person for 4 slots on each board; it doesn't matter where. This takes care of 4 of the 5 persons that are common to each pair of clubs (1-2; 2-3; and 1-3):

Club 1: A B C D __ __ __ __
Club 2: A B C D __ __ __ __
Club 3: A B C D __ __ __ __

Now you can fill in the fifth and sixth slots on each board with the fifth member common to each pair. And that means that the two positions left must be occupied by students who are members of only one club.

The results look like this:

Club 1: A B C D E F H K
Club 2: A B C D E G I L
Club 3: A B C D F G J M

Since each distinct letter represents a distinct person, just count up the number of distinct letters to get the number of distinct persons on the boards. The total number of people represented is the number of letters from A to M, and a quick count of the letters on the chart will show that this is 13. So a total of 13 students are members of one or more clubs, making **(B)** correct.

ODDBALL WORD PROBLEMS PRACTICE SET 2

As if there weren't enough real math in the world, the test makers sometimes make up their own, "phony" math. Don't let it throw you. The question will always provide the information you need.

Questions 4–5 refer to the following definition.

> The "connection" between any two positive integers *a* and *b* is the ratio of the smallest common multiple of *a* and *b* to the product of *a* and *b*. For instance, the smallest common multiple of 8 and 12 is 24, and the product of 8 and 12 is 96, so the connection between 8 and 12 is $\frac{24}{96} = \frac{1}{4}$.

4. What is the connection between 12 and 21?
   (A) $\frac{1}{9}$
   (B) $\frac{1}{7}$
   (C) $\frac{1}{3}$
   (D) $\frac{4}{7}$
   (E) $\frac{1}{1}$

5. The positive integer *y* is less than 20 and the connection between *y* and 6 is equal to $\frac{1}{1}$. How many possible values of *y* are there?
   (A) 7
   (B) 8
   (C) 9
   (D) 10
   (E) 11

Explanations: Practice Set 2

4. C

When a problem includes a special term or symbol, just follow the instructions that define it. There are two parts to a "connection": the smallest common multiple and the product. To get the smallest common multiple of 12 and 21, break each number down into its prime factors and multiply them together, counting common factors only once: $12 = 2 \times 2 \times 3$, and $21 = 3 \times 7$, giving you $2 \times 2 \times 3 \times 7$ for the least common multiple. The product of 12 and 21 is $(2 \times 2 \times 3) \times (3 \times 7)$. Therefore, the "connection" is $\frac{2 \times 2 \times 3 \times 7}{2 \times 2 \times 3 \times 3 \times 7}$, which reduces to $\frac{1}{3}$. Notice how easy it is to reduce the fraction when both the numerator and denominator are broken down into factors. **(C)** it is.

5. A

If the connection between y and 6 is $\frac{1}{1}$, then the smallest common multiple of y and 6 must equal the product $6y$. The lowest common multiple of two numbers equals the product of the two numbers only when there are no common factors (other than 1). Since y is a positive integer less than 20, check all the integers from 1 to 19 to see which ones have no factors greater than 1 in common with 6: 1, 5, 7, 11, 13, 17, and 19. So there are 7 possible values for y. **(A)** is correct.

And how about a final pair, before leaving Oddball Word Problems for good?

ODDBALL WORD PROBLEMS PRACTICE SET 3

9	8	6	3

6. The figure above shows an example of a 4-digit identification code used by a certain bank for its customers. If the digits in the code must appear in descending numerical order, and no digit can be used more than once, what is the difference between the largest and the smallest possible codes?

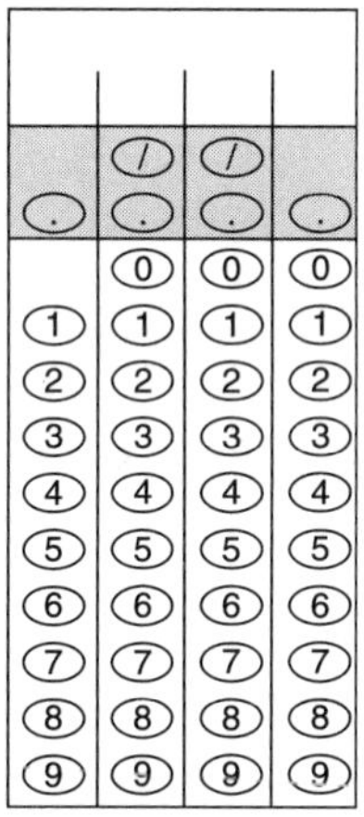

7. A machine is made up of two components, *A* and *B*. Each component either works or fails. The failure or nonfailure of one component is independent of the failure or nonfailure of the other component. The machine works if at least one of the components works. If the probability that each component works is $\frac{2}{3}$, what is the probability that the machine works?

(A) $\frac{4}{9}$

(B) $\frac{1}{2}$

(C) $\frac{2}{3}$

(D) $\frac{5}{6}$

(E) $\frac{8}{9}$

Explanations: Practice Set 3

6. 6666

You need the difference between the largest and smallest possible codes. A digit cannot be repeated, and the digits must appear in descending numerical order. The largest such number will have the largest digit, 9, in the thousands' place, followed by the next largest digits, 8, 7, and 6, in the next three places, so 9,876 is the largest possible number. For the smallest, start with the smallest digit, 0, and put it in the ones' place. Work up from there—you end up with 3,210 as the smallest possible code. The difference between the largest and smallest codes is 9,876 – 3,210 = **6666**, the correct answer on this one.

7. E

The fastest way to do this is to find the probability that neither component works, and subtract that from 1. Since the probability of a component working is $\frac{2}{3}$, the probability of a component not working is $1 - \frac{2}{3} = \frac{1}{3}$. Therefore, the probability that neither component works is $\frac{1}{3} \times \frac{1}{3} = \frac{1}{9}$, and the probability that the machine works is $1 - \frac{1}{9} = \frac{8}{9}$. **(E)** wins.

CHAPTER TWENTY

SAT Word Problems Practice Set and Explanations

Notes:

(1) Calculator use is permitted.

(2) All numbers used are real numbers.

(3) Figures are provided for some problems. All figures are drawn to scale and lie in a plane UNLESS otherwise indicated.

Reference Information

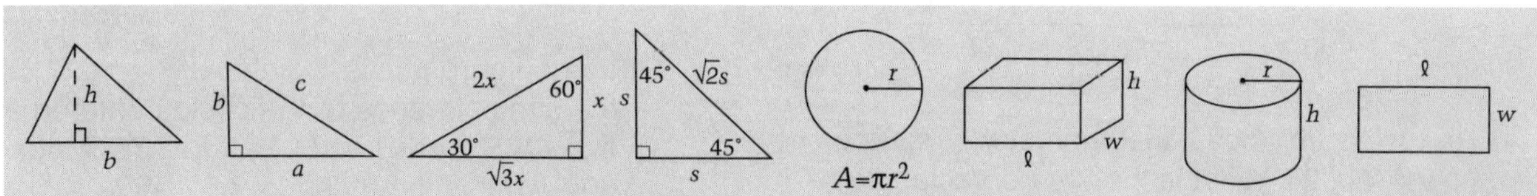

$A=\frac{1}{2}bh$ $c^2 = a^2 + b^2$ Special Right Triangles $A=\pi r^2$ $C=2\pi r$ $V=\ell wh$ $V=\pi r^2 h$ $A=\ell w$

The sum of the degree measures of the angles of a triangle is 180.
The number of degrees of arc in a circle is 360.
A straight angle has a degree measure of 180.

1. Dr. Hasenpfeffer's physics midterm has 60 questions. He scores the test as follows: for each correct answer, he gives 2 points; for each wrong answer, he subtracts $\frac{2}{3}$ of a point; for unanswered questions, he neither gives nor subtracts points. If Denise scored a 68 and did not answer 2 of the questions, how many questions did she answer correctly?

   (A) 34
   (B) 36
   (C) 38
   (D) 40
   (E) 42

2. A bag of candy contains only nut chewies and marshmallow delights. There are twice as many nut chewies as marshmallow delights. The nut chewies are either pecan or cashew and there are $\frac{1}{3}$ as many cashew chewies as there are peanut chewies. If Julie selects one piece of candy at random, what are the odds that she picks a cashew chewy?

   (A) $\frac{1}{6}$
   (B) $\frac{1}{3}$
   (C) $\frac{1}{2}$
   (D) $\frac{2}{3}$
   (E) $\frac{2}{5}$

3. Five runners run in a race. The runners who come in first, second, and third place will win gold, silver, and bronze medals respectively. How many possible outcomes for gold, silver, and bronze medal winners are there?

   (A) 5
   (B) 10
   (C) 15
   (D) 30
   (E) 60

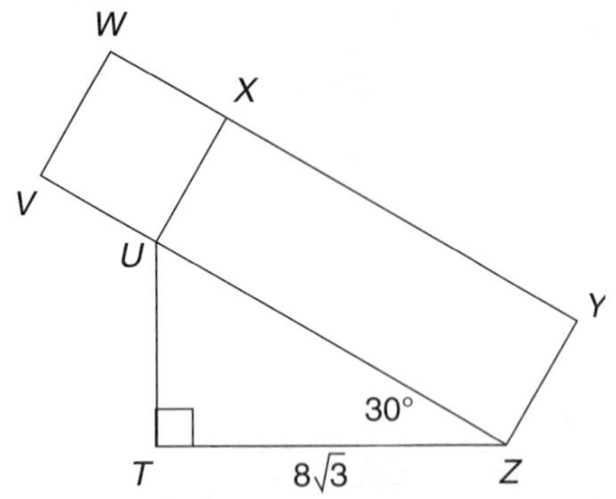

4. In the figure above, the perimeter of square *UVWX* is 24. What is the area of rectangle *UXYZ*?

   (A) 48
   (B) $48\sqrt{3}$
   (C) 96
   (D) $72\sqrt{3}$
   (E) 192

5. In a certain club, the average age of the male members is 35 and the average age of the female members is 25. If 20 percent of the members are male, what is the average age of all the club members?

   (A) 26
   (B) 27
   (C) 28
   (D) 29
   (E) 30

6. In a group of 50 students, 28 speak English and 37 speak Spanish. If five members of the group speak neither language, how many speak both English and Spanish?

   (A) 16
   (B) 17
   (C) 18
   (D) 19
   (E) 20

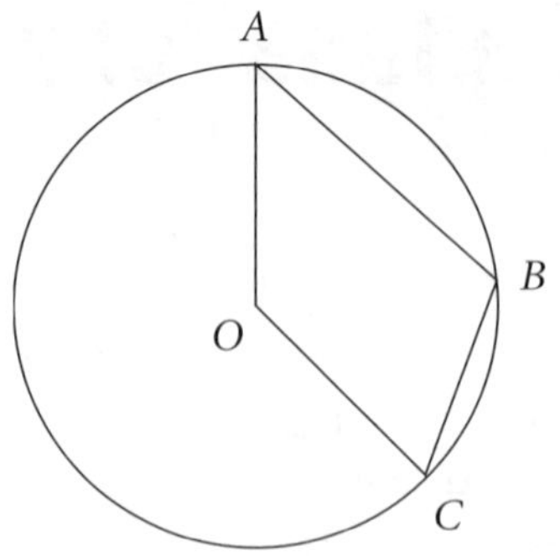

7. In the figure above, points *A*, *B*, and *C* lie on the circumference of the circle centered at *O*. If $\angle OAB$ measures 50° and $\angle BCO$ measures 60°, what is the measure of $\angle AOC$?

   (A). 110°
   (B) 120°
   (C) 130°
   (D) 140°
   (E) 150°

8. From 1980 through 1990, the population of City *Q* increased by 20 percent. From 1990 through 2000, the population increased by 30 percent. What was the combined percent increase for the period 1980–2000?

   (A) 25%
   (B) 26%
   (C) 36%
   (D) 50%
   (E) 56%

9. The line that passes through the points (1, 1) and (2, 16) in the standard (x, y) coordinate plane is parallel to the line that passes through the points (–10, –5) and (a, 25). What is the value of a ?

(A) –8
(B) 3
(C) 5
(D) 15
(E) 20

10. Maura drives to work, a distance of 30 miles, in 40 minutes. She takes the same route to return home. If her average speed on the trip home is half as fast as her average speed on the trip to work, what is her average speed, in miles per hour, for the entire round trip?

(A) 22.5
(B) 30
(C) 35
(D) 40
(E) 45

Year	Income
1995	\$20,000
1996	\$25,000
1997	\$30,000
1998	\$33,000
1999	\$36,000
2000	\$44,000

11. The table above displays Jamie's income for each of the years 1995–2000. Which of the years 1996–2000 shows the greatest percent increase over the previous year?

(A) 1996
(B) 1997
(C) 1998
(D) 1999
(E) 2000

12. The formula for converting a Fahrenheit temperature reading to Celsius is $C = \frac{5}{9}$ (F – 32), where C is the reading in degrees Celsius and F is the reading in degrees Fahrenheit. Which of the following is the Fahrenheit equivalent to a reading of 95° Celsius?

(A) 35° F
(B) 53° F
(C) 63° F
(D) 203° F
(E) 207° F

13. A bowler plays five games and scores 140, 130, 165, 140, and 195 on those games. Which of the following is true of these scores?

I. The median is higher than the mode.
II. The average (arithmetic mean) is higher than the median.
III. The average (arithmetic mean) is higher than 150.

(A) None
(B) III only
(C) I and II only
(D) II and III only
(E) I, II, and III only

14. The formula for the lateral surface area S of a right circular cone is $S = \pi r\sqrt{r^2 + h^2}$, where r is the radius of the base and h is the altitude. What is the lateral surface area, in square feet, of a right circular cone with base radius 3 feet and altitude 4 feet?

(A) $3\pi\sqrt{5}$
(B) $3\pi\sqrt{7}$
(C) 15π
(D) 21π
(E) $\frac{75\pi}{2}$

15. Two airplanes are 300 miles apart and flying directly toward each other. One is flying at 200 miles per hour, and the other at 160 miles per hour. How many minutes will it take for the two planes to meet?

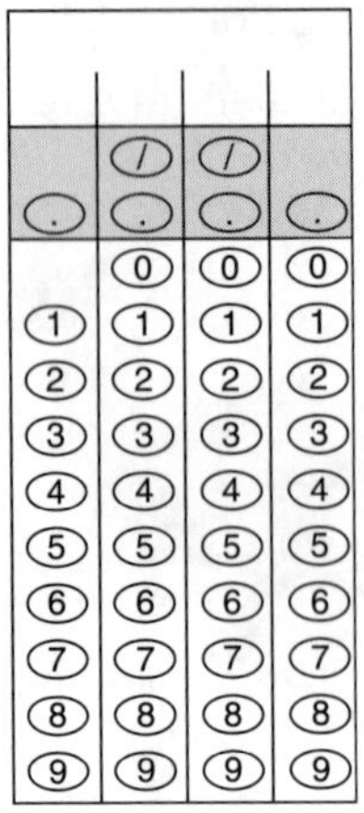

16. John is trying to remember a three-digit identification number. He knows that one of the last two digits in the number 138 is wrong, but he's not sure which. He also knows that all the digits in the identification number are distinct. If he were to start trying all the combinations that fit these conditions, what is the probability he would get the right combination on the first try?

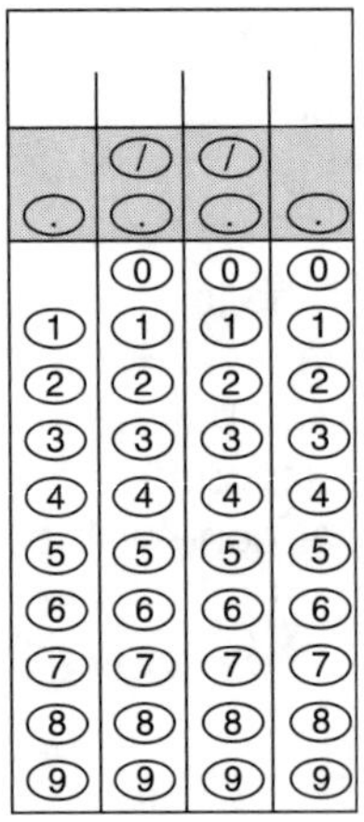

17. Alex wishes to plant three different fruit trees in his front yard. He has five different types of fruit trees he can choose from: cherry, plum, apple, peach, and pear. How many different combinations of fruit trees are possible?

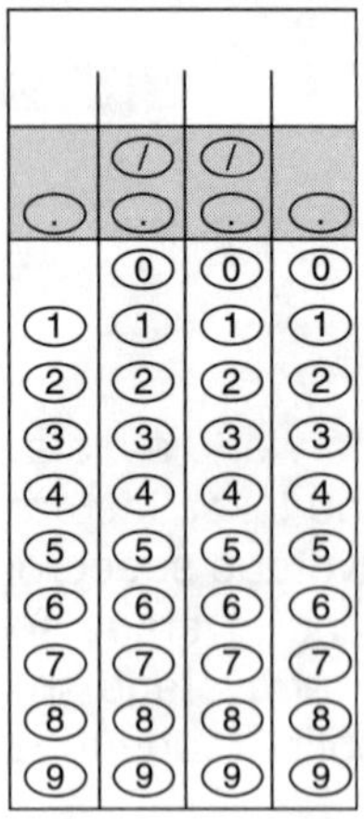

18. The length of each side of square *A* is increased by 100 percent to make square *B*. If the length of each side of square *B* is increased by 50 percent to make square *C*, by what percent is the area of square *C* greater than the sum of the areas of squares *A* and *B*? (Disregard % sign when gridding your answer.)

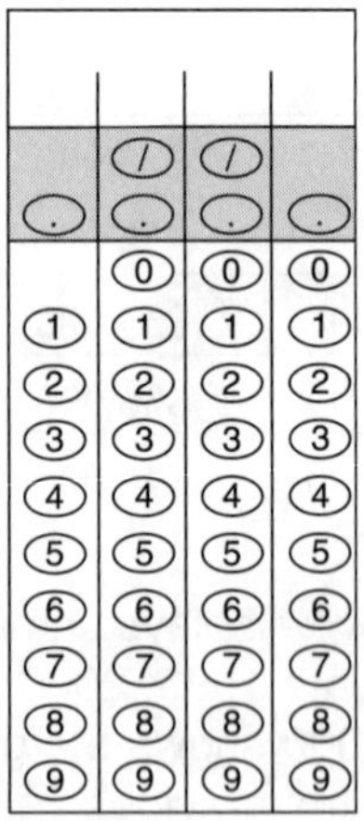

19. Carla is having a dinner party and is inviting 5 guests, 3 boys and 2 girls. Carla knows that she needs to sit at the head of the table, but hasn't decided on fixed seats for anyone else. If she decides not to sit any of her guests next to someone else of the same gender, how many different seating arrangements are possible?

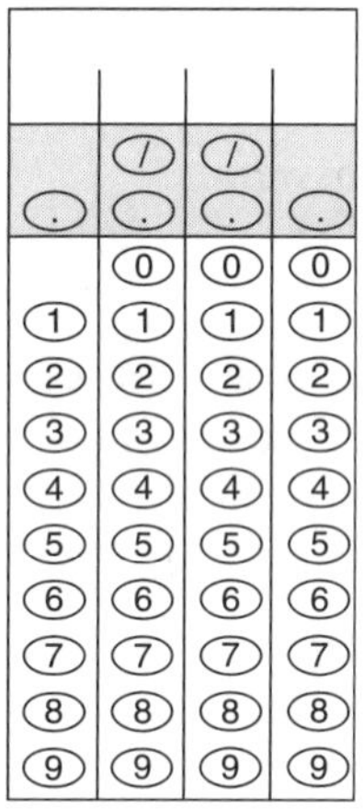

20. If the median value in a set of five *different* positive integers is 12 and the average (arithmetic mean) is 13, what is the greatest possible value of one of the integers in the set?

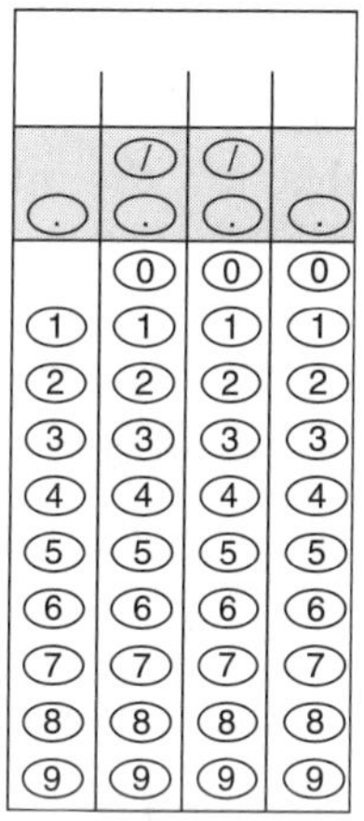

EXPLANATIONS

1. D

The long way to solve this problem is to pick variables for correct and incorrect answers, form two equations, and solve for the number of correct answers. It's quicker to backsolve this one. Denise answered 58 of 60 questions. Start with **(C)**. If she answered 38 correctly, she answered 20 incorrectly. $2(38) - \frac{2}{3}(20) = 62\frac{2}{3}$. This is less than 68, so Denise must have answered more questions correctly. Try **(D)**. If she answered 40 correctly, she answered 18 incorrectly. $2(40) - \frac{2}{3}(18) = 68$.

2. A

This is a probability question, but before we can plug into the basic probability formula, we need to figure out the number of the various candy types. The easiest way to do this is to pick a number for our smallest value and work backwards. We are told that there are two types of candy, nut chewies and marshmallow delights. There are twice as many nut chewies as marshmallow delights. From here, the category of nut chewies is narrowed down further. It seems the nut chewies can be either peanut or cashew and there are $\frac{1}{3}$ as many cashew chewies as peanut chewies. Cashew seems like the smallest number so far, so let's assign a value to it. If we say that there is 1 cashew chewy, there are $\frac{1}{3}$ as many cashew chewies as peanut chewies, so there must be 3 peanut chewies. So together, there are 4 nut chewies. We know that there are twice as many nut chewies as marshmallow delights and so there must be only 2 marshmallow delights. Now that we have our numbers straight, we can plug into the probability formula:

$$\text{Probability} = \frac{\text{\# of desired outcomes}}{\text{\# of possible outcomes}}$$

Since we are trying to find the probability of selecting a cashew chewy, the number of cashew chewies is the number of desired outcomes and the total number of pieces of candy is the number of possible outcomes:

$$\frac{\text{\# of desired outcomes}}{\text{\# of possible outcomes}} = \frac{1}{6}$$

(A) is the correct answer.

3. E

Any of the 5 runners could come in first place, leaving 4 runners who could come in second place, leaving 3 runners who could come in third place, for a total of $5 \times 4 \times 3 = 60$ possible outcomes for gold, silver and bronze medal winners.

4. C

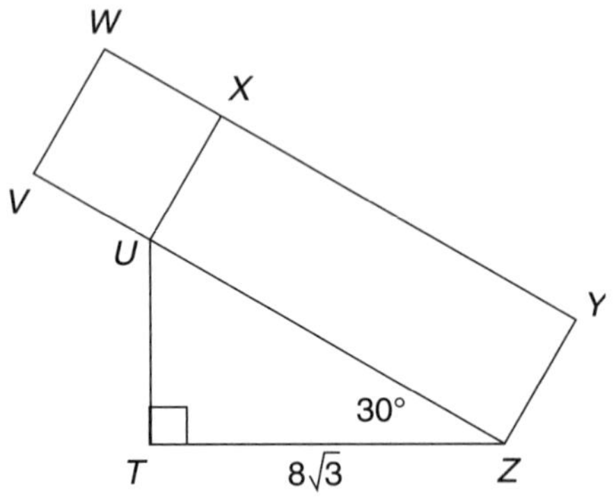

We want to find the area of rectangle *UXYZ*. The area of any rectangle is length times width. *UZ* represents the length of rectangle *UXYZ* and *UX* represents the width. So let's find the length *UZ*. In right triangle *UZT*, *UZ* is the hypotenuse. One angle of the right triangle is 90° and another is 30°, so the third angle has a measure of 180° – 90° – 30°, or 60°, making this is a 30-60-90 triangle. In a 30-60-90 triangle, the sides have lengths that are in the ratio $1 : \sqrt{3} : 2$. In this right triangle, leg *TZ*, which is opposite the 60° angle has length $8\sqrt{3}$. The leg of a 30-60-90 right triangle that is opposite the 60° angle corresponds to the middle term in the $1 : \sqrt{3} : 2$ ratio. So the short leg of right triangle *TUZ* is equal to 8, and the hypotenuse *UZ* is equal to 16. Now let's find the width *UX* of rectangle *UXYZ*. The perimeter of square *UVWX* is 24. The perimeter of any square is 4 times the length of any side. Since the perimeter of square *UVWX* is

24, the width UX has length $\frac{24}{4}$ or 6. So the length UZ of rectangle $UXYZ$ is 16 and the width UX of this rectangle is 6; the area of rectangle $UXYZ$ = length $\times$ width, which is 16×6, or 96. **(C)** is correct.

5. B

The overall average is not simply the average of the average ages for male members and female members. Because there are a lot more women than men, women carry more weight, and the overall average will be a lot closer to 25 than 35. This problem's easiest to deal with if you pick particular numbers for the females and males. The best numbers to pick are the smallest: Say there are 4 females and 1 male. Then the ages of the 4 females total 4 times 25, or 100, and the age of the 1 male totals 35. The average, then, is (100 + 35) divided by 5, or 27.

6. E

Out of the 50 students, 45 speak Spanish or English. If you add the number of English speakers and the number of Spanish speakers, you get 28 + 37 = 65. But there are only 45 students who speak Spanish or English, so 65 – 45 = 20 of them are being counted twice because those 20 speak both languages.

7. D

The key to solving this problem is to draw in OB and fill in the angle measures for the angles you are given:

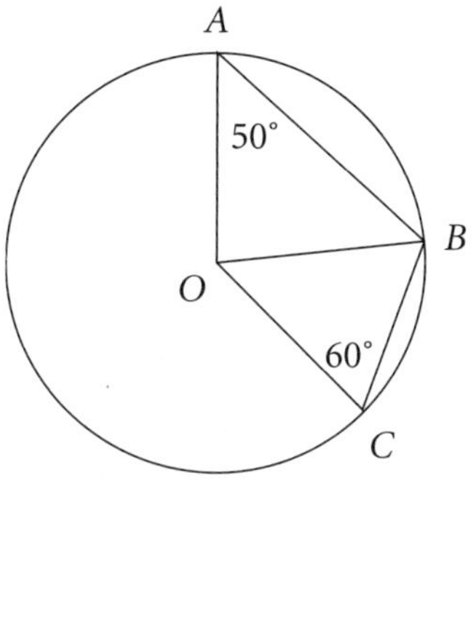

Because OA, OB, and OC are all radii of the same circle, $\triangle AOB$ and $\triangle BOC$ are both isosceles triangles, and therefore both have equal base angles:

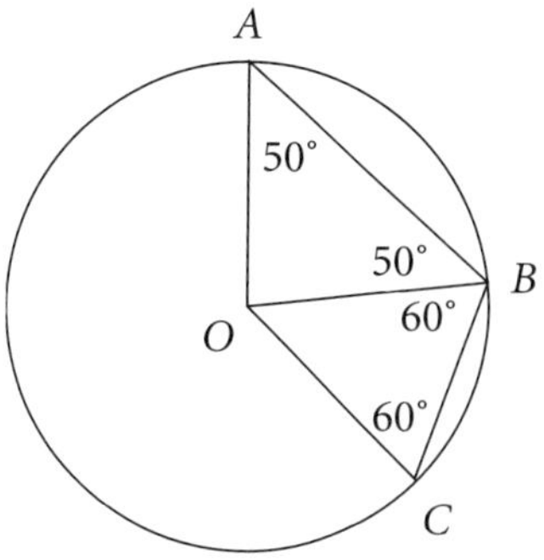

Using the fact that the 3 interior angles of a triangle add up to 180°, you can figure out that the vertex angles AOB and BOC measure 80° and 60°, respectively, as shown:

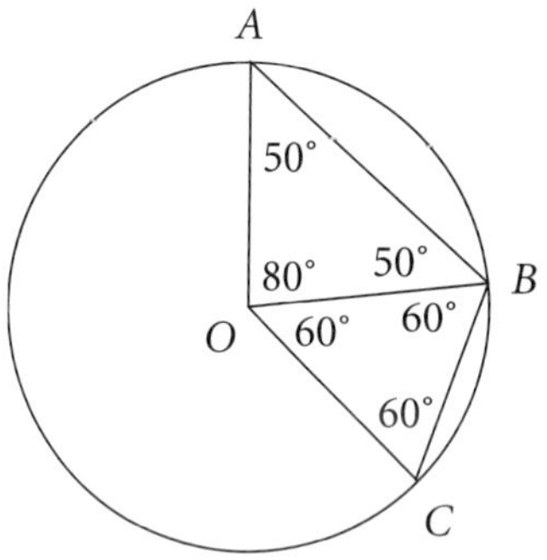

$\angle AOC$ measures 80° + 60° = 140°

8. E

You know by now to be careful with combined percent increases. If you just add 20% and 30% to get 50%, you fall into the test maker's trap. The best way to do a problem like this one is to pick a number for the original whole and just see what happens. And, as usual, the best number to pick here is 100.

If the 1980 population was 100, then a 20 percent increase would put the 1990 population at 120. Now, to figure the 30% increase, multiply 120 by 130%:

$$x = 1.3(120)$$

$$x = 156$$

Since the population went from 100 to 156, that's a 56% increase.

9. A

Parallel lines have the same slope. Use the first pair of points to figure out the slope:

$$\text{Slope} = \frac{y_2 - y_1}{x_2 - x_1} = \frac{16 - 1}{2 - 1} = 15$$

Then use the slope to figure out the missing coordinate in the second pair of points:

$$\text{Slope} = \frac{y_2 - y_1}{x_2 - x_1}$$

$$15 = \frac{25 - (-5)}{a - (-10)}$$

$$15 = \frac{30}{a + 10}$$

$$15a + 150 = 30$$

$$15a = -120$$

$$a = -8$$

10. B

Maura drives to work in 40 minutes, but returns home at half that speed. Common sense, or else the distance formula $R \times T = D$, should tell you that if she travels home at half the speed, it will take her twice as long, or 80 minutes, to return home. So the entire round trip will take 40 + 80 = 120 minutes, or 2 hours, and the entire distance she travels is 60 miles. Thus her average speed for the entire trip, in miles per hour, is $\frac{60 \text{ miles}}{2 \text{ hours}}$, or 30 miles per hour.

11. A

The greatest dollar increase came in 1999–2000, but that's not necessarily the greatest percent increase. The \$5,000 increase for 1995–96 is an increase of $\frac{1}{4}$, or 25%. The \$5,000 increase the following year is an increase of just $\frac{1}{5}$, or 20%. You don't even have to give much thought to the \$3,000 increases of the next 2 years—but what about the \$8,000 increase in 1999–2000? \$8,000 out of \$36,000 is less than $\frac{1}{4}$, so there's no need to calculate the percent; the 1995–96 increase wins.

12. D

This looks like a physics question, but in fact it's just a "plug in the number and see what you get" question. Be sure you plug 95 in for C (not F):

$$C = \frac{5}{9}(F - 32)$$

$$95 = \frac{5}{9}(F - 32)$$

$$\frac{9}{5} \times 95 = F - 32$$

$$171 = F - 32$$

$$F = 171 + 32 = 203$$

13. D

You should begin by rearranging the scores in ascending order: 130, 140, 140, 165, 195.

The resulting middle number, 140, is the median, and since 140 is the only recurring number, it is also the mode. Thus statement I is not true and **(C)** and **(E)** are out.

It looks like we're going to have to calculate the average:

$$\text{Average} = \frac{\text{Sum}}{\text{\# of terms}} =$$

$$\frac{130 + 140 + 140 + 165 + 195}{5} = \frac{770}{5} = 154$$

So statements II and III are both correct, and **(D)** is the answer.

14. C

This looks like a solid geometry question, but in fact it's another "plug in the numbers and see what you get" question.

$$S = \pi r\sqrt{r^2 + h^2}$$

$$= 3\pi\sqrt{3^2 + 4^2}$$

$$= 3\pi\sqrt{9 + 16}$$

$$= 3\pi\sqrt{25}$$

$$= 3\pi \times 5$$

$$= 15\pi$$

15. 50

The distance formula tells you that Distance = Speed × Time, or, as might be more useful in this case, Time = $\frac{\text{Distance}}{\text{Speed}}$. It would take the same amount of time for a plane traveling 200 mph and a plane traveling 160 mph to meet as it would if one plane were standing still and the other traveling at 200 + 160 = 360 mph. It would take a plane traveling at 360 mph $\frac{300}{360} = \frac{5}{6}$ hours = 50 minutes, to travel **300** miles.

16. 1/14 or .071

The wording on this problem is tricky, so take it one piece at a time. To find the probability that John gets the right combination on the first try, you have to find the number of possible combinations.

You know that one of the last two digits in 138 is correct and the other is incorrect. You also know that all the digits are distinct; that is, none of the digits are the same. So what possibilities are there? If 3 is correct, then 8 is wrong and the possible options are 130, 132, 134, 135, 136, 137, and 139. (Note there was no 131 and 133, since the digits must be distinct, and no 138, since you already know that is wrong.) Similarly, if 8 is the correct digit, the possibilities are 108, 128, 148, 158, 168, 178, and 198. All told, there are 14 possibilities.

If there are 14 possibilities, the probability that he gets the right combination on the first try is 1 in 14, or **1/14** (which can also be written **.071**).

17. 10

Here you want to choose three different trees out of five possibilities. So go ahead and call the trees A, B, C, D, and E. Now start listing out the possibilities systematically. One trick is to list out the possibilities in alphabetical order starting with ABC, and to work your way through the possibilities:

ABC
ABD
ABE
ACD
ACE
ADE
BCD
BCE
BDE
CDE

Thus there are a total of **10** possible combinations.

18. 80

The best way to solve this problem is to pick a value for the length of a side of square *A*. We want our numbers to be easy to work with, so let's pick 10 for the length of each side of square *A*. The length of each side of square *B* is 100 percent greater, or twice as great as a side of square *A*. So the length of a side of square *B* is 2 × 10, or 20. The length of each side of square *C* is 50 percent greater, or $1\frac{1}{2}$ times as great as a side of square *B*. So the length of a side of square *C* is $1\frac{1}{2} \times 20$ or 30. The area of square *A* is 10^2, or 100. The area of square *B* is 20^2, or 400. The sum of the areas of squares *A* and *B* is 100 + 400, or 500. The area of square *C* is 30^2, or 900. The area of square *C* is greater than the sum of the areas of squares *A* and *B* by 900 – 500, or 400. By what percent is the area of square *C* greater than the sum of the areas of squares *A* and *B*? $\frac{400}{500} \times 100\%$, or **80%**.

19. 12

This is a tricky seating arrangement question, so think about it systematically. It may also help to draw a diagram here. If Carla is seated at the head of the table, and no two people of the same gender may sit next to each other then our seating arrangement must look something like this:

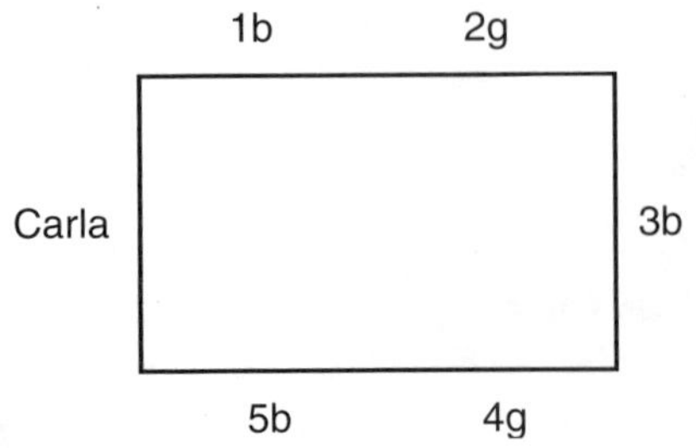

Now let's work our way around the table and figure out how many different arrangements are possible. Moving clockwise around the table, we know that seat 1 must be occupied by a boy, and there are 3 different boys who could fill this spot. Seat 2 must then be a girl. There are 2 different girls who could fill this spot. Seat 3 is another boy. Now that one of the boys is seated (next to Carla), only 2 boys remain for this seat. Seat 4 is a girl, and only one girl remains to sit here. Finally, only one boy remains for seat 5 next to Carla. To find the answer, multiply these possibilities. $3 \times 2 \times 2 \times 1 \times 1 = \mathbf{12}$

20. 37

The median is the number in the middle after the numbers have been arranged in ascending order.

The average is the $\frac{\text{sum of all the terms}}{\text{\# of terms}}$

So, given the average is 13 we know that the sum of all the terms is the average times the number of terms, or $13 \times 5 = 65$

And we know from the median that the terms arranged in ascending order are:

__, __, 12, __, __

We want to make one of the terms as *big* as possible, so that means we want to make all the other terms as *small* as possible. Since all the terms are *different* positive integers, when we minimize the other terms we get:

1, 2, 12, 13, __

And since the sum of the terms is 65, that means the fifth term is **37**, which is the correct answer.